Making Knowledge

Journal of the Royal Anthropological Institute Special Issue Book Series

The Journal of the Royal Anthropological Institute is the principal journal of the oldest anthropological organization in the world. It has attracted and inspired some of the world's greatest thinkers. International in scope, it presents accessible papers aimed at a broad anthropological readership. We are delighted to announce that their annual special issues are also repackaged and available to buy as books.

Volumes published so far:

Making Knowledge: Explorations of the Indissoluble Relation between Mind, Body and Environment, edited by Trevor H.J. Marchand

Islam, Politics, Anthropology, edited by Filippo Osella and Benjamin Soares

The Objects of Evidence: Anthropological Approaches to the Production of Knowledge, edited by Matthew Engelke

Wind, Life, Health: Anthropological and Historical Perspectives, edited by Elisabeth Hsu and Chris Low

Ethnobiology and the Science of Humankind, edited by Roy Ellen

MAKING KNOWLEDGE

EXPLORATIONS OF THE INDISSOLUBLE RELATION BETWEEN MIND, BODY AND ENVIRONMENT

EDITED BY TREVOR H.J. MARCHAND

WILEY-BLACKWELL

A John Wiley & Sons, Ltd., Publication

Royal Anthropological Institute

This edition first published 2010
© 2010 Royal Anthropological Institute of Great Britain & Ireland
Originally published as Volume 16, Special Issue May 2010 of *The Journal of the Royal Anthropological Institute*

Blackwell Publishing was acquired by John Wiley & Sons in February 2007. Blackwell's publishing program has been merged with Wiley's global Scientific, Technical, and Medical business to form Wiley-Blackwell.

Registered Office
John Wiley & Sons Ltd, The Atrium, Southern Gate, Chichester, West Sussex, PO19 8SQ, United Kingdom

Editorial Offices
350 Main Street, Malden, MA 02148-5020, USA
9600 Garsington Road, Oxford, OX4 2DQ, UK
The Atrium, Southern Gate, Chichester, West Sussex, PO19 8SQ, UK

For details of our global editorial offices, for customer services, and for information about how to apply for permission to reuse the copyright material in this book please see our website at www.wiley.com/wiley-blackwell.

The right of Trevor H.J. Marchand to be identified as the author of the editorial material in this work has been asserted in accordance with the UK Copyright, Designs and Patents Act 1988.

Wiley also publishes its books in a variety of electronic formats. Some content that appears in print may not be available in electronic books.

Designations used by companies to distinguish their products are often claimed as trademarks. All brand names and product names used in this book are trade names, service marks, trademarks or registered trademarks of their respective owners. The publisher is not associated with any product or vendor mentioned in this book. This publication is designed to provide accurate and authoritative information in regard to the subject matter covered. It is sold on the understanding that the publisher is not engaged in rendering professional services. If professional advice or other expert assistance is required, the services of a competent professional should be sought.

Library of Congress Cataloging-in-Publication Data

Making knowledge : explorations of the indissoluble relation between mind, body and environment / [edited by] Trevor H.J. Marchand.
        p. cm.—(Journal of the royal anthropological institute special issue book series ; 4)
        Includes bibliographical references and index.
    ISBN 978-1-4443-3892-8 (pbk.)
  1. Philosophical anthropology.   2. Knowledge, Theory of.   3. Mind and body.   4. Cognition and culture.   I. Marchand, Trevor H.J.

    BD450.M26265 2011
    306.4′2—dc22

                                                                                    2010040512

A catalogue record for this book is available from the British Library.

Set in 10/12pt Minion by Toppan Best-set Premedia Limited
Printed in Malaysia

1   2010

Contents

Notes on contributors

Emma Cohen is a researcher in the Research Group for the Comparative Cognitive Anthropology attached to the Max Planck Institute for Evolutionary Anthropology, Leipzig, and the Max Planck Institute for Psycholinguistics, Nijmegen. She has conducted fieldwork on an Afro-Brazilian religious tradition in Belém, northern Brazil, focusing primarily on concepts, behaviours, and practices associated with spirit possession. Her publications include *The mind possessed* (Oxford University Press, 2007). She is currently researching the ways people (across cultural and religious contexts) represent the relationship between minds, bodies, and persons. *Research Group for Comparative Cognitive Anthropology, Max Planck Institute for Evolutionary Anthropology, Leipzig, Germany.*

Roy Dilley is Professor of Social Anthropology and Dean of the Faculty of Arts at the University of St Andrews. He specializes in the study of Haalpulaaren (Tukulor) social organization and culture in Senegal, and published *Islamic and caste knowledge practices among Haalpulaaren, Senegal: between mosque and termite mound* (Edinburgh University Press for the International African Institute, 2004). Other research interests include anthropological theory and cultural economics, and he is editor of two thematic collections entitled *Contesting markets: analyses of ideology, discourse and practice* (Edinburgh University Press, 1992) and *The problem of context* (Berghahn, 1999). *Department of Social Anthropology, University of St Andrews, St Andrews, Fife, UK.*

Greg Downey is Senior Lecturer in Anthropology at Macquarie University. His research bridges cultural anthropology with biological and neurological studies of sport and embodied knowledge. He is author of *Learning capoeira: lessons in cunning from an Afro-Brazilian art* (Oxford University Press, 2005) and co-editor (with M. Fisher) of *Frontiers of capital: ethnographic reflections on the New Economy* (Duke University Press, 2006). He is completing a monograph on *The athletic animal* with support from the Wenner-Gren Foundation. *Department of Anthropology, Macquarie University, Sydney, Australia.*

Tim Ingold is Professor of Social Anthropology at the University of Aberdeen. He has conducted fieldwork among Saami and Finnish people in Lapland, and has written extensively on comparative questions of environment, technology, and social organization in the circumpolar North; evolutionary theory in anthropology; biology and history; the role of animals in human society; and issues in human ecology. He is currently exploring the interface between anthropology, archaeology, art, and architecture, and his latest book is *Lines: a brief history* (Routledge, 2007). *Department of Anthropology, School of Social Science, University of Aberdeen, Aberdeeen, UK.*

Dr Nicolette Makovicky is Lecturer in Russian and Eastern European Studies at the School of Interdisciplinary Areas Studies, University of Oxford. She obtained her PhD in Anthropology at University College London, followed by a Junior Research Fellowship at Wolfson College, Oxford. Her research considers the impact of socio-economic reforms and EU-integration on historically embedded modes of economic activity in Central Europe. Examining the political and social context of production and innovation in textile crafts since the early 20th century, she has a particular theoretical interest in processes of value creation, work ethics, entrepreneurialism, gender and citizenship in post-socialist society. An external tutor in the department of the History of Design at the Royal College of Art since 2007, she has also published on the relationship between craft, modernity and ideology, as well as memory and the domestic interior. *Wolfson College, Oxford, Oxford, UK.*

Trevor H.J. Marchand is Professor of Social Anthropology at the School of Oriental and African Studies, where he teaches the anthropology of space, place, and architecture. He has conducted fieldwork with masons in Arabia and West Africa, and as an ESRC Fellow (2005-8) he studied training and practice among English woodworkers. His research focuses on embodied cognition and communication and he is the author of *Minaret building and apprenticeship in Yemen* (Curzon, 2001) and *The masons of Djenné* (Indiana University Press, 2009), and co-producer of the documentary film *Future of mud* (2007). *Department of Anthropology, School of Oriental and African Studies, London, UK.*

Anna Odland Portisch is a Postdoctoral Associate of SOAS, where she also received a Ph.D. for her studies among the Kazakh of western Mongolia. Her research examines learning and skill-based knowledge in felt-craft production, and her work is focused on apprenticeship, cognition, and identity formation. She recently curated an exhibit on Kazakh textiles for the SOAS Brunei Gallery, and was an ESRC Fellow at Brunel University, where she lectured on anthropological and psychological perspectives on learning. *School of Oriental and African Studies, London, UK.*

Konstantinos Retsikas is Lecturer in Anthropology of South East Asia at SOAS. His research focuses include phenomenology, identity, and Islam. Recent publications include 'The Semiotics of violence: ninja, sorcerers and state terror in post-Soeharto Indonesia', *Bijdragen tot de Taal-, Land- en Volkenkunde* (2006) and 'Knowledge from the body: fieldwork, power, and the acquisition of a new self' in *Knowing how to know: fieldwork and the ethnographic present* (eds) N. Halstead, E. Hirsch & J. Okely (Berghahn, 2008). *Department of Anthropology and Sociology, School of Oriental and African Studies, University of London, London, UK.*

Tom Rice received his Ph.D. in social anthropology from Goldsmiths and was a postdoctoral Research Fellow at the University of Cambridge. He is currently a Teaching Fellow at the University of Exeter. His research explores the sonic environments of institutions and the types of auditory knowledge used and applied in these settings. He has published articles on 'auditory anthropology' in *Anthropology Today*, *Critique of Anthropology*, and *The Senses and Society*. *Room 313, Department of Sociology and Philosophy, University of Exeter, Exeter, UK.*

Soumhya Venkatesan is a Lecturer in Social Anthropology at the University of Manchester. Based on fieldwork with Muslim mat-weavers in South India and carpet-weavers in Bukhara, her research focuses on materiality and the relationship between people and things, and explores issues of embodiment and the transmission of skills. Her present research on Indian potters and sculptors of venerated idols considers the relation between makers and objects. She is currently preparing a book manuscript based on her doctoral research. *Social Anthropology, University of Manchester, Manchester, UK.*

Preface

TREVOR H.J. MARCHAND *School of Oriental and African Studies*

In 2005, with funding from the Economic and Social Research Council (ESRC), I commenced a new project with woodworkers in East London that built upon my previous studies of building-craft knowledge and apprenticeship in Yemen and Mali. In addition to the fieldwork and theoretical investigations into motor cognition and embodied forms of communication, the project also allowed me to invite anthropologists with shared interests in skill-learning to present their research in a seminar series and a subsequent one-day workshop, both hosted at the School of Oriental and African Studies (SOAS) in 2007. This volume grows out of the proceedings of that programme, initially titled *The transmission of knowledge.*

It is now three decades, and longer, since the works of Foucault (1977), de Certeau (1984), and especially Bourdieu ushered 'everyday knowledge and practice' to the fore of the social science agenda, and this focal concern is retained by the volume contributors. But while participants in the seminars and workshop gratefully acknowledged Bourdieu's seminal role in excavating Mauss's 'techniques of the body' (Mauss 1934) and developing a theory of habitus (Bourdieu 1977), they were invited to consider the limitations of 'practice theory' (e.g. Bloch 1991; Farnell 2000; Jenkins 1992) in advancing their own empirically based accounts of learning, situated practice, and embodied cognition. A project statement and set of questions framed the seminar programme. In particular, participants were asked to consider: How might social anthropologists effectually chronicle manifestations of human knowledge that 'exceed language', including bodily and perceptual practices? In which ways can 'know-how' be cogently described and represented in our ethnographic accounts? How, and under what circumstances, are new practices taken up and honed? And by what combination of cognitive and social mechanisms do they become stabilized as 'memory' or 'habits' that are consciously or unconsciously enacted? What drives improvisation in activity? And how do innovations in practice become publicly recognized and validated? How are different domains of knowledge co-ordinated within the mind-body complex, thereby resulting in both intelligent and intelligible performance? How are different ways of knowing variously communicated and interpreted by participating members within fields of practice? And crucially, how might we appropriately account for the necessary but ever-changing relations of learning to the physical and social environment in which it unfolds?

The follow-up workshop provided an intensive forum for seminar speakers and an invited panel of discussants to present and debate issues of theory and method, and consider anthropology's current and future contributions to the enduring, cross-disciplinary study of human knowledge. During the roundtable session we critically assessed the word 'transmission' and debated its appropriateness for accurately describing the myriad of complex ways in which knowing is articulated, acquired, and transformed *in situ*, involving communities of actors engaged in co-ordinated (and sometimes discordant) practices and communication. In the social sciences, 'transmission' has been regularly employed as a shorthand for the combined processes of teaching and learning, or for the operations of socialization and enculturation across generations, and several contributing authors rightfully use the term in this manner. But it can also bear problematic connotations of mechanical reproduction and homogeneous transferral of facts and information from one head (or body) to another. Lave has argued that 'transmission and internalization [are not] the primary mechanisms by which culture and individual come together', proposing instead 'that activity, including cognition, is socially organized and quintessentially social in its very existence, its formation and its ongoing character' (1988: 177). In wanting the title of our collective work best to convey our shared aims in representing learning and knowing, I have renamed the volume *Making knowledge*. 'Making', I feel, more accurately captures the processes and durational qualities of knowledge formation; and rather than being suggestive of hierarchical and methodical transfer, it fosters thinking about knowledge as a dialogical and constructive engagement between people, and between people, things, and environment.

This special volume of the *JRAI* features the works of leading scholars who promote bold, innovative approaches to understanding the nature and social constitution of human knowing. Notably, the theme, 'making knowledge', is not an intended revival or perpetuation of the 'anthropology of knowledge' subfield that emerged in the 1970s. Rather, the collection represents a concerted investigation into the core activity of all anthropology: namely 'the making of knowledge about the ways other people make knowledge'. The ethnography, theory, and methods presented expose possibilities for interdisciplinary collaboration and lay solid foundations for further investigations into embodied cognition and conceptual thinking. Ideas are couched in long-term, worldwide fieldwork; and a host of intriguing commonalities and differences emerge across the collection. All the authors are deeply unified in their concern for the appropriate study and representation of knowledge in its diverse forms and expression. Knowledge is explored both in its various modes of articulation (i.e. motor, sensory, and propositional) and in its range of social, cultural, and material manifestations. Conclusively, knowledge and practice are not fixed; nor are they hostage to unconscious reproduction. Rather what the chapters demonstrate is that our human knowledge, like our physical bodies, is constantly reconfigured in the activities and negotiations of everyday work and life.

I thank the seminar speakers and workshop discussants for their co-operation in realizing this project, and the ESRC for their generous funding (Res-000-27-0159). The workshop discussants included Emma Cohen, Anna Portisch, and Charles Stafford. Chapter contributions from Cohen and Portisch are included in this collection. Regrettably, Rita Astuti, Susanne Kuechler, and Harry West had to withdraw from publication, but their individual contributions to the seminar series were highly valued. I also thank Richard Fardon and my fellow colleagues at SOAS for their support throughout the seminar series; and the students of SOAS and other colleges who regularly attended and enlivened the discussions with shrewd insights and penetrating questions. Finally, I thank Julia Elyachar and an anonymous reviewer for their valuable comments on an earlier draft of the volume, and Justin Dyer for his meticulous copy-editing.

REFERENCES

BLOCH, M. 1991. Language, anthropology and cognitive science. *Man* (N.S.) **26**, 183-98.

BOURDIEU, P. 1977. *An outline of a theory of practice* (trans. R. Nice). Cambridge: University Press.

DE CERTEAU, M. 1984. *The practice of everyday life* (trans. S. Rendall). Berkeley: University of California Press.

FARNELL, B. 2000. Getting out of the habitus: an alternative model of dynamically embodied social action. *Journal of the Royal Anthropological Institute* (N.S.) **6**, 397-418.

FOUCAULT, M. 1977. *Discipline and punish: the birth of the prison* (trans. A. Sheridan). New York: Smith.

JENKINS, R. 1992. *Pierre Bourdieu*. London: Routledge.

LAVE, J. 1988. *Cognition in practice: mind, mathematics and culture in everyday life*. Cambridge: University Press.

MAUSS, M. 1934. Les techniques du corps. *Journal de Psychologie* **32**, 3-4. (Reprinted in his *Sociologie et anthropologie*. Paris: Presses Universitaires de France, 1936.)

Introduction: Making knowledge: explorations of the indissoluble relation between mind, body, and environment

TREVOR H.J. MARCHAND *School of Oriental and African Studies*

> Again, of all the things that come to us by nature we first acquire the potentiality and later exhibit the activity (this is plain in the case of the senses; for it was not by often seeing or often hearing that we got these senses, but on the contrary we had them before we used them, and did not come to have them by using them); but the virtues we get by first exercising them, as also happens in the case of the arts as well. For the things we have to learn before we can do them, we learn by doing them, e.g. men become builders by building and lyreplayers by playing the lyre; so too we become just by doing just acts, temperate by doing temperate acts, brave by doing brave acts.
>
> Aristotle, *Nicomachean ethics*, book 2, chapter 1: 31-2

In the above quote, Aristotle concisely describes the combination of nature and nurture that *is* us. As a species, we are composed, in part, of innate capacities – perceptual, cognitive, and motor – that engage us with the world of which we are a part, and thereby enable us to survive, adapt, and thrive. By contrast, 'arts and virtues' are not endowed, but realized and reinforced in practice. Anthropological studies of knowledge have traditionally concentrated on the by-products of nurture, consigning the discovery of 'nature' to the pure and applied sciences. Recent decades, however, have witnessed growing porosity in the boundaries that divide the social and natural sciences. There is widening recognition that nature or nurture should not be studied in isolation, for their interdependence is not trivial, but vital; and the processes by which they operate, and the effects that they yield, are not bounded, but coalesce.

The principal aim of this volume is to progress anthropology's thinking about human knowledge through exploration of the interdependence of nurture with nature; and more specifically the interdependence of minds, bodies, and environment. In their individual pursuits on the topic, several authors delve variously into the fields of cognitive studies, philosophy of mind, psychology, neuroscience, biology, and medicine, and others join their anthropological method to history, classical philosophy, and emergent ideas from the field of craft. While emphases on the roles played by environment and context in the processes of knowledge-making vary between the chapters, all draw the sentient, practising, tool-wielding body into the core of their work. The reader should not anticipate definitive answers to eternal questions of 'How do we know?' and 'How do we come to know?' But it is hoped that the ideas, ethnographic case studies, and anthropological perspectives presented here will abet deeper, better-informed questioning about knowledge, and stimulate interdisciplinary approaches to the study of learning, thinking, and practice.

I begin this introductory chapter with an overview of the (often conflicting) positions that dominated the 'anthropology of knowledge' in the closing decades of the last century. I continue with a discussion of the recent convergences between cognitivists, phenomenologists, and practice theorists that have generated a more inclusive space for 'thinking about knowing' in complex and productive ways. The contributing chapters exemplify this new general direction. And though the authors may diverge in theory and method, there is mutual recognition that knowledge-making is a dynamic process arising directly from the indissoluble relations that exist between minds, bodies, and environment.

In the following section, I reflect on my own studies with craftspeople in order to introduce several key issues regarding apprenticeship as both a mode of learning and a field method. In doing so, my aim is not to promote apprentice-style fieldwork as the paramount method for inquiries into knowledge. Rather, apprenticeships of one form or another were taken up by the majority of authors included in this collection, and as a field method it is explicitly geared toward the study of learning in practical contexts where verbal communication is frequently (but not categorically) of secondary import to physical skill and display.

Next, the idea that 'cognition is individual' is established, but it is equally conceded that 'making knowledge' is a process entailing co-ordinated interaction between interlocutors and practitioners with their total environment. As a minimum, the latter consists of artefacts, tools-to-hand, and raw materials; space, place, and architecture; paths and boundaries; time-frames and temporal rhythms; light, darkness, and weather. As sentient beings, we are engaged with a changing array of environmental factors at every given moment, all of which impact the thoughts we think and the actions we produce. But it would be near impossible to take comprehensive stock of the role played by every contextual element in an account of knowledge-making. Thus, not surprisingly, the authors bring focused attention to those they deem salient to the particular working, learning, or life-world environment under study: for example, the stethoscope, lace-making diagrams, woodworking tools, weaving looms, yarns and needles, the ground on which we walk, and the winds that blow as we journey. Before concluding with a summary of the scope and contents of this volume, I briefly present a theory of 'shared production' in knowledge-making that draws upon recent literature in cognitive linguistics and neuroscience. Making knowledge, after all, is an ongoing process shared *between* people and *with* the world.

Anthropology and knowledge: toward an interdisciplinary approach

The study of knowledge is the *sine qua non* of social and cultural anthropology. What people say and do, what they believe, and how they organize and classify the phenomena of their worlds have constituted the core foci of the discipline throughout its manifold developments (D. Boyer 2005: 141-2; D'Andrade 1995: 5-7). The post-structural turn advanced deliberations on the relations of knowledge to power, and promoted broader definitions of 'discourse' that encompass practice and performance in addition to spoken and textual exchange. But despite decades of meticulous study about the ways in which knowledge is articulated and made manifest in innumerable contexts, the majority of anthropological analyses stop short of providing satisfying explanation (or approximations) of how learning, knowing, and practice actually occur, take shape, and continually transform *with* situated bodies and minds. Fieldworkers customarily record *what* their subjects know, but they are less inclined to delve into questions of *how* we come to know as humans. The relevance of Malcolm Crick's observation made more than a quarter-century ago endures: '[A]nthropologists speak of the creation of knowledge, of thought, and consciousness without detailing any processes or mechanisms' (1982: 291). Both the phenomenological experience that accompanies doing and the human biological processes – anatomic and neurological – that are integral to learning and practice are sidelined by mainstream anthropology (Downey 2005: 207). And despite emphases on issues of agency, resistance, and performance, ethnography tends to omit histories of individuals and their unique accretion of experience; their physical, perceptual, or cognitive developments, as well as the corresponding limitations or deteriorations; and the particular dynamics that animate nested communities of practice within larger social groupings. Collectively, these give rise to the ongoing ways that individuals acquire skill and enhance 'personal style'. Harris appositely proposes a pursuit of 'knowing as an ongoing process' rather than 'knowing as certainty' and, in so doing, he urges us to 'move away from methods understood as formal procedures and tools ... [toward] an artisanal approach to anthropology' (2007: 4 and 12; see also Ingold 2008: 85-6).

In the early 1980s, Crick called for the forging of 'serious links with the neurobiological sciences' in order to progress anthropology's study of knowledge (1982: 296). This challenge was echoed by Victor Turner (1983), who promoted interdisciplinary synthesis, arguing that recent work emerging from neurology was potentially beneficial to our understandings of religious belief and ritual. By the 1980s, the brain sciences were delivering results that promised imminent answers to age-old questions about memory, belief formation, and consciousness, and some anthropologists took these new ideas and findings on board. Charles Laughlin, for example, coined his approach to the study of consciousness 'neurophenomenology' (Laughlin, d'Aquili & McManus 1990). Though thought-provoking, the theory and method provided no substantial insights into the workings of the brain, and had minimal impact on mainstream anthropology. Other more resolutely cognitive anthropologists, such as Scott Atran (Atran, Medin & Ross 2006), Pascal Boyer (1999; 2001), Lawrence Hirschfeld (2006), Dan Sperber (1994; 2001), and John Tooby (Cosmides & Tooby 1994), have merited considerably more attention – both appreciative and critical – for their bold, formal approaches to the mechanics of thought and activity. These authors borrow variously from philosophy of mind, cognitive science, neuroscience, psychology, and evolutionary theory in order to assemble models of 'massive modularity', to map domain specificity, and to describe special-purpose cognitive devices. These structures and mechanisms purportedly enable us to have mental states, intentions, and beliefs; process environmental data and construct meaning; and economically execute the broad range of tasks and skills that are within our capacities. Pascal Boyer acknowledges, however, that 'cognitive science is most helpful in describing and explaining "ideational culture", that is, the set of mental representations entertained by members of a particular group that makes that group different from other' (1999: 206). But by limiting the focus to 'ideational culture', and by underestimating the mutual dependencies between internal apparatuses and the world in which people live and the acting bodies with which they learn, cognitive modelling constricts description and explanation, and risks presenting only caricatures of human knowledge. In a deliberate turn against 'internalization', Jean Lave and Etienne Wenger's influential study on situated learning advocates, by contrast, a thinking about learning as 'increasing participation in communities of practice [that] concerns the whole person acting in the world' (1991: 49).

Similarly, Tim Ingold has countered such cognitivist approaches, maintaining that human beings are not devices for processing 'information'. Rather, knowledge consists foremost of skill and is realized in 'fields of practice' (2001: 114). Ingold's position is not adverse to biological explorations of our humanity *per se*, but he cautions ardently against scientific theory that entrenches a dualism of 'inner self' versus 'public world'. He likewise makes a formidable case against the neo-Darwinian theory underpinning much cognitive theory in its 'classical' guise, disclosing the circularity of its reasoning. 'Organic form is generated, not expressed, in development', he states, and it arises as 'an emergent property of the total system of relations set up by virtue of the presence and the activity of the organism in its environment' (2001: 122). With compatible reasoning, Christina Toren insists that 'the human mind cannot be analogous to a set of computer programs', but rather 'our cognitive processes are *constituted* through our embodied engagement in the world and predicated on inter-subjectivity' (1993: 467, original emphasis). Living and knowing are the same thing, she claims, so the biology of cognition (and the possible existence of some forms of domain specificity) is necessarily a manifestation of historically located subjects (1993: 466). Moreover, in the case of the 'historically located' field researcher, Harvey Whitehouse considers how it is that we are susceptible to our hosts' ways and understandings of appropriate behaviour. He writes against the idea that it is 'the outcome of a shared "bridgehead" of genetically determined modules' (1996: 113). Rather, what we and our hosts share in common is a 'capacity for learning, against a rich and intricate background of prior learning' (1996: 113).

At the turn of the millennium, Emily Martin took a decidedly contrasting position to that voiced by Crick and Turner, warning of the threat posed by 'neuroreductionism' to social and cultural anthropology, and its power to efface 'context' from our understandings of what it is to be human. She writes that in computational neuroscience models (e.g. Churchland & Churchland 1998; Lakoff & Johnson 1999) 'individuals communicate, brain to brain, like nodes in a network, not like elaborately *interwoven threads* in a vibrant *cultural tapestry*' (Martin 2000: 584, my emphasis). To be sure, reductionism in any guise renders only impoverished accounts of how people come to know what they know. The variability, dynamic nature, and situatedness of knowledge demand theoretical complexity and careful consideration of the multiple (possibly innumerable) factors that exist both within and without the individual, and of the spatial and temporal arrangements in which these interact. But I contend that imagery such as 'interwoven threads' and 'cultural tapestry' lends no greater clarification to questions about the communication and learning of knowledge than do the computing metaphors used by many cognitive researchers and neuroscientists to theorize about the brain. Martin's window onto the neurosciences is slightly polemical, failing to credit influential works of leading cognitive scientists and philosophers – Putnam (1988) and Searle (1998) excepted – who take context and complexity seriously, and whose findings, in turn, might actually enrich the field of our own inquiries.

In their writings on the 'embodied mind' nearly a decade earlier, Francisco Varela, Evan Thompson, and Eleanor Rosch already noted that the cognitive sciences have 'slowly drifted away from the idea of mind as an input-output device that processes information toward the idea of mind as an emergent and autonomous network' (1991: 151). Cognitive philosopher Jerry Fodor, author of the modularity thesis (1983), argues adamantly against 'massive modularity' (as formulated in, for example, Cosmides & Tooby 1994, and Sperber 1994) and the over-extension of computational models to explain 'mind'. While maintaining a modular explanation limited to perceptual apparatuses, he insists that cognitive science (and thereby cognitive anthropology) must live with the fact that most thinking is non-modular; and that our higher-order thought processes are very likely inexplicable, at least within the computational paradigm (Fodor 2000). As an attuned anthropologist to these debates, Whitehouse notes that 'most recent models in neuroscience and artificial intelligence describe relatively domain-general processes of learning' versus innate, hard-wired domains (2001a: 5). Supported by Gerald Edelman's neurological research (1992), Whitehouse challenges the modularity thesis that 'child development follows a genetically specified schedule' (1996: 105). Instead, he argues that the 'developmental sequence results from the reinforcement of certain firing patterns through experience', and thus 'engagement with the environment is not a process of *instruction* (as in conventional computer-like processes), but of *natural selection*' (1996: 106, original emphasis). 'Emergentist' alternatives in cognitivism, such as that proposed by Andy Clark, are credited with taking the kind of encompassing, non-reductive approach that may be necessary (Ingold 2001: 114). The goal of Clark's thesis is to expel residual Cartesianism from cognitive studies by espousing a theory of 'extended mind' that accounts for interacting brain, body, and physical and social environments in equal measure (Clark 1997).

Mauro Adenzato and Francesca Garbarini are a part of that new school of neuroscience which is expanding its frontiers and searching for explanations beyond computational models. They confidently assert that second-generation cognitive sciences have surpassed the functionalist metaphor of the brain as a syntactic information-processor akin to the Turing machine. Acknowledging 'that cognitive processes are rooted in the neuroanatomic substrate', they follow the ideas of Clark and of Varela, Thompson, and Rosch in describing mind as 'an emerging property of the brain' (Adenzato & Garbarini 2006: 748). Drawing on a spectrum of source material that includes Rizzolatti and Craighero's research on the mirror-neuron system (2004), Merleau-Ponty's phenomenology of perception (1962), and Ingold's studies of skills (2000), Adenzato and Garbarini explore the indispensable relationship between an organism and its environment. Their perspective of 'embodied cognition', shared by a cross-disciplinary community of scholars, views mind as a biological system rooted 'in body experience and interwoven with action and interaction with other individuals' (2006: 748). The biological, environmental and social are thereby integrated within a unified framework of analysis. In an analogous manner, neurologist Frank Wilson's meticulous study of the hand (1998) marshals neuroscience, anatomy, psychology, and his own ethnographic accounts of puppeteers, musicians, and other practitioners to construct a lucid portrayal of the evolution and skilled intelligence of human hands at work in various settings and on diverse tasks.

So, despite Martin's anxieties over computational analytic hegemony, anthropologists should derive satisfaction from the fact that our practice of fieldwork and studies *with* people, and our principal concerns with history, context, and environment in the study of 'being human', have taken root in prominent quarters of the brain sciences. An inclusive research space that productively accommodates 'neurological, psychological, and sociological theories' (Whitehouse 2001*b*: 221) is on the horizon, offering precious opportunity for academic collaboration on enduring questions about human ways of learning and knowing, the nature of agency and consciousness, and the mind-body relation. Oliver Sacks was a key emissary in emphasizing the value of ethnographic fieldwork in neurological studies of mind (e.g. 1996). In exchange, anthropologists pioneering the subfield of neuroanthropology are exploring the potential contributions that neuroscience can make to our discipline. Paul Mason (2007) eloquently states that the focal concern for neuroanthropology is 'the reiterative causality between brain, culture and the environment'.

Greg Downey (2005; 2007; this volume) and I (Marchand 2001; 2003*a*; 2007*a*; this volume) have also probed the productive interface between anthropology and neuro-science in our respective studies of the Afro-Brazilian martial art of capoeira and building crafts. Current research on the aforementioned mirror-neuron system – a network of brain areas in the pre-motor and parietal cortices that is activated by both producing and recognizing the same object-orientated movement performed by the self or others (Arbib & Rizzolatti 1997; Rizzolatti, Fogassi & Gallese 2001) – has enabled us to conceptualize more clearly the sorts of imitative learning that we and our fellow practitioners engage in either in the *roda* (capoeira ring) or at the construction site. Studies of motor cognition, and especially research into the relation between motor execution and simulation (e.g. Jeannerod 1994; 2006), have propelled our individual thinking about the mind-body complex; the fluid composition and mechanics of 'intelligent action' and the 'uncoordinated' trials of novices; and the nature of embodied communication and the cognitive interface between 'seeing' and 'doing'. In short, scientific learning about the brain in combination with ethnographic field data gathered by observation, interview, or direct phenomenological engagement with environment, actors, and activities can mutually contribute to the formulation of new questions in the search for more nuanced understandings of human being, learning, and knowledge.

Rita Astuti, too, has asserted that participant observation, linguistic proficiency, and a systematic method for recording ethnographic data are essential, but not entirely sufficient, for exploring and describing the ways knowledge is manifested. To sustain the 'innovative spirit with which Malinowski created our discipline', she advises that we 'be prepared to advance our methodology by co-operating with other disciplines' (2001: 443). In studies with the Vezo of Madagascar, Astuti's novel insights into the relation between implicit and explicit knowledge arise from a constructive engagement with cognitive psychology (2001: 432). But her call for interdisciplinarity, I believe, is not about relegating anthropology to partnerships solely with branches of the brain sciences. Rather, more generally, anthropologists are urged to be critically aware and responsive to the methods and findings of the other disciplines with equally vested interests in human learning and knowing such as philosophy, linguistics, sociology, psychology, and educational studies. In doing so, we stand to benefit from different but complementary expertise and thereby enhance our own understandings and explanations. For certain, there is no singular trajectory in this pursuit, or ideal interdisciplinary arrangement. Learning about learning and coming to know about knowing are colossal tasks beyond the scope of any one enterprise. Frederick

Barth concluded his Mintz Lecture on *An anthropology of knowledge* with a similar message: '[T]o unravel more of the processes and dynamics of the human varieties of knowledge, it seems that we have an unending program of discovery and analysis ahead of us' (2002: 11).

An aim of the present volume is to contribute to this programme of discovery and analysis. Nigel Rapport and Mark Harris have noted that 'ways of knowing' include both 'modes of knowing' and 'pathways to knowing' (2007: 327). The ideas formulated here engage reflectively with both. Each chapter advances anthropology's engagement with 'knowing' in a novel manner through cutting-edge interdisciplinary research, innovative field methodology, or the charting of unexplored territory in the discipline – and in several cases, a daring combination of all three. A mode of engaged anthropological inquiry stands firmly at the core of the work. Anthropology, Ingold reminds us, is not a study *of*, but a study *with*: 'Immersed with [people] in an environment of joint activity, [anthropologists] learn to see things (or hear them, or touch them) in the ways their teachers and companions do' (2008: 82). Indeed, for several contributing authors, an apprentice-style method of 'learning about practice by practically doing' nurtures truly 'embodied' discoveries about the temporal, social, and physical processes that are inseparable from acts of learning and communicating knowledge (see also Dilley 1989; O'Connor 2005; Sinclair 1997; Stoller 1989; Wacquant 2004). 'How do we know?' (or not) and 'How do we come to know?' are driving questions in these explorations. There is nothing new in either the quest or the questions posed – in fact they are refreshingly timeless. What are new are the ways and the contexts in which the contributors investigate situated and inter-subjective practices in 'making knowledge'.

Doing to learn and learning to do

In a previous incarnation as an architecture student, I had the good fortune of working summers as a building inspector, and later of overseeing the construction of my residential designs. During those work experiences, I was regularly struck by the way that site carpenters carried out often-complicated tasks with a Spartan economy of words – and typically with minimal reference to my carefully prepared plan drawings. I recall observing a junior carpenter eyeballing his supervisor for cues while endeavouring to co-ordinate the pattern of his own activities after those of the old man. I, too, enjoyed making things, and my surfacing queries about the carpenters' on-site learning resonated with my as-yet-crude musings about intelligent practice and 'knowledge beyond language'. I therefore came to anthropology to research these questions and have worked ever since alongside craftspeople, learning their skills while learning about their learning and their lives. Having apprenticed with Yemeni minaret-builders in the city of San'a (2001) and Malian mud masons in the town of Djenné (2009), I commenced a new study in 2005 with carpentry trainees at the Building Crafts College in East London (Marchand in preparation). In this section, I reflect upon aspects of my own field experiences and theoretical interests in order to draw out some of the general issues and questions about apprenticeship, learning, and the transmission of knowledge that are addressed more comprehensively and site-specifically in the contributing chapters.

Two years of fieldwork at the Building Crafts College consisted of daily participation as a trainee in the fine woodwork programme. In addition to National Vocational Qualifications (NVQ) and a City & Guilds Diploma, I earned a solid skill base in joinery and furniture-making, and became a member of a professional community of crafts-people. A principal objective of the study was to arrive at a clearer understanding and description of the sort of embodied cognition and communication I was witness to, and regularly immersed in, at the workshop. An apprentice-style method, like that used by Roy Dilley, Greg Downey, Nicolette Makovicky, Anna Portisch, Tom Rice, and Soumhya Venkatesan (all this volume), squarely situated me as a subject within my study, and compelled me to reflect carefully upon my own ways of learning and exercising what I was coming to know as a practitioner. It also plunged me into the daily interactions and social politics at college; and engaged me directly with co-operative strategies and competitive struggles between trainees. As a member of that group, I was subject to college authority and subordinate to the expert status of my instructors, and to the advanced know-how of some colleagues.

Unlike a mason's apprenticeship in Yemen or Mali, my London training was seg-regated from the everyday operations and economies of a construction site. As paying students, we attended college to learn; and, as college employees, instructors were there primarily to teach. Categories of persons, and their corresponding roles and duties, were more starkly delineated and differentiated than those on the Arabian and West African construction sites, where making buildings – not qualified individuals – is the priority. In those locations, the collective activity of constructing with homogeneous palettes of building materials, a limited kit of tools, and uncomplicated methods generates a more porous division of labour in practice, if not necessarily in job titles and rank. College tasks, by contrast, were mainly individual: each student making, for instance, his or her own casement window, panel door, or staircase; and by the second year producing pieces of furniture and resolving individual designs with different arrays of timbers, tools, and cabinetry methods. Timescales for the completion of projects also varied depending on the trainee's levels of aptitude, motivation, and physical stamina, as well as on their commitments outside college. Such circumstances contributed to less interdependence among trainees and a more competitive individualism than witnessed among site apprentices and labourers.

The college curriculum is formally structured in accordance with government cri-teria, and includes separate theory components, textbooks, and written examinations. The vast majority of technical teaching and learning was nevertheless achieved with a paucity of oral explanation or textual instruction, and more readily relied upon demonstration, imitation, and repeated practice. Words and utterances were regularly used for deictic purposes: to highlight the salient aspects of a tool-wielding practice; to stress particular bodily positions and postures; or to draw attention to aspects of a tool or qualities of the timber being worked. This does not imply that the workshop was a Carthusian atelier – silent but for the industrious tapping of tools. By contrast, the buzz of conversation was constant, and biting banter ricocheted from one work-bench to the next. As I was born and raised in Canada, my fieldwork was also a steep socialization into 'English' culture, conduct, and humour. Indeed, like Yemeni and Malian building sites, the workshop was not merely a space for technical learning; it was an arena for competing masculinities and femininities, and a forum for asser-tions of ethnicity and race, as well as social class. Michael Herzfeld aptly notes that, in qualifying 'apprenticeship', any attempt to separate the social from the technical 'is in some sense a Cartesian convenience' (2007: 96). Talk across workbenches and over canteen lunches frequently included deliberations on craft ethics, environmental issues, and utopian ideals of satisfying work; and these concerns informed the ongoing constructions of identity, practice, and aspirations of the men and women I trained with (Marchand 2007*b*; also Wacquant on pugilistic pedagogy, 2004: 111).

Like college pupils, Yemeni and Malian apprentices also pay for training, but with the free or cheap labour they supply, not cash. Disciplined comportment and obedience improve prospects of establishing a career in the trade and of inheriting work and clientele. Acquiring skills is mandatory for any who wish to stay employed or ascend the ladder of command, but for apprentices and masons alike, learning is largely a by-product of participating in the work programme and instances of explicit teaching are exceptional. As Howard Becker (1972) observes, apprentices have responsibility in organizing their own curriculum and recruiting necessary teaching or guidance from superiors. Motivated individuals must identify what they need to know (including craft technique, business skills, appropriate conduct, trade secrets, powerful benedictions, etc.), strategize their physical position in proximity to mentors, and tactically seize opportunities that provide access to practice. In Djenné, a degree of questioning is tolerated, but less so in Sanʿa, where a rigid patriarchal order curtails easy interaction between junior and senior members of the work team, and questioning is interpreted as a challenge to authority (also Goody 1989: 252-3). Navigating access to the right examples and discovering how things are done are valuable skills in themselves, and are mastered only through years of determined experience, as any field researcher knows.

In the eyes of my minaret and mud mason colleagues, the prized fruits of their labours are the structures that they make, the financial remunerations they receive, and the mason-subjects formed under their guidance. Though they seldom 'teach' in an overt manner, they readily acknowledge the instrumental need to equip younger generations with skills in order to sustain a qualified workforce, perpetuate craft know-how, and preserve the architectural heritage of their respective towns (both of which are UNESCO World Heritage sites).[1] By way of example, a site master's activities communicate skilled know-how and, above all, adeptness in calculation and production. The workplaces that they organize and manage offer site opportunities for ambitious individuals actively to learn by doing – and by doing, earn a living. In similar ways that the dance studio (Dyck & Archetti 2003: 10), the capoeira *roda* (Downey 2005), and the gymnasium (Wacquant 2004) are places of 'collective teaching', so too is the building site. Activities are carried out in a co-ordinated manner between individuals, and each participant is a 'potential visual model' (Wacquant 2004: 113). Building-craft apprentices effectively 'steal with their eyes' (Herzfeld 1995: 139-40; 2004: 107) and other perceptual senses, and improvise imitative and experimental responses to the surrounding tasks and activities that demand their involvement (Hallam & Ingold 2007). Practice and understanding unfold dialogically with one another, and as a new posture, gesture, or action is 'apprehended-comprehended', it serves as 'the support, the materials, the tool that makes possible the discovery and thence the assimilation of the next' (Wacquant 2004: 118).

The ways that we, as humans, 'apprehend' and 'comprehend' physical activity begs further investigation. As anthropologists in the field, we can bear witness to, or experience first-hand, physical practices; and we can draw upon the conceptual knowledge we gain about the context in which they occur to enrich our interpretations of those phenomena with social, cultural, and historical significance. But by relying solely on participant observation, oral accounts, or ethnographic reasoning, we limit our insights into the cognitive and anatomical processes involved in learning and doing. In my estimation, detailed sketches are needed – like those composing this volume – of the mutual dependencies between biology, society, and environment. In drawing variously upon expertise from the brain sciences, linguistics, philosophy of mind, psychology, or phenomenology, many of the present chapters strive to understand what goes on 'inside' us without losing sight of what happens 'outside'. The ideal places for this exploration, as the authors demonstrate, are sites of everyday practice and communication. Together, practitioners and interlocutors structure their places of learning through activity and dialogue in the spaces they define and organize; along their pathways of movement (Ingold); and with the tools, implements, and artefacts they use, create, and destroy. Making knowledge – or ignorance (Dilley) – is a constant process in capoeira training (Downey), auscultation classes (Rice), and carpentry workshops (Marchand); within the homes and communities of *syrmaq*-makers (Portisch), lace-makers (Makovicky), and weavers (Venkatesan; Dilley); and in everyday constructions of ethnicity and distinction (Retsikas).

Since Michael Coy's edited work on 'apprenticeship' as both research topic and field method (1989), apprenticing as a means of inquiry has been safely secured within anthropology's canon of standard practice, spurring some to pursue topics that complement personal as well as scholarly interests. Apprenticing and direct participation enable academics to acquire some level of first-hand experience, and possibly 'expertise', in the practices that they theorize and write about. Regular schedules of participation in (sometimes monotonous or gruelling) exercises allow reflection on one's own learning, mistakes, and progress, as well as the pains and pleasures that accompany physical labour. In the exchange of 'toil' for 'ethnographic knowledge', fieldworkers are exposed viscerally to the learning environments and livelihoods of fellow workers, craftspeople, and athletes; and they are able to interact more competently within the multiple mediums and nuanced forms of communication that are employed in the transmission of skills and comportment (Marchand 2008). By adopting an explicitly apprentice-style method, or by actively engaging in the practices they study (see, e.g., Lee & Ingold 2006; Retsikas 2008), the contributors to this volume have developed their individual understandings about learning and knowing by 'doing' what they study. Cultivating such understanding, as they convincingly convey, demands long immersion, perceptual and kinaesthetic awareness, careful reflection, persistent questioning, and a constant probing of the complex and multiple factors that constitute any field of practice.

Shared productions of knowledge

In his foreword to Lave and Wenger's study *Situated learning*, William Hanks remarks that 'the apprentice's ability to understand the master's performance depends not on their possessing the same *representation* of it, or of the object it entails, but rather on their being engaged in the performance in congruent ways' (1991: 21, my emphasis). The idea that we learn through participation was embraced in studies of learning (Pelissier 1991) and apprenticeship, but the cognitive manner in which mental representations are individually constructed by co-practitioners and interlocutors has received comparatively little attention from anthropologists.

A theory of 'mental representations' (including acoustic, visual, olfactory, haptic, motor, propositional, etc.) implies that stimuli received from our total environment are cognitively and corporeally mediated. For example, in contemplating the processes of cultural transmission, Maurice Bloch writes that it 'is not a matter of passing on "bits of culture" as though they were a rugby ball being thrown from player to player. Nothing is passed on; rather, a communication link is established which then requires an act of re-creation on the part of the receiver'. And this act of re-creation, he goes on to suggest, entails an integration of the original stimulus 'into a different mental universe' (2005: 97). Bloch is not suggesting that we are separated from the social and physical environment in which we exist; but rather, *how we know* and *what we can know* or *experience* of the world (including ourselves) is always and necessarily a product of our species-specific perceptual apparatuses, cognitive architecture, and biological constitution, which, together, give us life and enable us to survive. Ethnographic studies of knowledge-making aptly demonstrate that perceptual abilities are sharpened or deteriorate during the course of people's lives, livelihoods, and pastimes (Grasseni 2007; Rice, this volume); synaptic networks and neural pathways are established and modified through practice, experience, disease, or ageing (Downey 2005; Whitehouse 1996); and anatomical constitution is (re)configured, minimally, in activity (or lack thereof) (Ingold, Retsikas, Venkatesan, this volume). The fact that biological constitutions evolve, change, and decline buttresses the claim that experiencing (and thus learning and knowing) is individual, and is likewise temporally situated (Rapport & Harris 2007). But at the same time, acts of making knowledge are always and necessarily realised *in* interaction with others and with the world.

In the passage below, I offer a straightforward example of the way that knowledge is made, updated, and constantly reconfigured in the flux of everyday interactions, and I briefly outline a possible explanation of the individual cognitive processes involved in what has been coined a 'shared utterance' (Purver & Kempson 2004). My aim more generally is to convey the sorts of theoretical concerns that inspired this project and that are taken up in various and divergent ways by the contributing authors.

In linguistics, the term 'shared utterance' describes the phenomenon whereby one interlocutor interrupts the verbal utterance of another in order to complete a statement or, more saliently, an 'idea' (i.e. mental representation) that both speaker and hearer are incrementally constructing in the real time of dialogue. A sample of conversation from the college carpentry workshop where I trained illustrates this point:

> *Instructor (♀):* I think oak is the right choice for this design. The trouble with oak is it's ...
> *Trainee (♂):* Expensive! Yes, I realized that when I went to price it up.

Speakers and listeners fluidly swap roles in this manner, whereby the producer of an utterance becomes the parser (whose cognitive task is incrementally to assign context-dependent interpretation to the words of a string as they are received on-line) from the moment that the listener takes over as speaker. In constructing an interpretation of an utterance as it is received on-line, it is possible (and normally desirable from the speaker's perspective) that the hearer is entertaining a representation that matches the communicative intent of the speaker. But the representation that a hearer constructs may also differ or diverge, thereby establishing the possibility for carrying the dialogue in new directions unanticipated by the initial speaker. In other words, if the parser interjects to take over as producer of the string, like in the above example, he may complete the statement with information that was not in the speaker's mind to convey. For instance, the instructor might have intended to complete her string with '... a bugger to work with', referring to the extreme hardness of oak timber. The trainee, however, cuts her off to complete the utterance with 'Expensive!', thereby laying the groundwork for a shift in conversation. The potential consequences of this are multiple. Interlocutors may, for instance, carry on talking 'past one another' without achieving parity in the semantic representations they individually construct, and ultimately failing to 'communicate'. Alternatively, the initial speaker, in this case the instructor, may choose to supply additional information to correct her interlocutor's intervention and re-establish her own intended message and meaning in the dialogue context. Or, interestingly, the first speaker may modify the initial 'idea' that she intended to communicate by parsing the input supplied by the intervening interlocutor and thereby constructing a revised or alternative representation. If so, then the dialogue may take a turn following the second speaker's lead, and so on. This last possibility, in particular, demonstrates that though the cognitive processes of interpretation are individual, the production of knowledge, as mental representations, is social. Knowledge is realized on-line: *in* communication and, more generally, *in* interaction. The dynamic nature of interaction presents constant opportunity for new and possibly divergent ways of thinking and speaking about things. Thus dialogue is not an articulation of fixed things already known, but rather it is a kind of 'knowing in progress'. The state of 'knowing' is one of constant flux, update, and transformation; and careful study of this reveals the underlying processes of social and cultural change.

The phenomenon of 'shared utterance' occurs frequently in spoken dialogue, but, equally, what might be coined 'shared performance' (Marchand 2007a) describes numerous practices. In obvious examples of playing sports, dancing, working, or making things together, practitioners regularly co-ordinate their activities, and at some point, mid-action, one may intervene and successively complete the motions of another's goal-directed sequence. In other words, co-practitioners swap roles as observers and generators (or parsers and producers) in performing tasks. We all regularly do so in the co-ordinated (and sometimes not-so-co-ordinated) tasks and activities that we do together, and that we have been doing since our days in the childhood nursery. Probing this seemingly mundane, everyday occurrence unleashes a multitude of questions concerning the ways that shared activity, and consequently shared productions of knowledge, is achieved. What are the processes (cognitive, motor, and otherwise) that enable an observer to leap to the conclusion of what their co-practitioner has in mind to do, intercept the activity, and complete the task? And how, like shared utterance, do parser-cum-producers introduce new directions to the motor-based interpretations that co-practitioners are simultaneously constructing as they work together, and thereby introduce change to skilled practice? And what role, too, does the environment of tools, materials, fellow actors, artefacts, and physical setting play in the interpretation and generation of activity?

The chapters in this work variously address such issues and questions through a combination of ethnography and theory. The theoretical reflections are not necessarily couched in cognitive, linguistic, or neurological research, but the individual approaches demonstrate a shared concern with the dynamic interaction between practitioners and their environment, and the consequent productions of knowledge and skill. The five chapters that comprise the first half of the volume present in-depth explorations of the mutually constituting activities of teachers and learners, and the role of the learning environment in forming pedagogies, identities, values, attitudes, and performance.

Teaching and learning

In the first chapter, Greg Downey directly addresses issues of motor understanding and imitation with his ethnographic research on capoeira. As a long-time practitioner of the Afro-Brazilian martial art, his own experiences and careful studies of training squarely challenge Bourdieu's theory of the habitus. Downey writes that hard divisions between propositional and embodied forms of knowledge are part of the same Cartesian legacy that propagates the assumption that perception and action are coded separately by the brain, and co-ordination of the two systems requires some type of overarching system, like the habitus (Bourdieu 1977; 1990). With lucid references to current neurological research, Downey carefully examines individual strategies of transmission and enskilment among his fellow practitioners to reveal the complexity and challenge involved in mimesis. Conscious and concerted effort is displayed, for instance, by the *Mestre* (teacher), who scaffolds student attempts to imitate by physically adjusting their postures and movements. For students, acquisition of capoeira techniques is characterized by its 'slow pace, inconsistency, and piecemeal' nature (p. 31). While some aspects of imitation are hard-earned, others proceed more automatically and entirely 'without theory'. Mirror-neuron theory demonstrates that we perceive motor activity in the same neural functions as we ourselves act, therefore requiring no symbolic mediation. In Downey's view, this makes everyday automatic activity a poor candidate for the sort of unifying treatment proposed by the habitus, and he calls its existence into rigorous questioning. The theory of a 'unified structuring structure is elegantly modernist and functional', he observes. In reality 'the human brain and body ... are baroque, cobbled together by evolution, biological processes, and individual development' (p. 32).

Tom Rice, too, emphasizes diversity in individual effort and creative strategizing that take place within a community of professional practitioners. As an 'honorary observer' and participant among medical trainees in London, Rice, in his research, focuses on the art of auscultation in cardiology. He carefully considers how biological constraints impact the transmission and acquisition of perceptual skills, and how training transforms perceptual apparatuses and modes of attention. Learning to listen and to identify types of heart murmurs form the core of stethoscopic training, and Rice's ethnography throws into relief a field of sensory practice and expertise little explored in anthropology. In contrast to more familiar depictions of the objectifying 'medical gaze', we learn that stethoscopic listening produces a sensation of being penetrated by the patient like a 'sonic draught reaching the head' (p. 46). Learning to tune one's ear to the body is highly individual and, like Downey's *Mestre*, course instructors scaffold students' perceptual enskilment in a variety of imaginative ways that include the use of visual representations for sounds, onomatopoeia, and CDs with audio recordings of murmurs. Medical students and practitioners develop ways for 'talking about' what they hear in order to establish consensus about diagnoses. Rice argues that this also serves to break down the subjective isolation of listening and to reinvent 'the stethoscopic auditory experience as a shared and communal one' (p. 51). As opposed to the homogenizing effect that the habitus purportedly has on the practices of a community (Sinclair 1997), Rice's ethnography demonstrates that perceptual practice is in fact a prime site for the production of difference, and that education in auscultation is an ongoing creative affair.

Like capoeira artists and medical trainees, craft skills are not fixed, but change and develop constantly throughout the lives of practitioners. Anna Portisch's study of *syrmaq* (felt carpet) production among Kazakh women in western Mongolia firmly supports Bernstein's observation that 'practice is a certain type of repetition without repetition' (1967: 134). Scarcity of tools and materials promotes improvisational strategies with things to hand, resulting in changing fashions and styles of the material artefacts; as well as constantly evolving techniques, physical actions, and attitudes. In learning technique, women also importantly learn how to assess their work-in-progress and to make responsive adjustments. Portisch illustrates that processes of evaluation and adjustment are continual and conscious, thereby challenging a central tenet of practice theory: namely that mastered practices are executed unreflectively. Mastery, we are told, is a measure of one's practised ability simultaneously to keep 'several aspects of an execution in one's awareness' (p. 72). The ethnography eloquently conveys how design and form emerge together dialogically *in* the practice of making. The production of decorative domestic textiles, however, is just one activity in the constellation of household chores that women attend to, and craft learning is thoroughly integrated with one's broader social formation as an active, productive member of the family and community. Because it is not carved out as a separate activity within distinct workspaces and timeframes, *syrmaq*-makers do not identify themselves as 'craftspeople'. Rather, like Soumhya Venkatesan's weavers (this volume), craft is merely part of the working schedule and something that women do. Portisch argues, however, that problem-solving strategies forge direct and pervasive relations between women's *syrmaq*-making practices and their surrounding social, material, and natural environment where solutions are sought and found. In this sense, these Kazakh women truly live their craft.

Nicolette Makovicky's comparative study with bobbin lace-makers in Slovakia highlights contrasting attitudes to craftwork and learning. Differing pedagogies, places, and purposes generate discrete practical and conceptual approaches to craft. Among those for whom the craft is essentially an economic enterprise, the intricate techniques of the trade are learned in the home and among kin. There is no formal method, but an apprentice's learning is centred on performing set actions with the bobbins and committing these movements to motor memory through repetitive practice. Makovicky observes that complex tasks are commonly learned by segmenting them into smaller components that can be mastered through repetition and subsequently reassembled in fluid and variegated activities. A maker's experience is gauged by her ability to monitor the progress of the lace without having to look at her hands. And, like Portsich's *syrmaq* production, patterns emerge in practice rather than being created *a priori*. Because of the inherent difficulty of articulating know-how with words, lace-makers produce schematic drawings to communicate movement. The ethnography juxtaposes the craftswomen's use of their drawings with collectors' interpretations of these sketches as 'a "store" or "carrier" of knowledge' (p. 89). The incentive for many collectors is the conservation of tradition, and those who attend evening classes to learn the craft expect instructors to teach skills necessary for reproducing motifs. This pedagogical emphasis on motif is contrasted with the craftswomen's stress on mastering movement, and Makovicky demonstrates how conflicting readings of the drawings as either artefact of knowledge or tool for guiding movement are reflected in the distinctive identities and evaluations of craft in the two communities.

By employing current research on motor cognition, my own study among practising carpenters builds upon dynamic syntax theory (Cann, Kempson & Marten

2005) to develop a model of embodied learning and communication. Neurophysiological theories demonstrate that third-party observers use the 'motor rules' embedded in their individual motor system to simulate the actions they observe. Motor simulation is the 'sense' or 'feeling' of executing an action without necessarily realizing it. In the workshop, for example, this occurs constantly when watching others perform tool-wielding exercises or while reflecting on one's own skilled activities. In other words, the motor system produces 'understanding *from* the body': effectively, understanding by 'doing', or by 'simulating' doing. Motor simulation also forms the basis for both imitation and learning new skills. Based on the premise that 'parsing' an activity, like 'generating' it, is accomplished in the motor domains, I show how both the observer and performer of an activity simultaneously and incrementally construct motor-based representations in the real time of practice. And when the observer's motor-based understanding is successful, his representations closely approximate that of the performer in terms of content and structure. Because this is so, the observer can race ahead to complete his motor simulation of the full activity before it is actually finished by the performer. He therefore may intervene and complete the task, and will do so to the extent that his experience and ability allow, and with a co-ordination of movements that compose his personal 'style'. Our human capacity for motor simulation makes embodied communication possible, and this, I argue, presents infinite opportunity for carrying the social production of skill-based knowledge in new, unforeseen directions.

Processes of knowing and not knowing
The integration of a phenomenological approach to the sensing body (Merleau-Ponty 1962) with other field methods and theories is shared by several authors in this volume. Explorations in the second half, however, are not necessarily located in the sorts of teaching-learning environments described in the first – though several are. Instead the focus here is more specifically on individual processes, strategies, and tactics of knowing – and not knowing – within broader environmental, social and political frames of reference. The idea that 'knowledge' is an ongoing activity rather than an object or definable entity is reinforced; and the chapters illustrate the fact that knowing is inseparable from everyday life and practice.

Becoming knowledgeable is not a matter of assembling information, Tim Ingold argues, but rather knowledge is formed in everyday activities and knowing is coterminous with our movement *through* the world. Ingold's chapter reveals the intrinsic, mutually constitutive relationships between the life-giving ground, the paths along which wayfarers move, and the medium of air, wind, and weather in which we exist. Kantian and Marxist ideas about the meaning and purpose of the 'ground' are discussed and contrasted, and Ingold refutes their respective notions that ground is the 'stage on which the play of our skills proceeds' or 'an instrument of [our] purpose' (p. 117). Taking a phenomenological approach to the issue, he proposes instead that ground is an infinitely variegated surface that is constantly regenerated and coming into being along with its inhabitants. The ground is kinaesthetically perceived and interpreted by walkers, and constitutes one of those 'essential supports for cognition that lie beyond the body and its brain' (p. 129). Footprints made by walkers form impressions that, in turn, are transformed by wind, rain, sun, and other footprints. The 'surface' of our life-world is therefore contrasted with the act of 'surfacing', which carries the intent of creating a hard boundary between what lies below and above, and metaphorically between the material and the mental. 'Wayfaring', too, is distinguished from 'transport', which carries mind and body across the ground and between fixed points on a map. Surface and wayfarer are seminal to Ingold's thesis that knowledge is not 'built' from data acquired at static positions or from carefully selected vantage-points, but 'grows' and changes with human subjects and the world through which they journey.

Like Downey, Konstantinos Retsikas squarely challenges Bourdieu's placement of the habitus entirely beyond the realm of conscious awareness. His study of Indonesian conceptions of personhood and the body demonstrates that principles of ethnic hierarchy are, at some level, manipulated in a knowing manner by Javanese, Madurese, and mixed populations. The chapter sets up an imagined dialogue between Bourdieu and the author's informants about the socially informed body. With rich ethnographic detail, Retsikas shows how concepts of Javanese and Madurese personhood are mutually composed through structured oppositions that can be succinctly summarized by the terms *halus* and *kasar*. These invoke qualities of 'finesse' and 'roughness', respectively, and may be employed to categorize an array of social, cultural, and environmental phenomena, including colour categories and styles of dress; kinaesthetic movements and terrains; tastes and agricultural origins of food; and the aural and oral qualities of speech. Retsikas argues, however, that it is not merely attributes, aesthetics, and practices that distinguish Javanese from Madurese, but more profoundly, the two are 'experienced as having different bodies' (p. 143). In this cultural context, formation of the body and person is believed to precede conception of the foetus, and to be at once social and biological. Indeed, biology is construed within the social, and conflation of the two seriously undermines a theory of habitus that seeks to explain how 'natural equality is transformed into social inequality'. Most provocatively, Retsikas considers the 'lack' of discourse about the mixed Javanese-Madurese population. He proposes that silence around issues of personhood, body, and practice within that group is vested in both a collective desire to objectify others and a conscious resistance to being objectified.

The theme of resistance is carried over in Soumhya Venkatesan's study among mat-weavers in the town of Pattamadai, India. Unlike the craftspeople described in earlier chapters, these individuals do not learn their trade with a passion for becoming 'weavers'. Similar to the village lace-makers in Makovicky's work, weaving is taken up for primarily economic reasons; and in contrast to the prestige gained by mastering auscultation (Rice), mat-weaving bears low status. Weaving, like the rolling of *beedis* (Indian cigarettes), is integral to household economies, and Venkatesan clearly demonstrates why studies of learning need to be in dialogue with an anthropology of work. With reference to Vygotsky's theory of 'proximal development', she describes how learning proceeds in piecemeal fashion devoid of any formalized pedagogy. Girls learn to weave at home through varied combinations of instruction, observation, imitation and 'having a go'. Improvisational problem-solving is enacted through the constant readjustments of actions and movements in response to the loom and materials. More than merely acquiring technical proficiency, regular participation in the activity exposes practitioners to social values and attitudes, and reinforces gendered identities and social class positions. 'Skill is an outcome', Venkatesan observes, 'not a prerequisite' (p. 161), and the skill provides poor women with some form of financial security. In stark contrast to the beautiful mats produced, weaving activity causes an assortment of physical pains and debilitating problems that are emphasized by women in discussing their work. Venkatesan documents the sensitive intervention of an NGO worker who designed an ergonomic loom, but the necessary changes to bodily practices were resisted and Pattamadai weavers quickly resorted to familiar tools and methods.

Roy Dilley's concluding chapter makes an important interjection in the discussion of knowledge by considering its relation to ignorance, and the manner in which both facets are cultivated and transmitted across generations. The chapter considers the ways that knowledge and ignorance are played out in specific social and political frames, and Dilley draws upon his apprenticing fieldwork with Senegalese craftsmen and studies of French colonial officers. He begins by pointing out that, like knowing, *not* knowing takes various forms, and in Western discourses these are subject to ethical evaluation. In the colonial setting of the French Sudan, officers' nescience regarding their surroundings and the local cultures was sometimes a case of simply 'not knowing', but ignorance was also intentionally fostered to keep 'deep-seated prejudices' intact. Early generations of officers relied on empirical experience for their knowledge, but a new breed from the 1920s onward was book-trained before arrival. These different ways of knowing came into conflict, and Dilley shows how claims and accusations of ignorance may be wielded as a 'moral weapon'. By contrast, his studies of craftspeople demonstrate that ways of knowing and *not* knowing are 'a precondition ... for the organization and distribution of relations of learning within specific contexts' (p. 171). Craft skills denote membership within inherited trades, and not having them is normally a function of social position and the local division of labour. Caste group members are believed to possess innate abilities for learning their craft, and those who lack the skill are conceived as 'constitutionally flawed' (p. 175). Dilley justly notes that anthropologists rarely consider what the absence of bodily knowledge entails, and he urges us to balance studies of learning and knowing with more thoughtful contemplations of ignorance.

Finally, in her postscript to the volume, Emma Cohen reiterates the need for anthropology to engage constructively with the expertise and findings of other disciplines in order to develop more robust accounts of knowledge-making practices. In a presentation of her studies with spirit mediums in Belém, Brazil, she addresses the question of how an individual's various forms of knowledge interact and inform one another in the processes of reasoning about possession. Cohen looks to research in human psychology to describe the ways that people's explanatory understandings of apparent contradictions are cognitively constructed, and how they are accommodated in memory. She contends that conventional psychological methods for studying learning and knowledge are relevant to anthropology's long-standing concern with cultural transmission. Neurological accounts, too, are highly significant, but Cohen warns that 'by leaping from culture to brains and back, and bypassing the cognition in between, we risk missing what is happening at the psychological and behavioural levels' (p. 190). Her postscript also poignantly suggests that the body plays a more crucial role in the making of *all* forms of knowledge than what can be revealed through ethnographic observation alone. With reference to emerging research in the cognitive sciences, she writes that what we know is 'reactivated via the partial simulation of the cognitive and bodily states, social interactions, and environmental situations that contributed to its acquisition' (p. 184). This implies that embodied knowledge is more than merely skilled practice and performance, and that the body plays a key role in the making and recall of a wide spectrum of knowledge, including the conceptual kind. If this is so, the need for an analytic framework that accounts for the complex relations of interdependence between minds, bodies, and environment is all the more necessary to our studies of society and culture.

NOTE

[1] See Marchand (2003b) for a discussion of the impact of UNESCO World Heritage status on local craft knowledge and practice in both San'a and Djenné.

REFERENCES

Adenzato, M. & F. Garbarini 2006. The *as if* in cognitive science, neuroscience and anthropology: a journey among robots, blacksmiths and neurons. *Theory & Psychology* **16**, 747-59.

Arbib, M. & G. Rizzolatti 1997. Neural expectation: a possible evolutionary path from manual skills to language. *Communication and Cognition* **29**, 393-424.

Aristotle 2004. *The Nicomachean ethics* (trans. J.A.K. Thompson). London: Penguin.

Astuti, R. 2001. Are we all natural dualists? A cognitive developmental approach. *Journal of the Royal Anthropological Institute* (N.S.) **7**, 429-47.

Atran, S., D. Medin & N. Ross 2006. Thinking about biology: modular constraints on categorization and reasoning in the everyday life of Americans, Maya and scientists. In *Biological and cultural bases of human inference* (eds) R. Viale, D. Andler & L. Hirschfeld, 97-130. London: Routledge.

Barth, F. 2002. An anthropology of knowledge. *Current Anthropology* **43**, 1-18.

Becker, H. 1972. A school is a lousy place to learn anything in. *American Behavioral Scientist* **16**, 85-105.

Bernstein, N.A. 1967. *The co-ordination and regulation of movement*. Oxford: Pergamon.

Bloch, M. 2005. A well-disposed social anthropologist's problem with memes. In *Essays on cultural transmission*, 87-101. Oxford: Berg.

Bourdieu, P. 1977. *An outline of a theory of practice* (trans. R. Nice). Cambridge: University Press.

——— 1990. *The logic of practice* (trans. R. Nice). Stanford: University Press.

Boyer, D. 2005. Visiting knowledge in anthropology: an introduction. *Ethnos* **70**, 141-8.

Boyer, P. 1999. Human cognition and cultural evolution. In *Anthropological theory today* (ed.) H.L. Moore, 206-33. Cambridge: Polity.

——— 2001. *Religion explained: the evolutionary origins of religious thought*. New York: Basic Books.

Cann, R., R. Kempson & L. Marten 2005. *The dynamics of language: an introduction*. Amsterdam: Elsevier.

Churchland, P. & P. Churchland 1998. *On the contrary: critical essays, 1987-1997*. Cambridge, Mass.: MIT Press.

Clark, A. 1997. *Being there: putting brain, body and world together again*. Cambridge, Mass.: MIT Press.

Cosmides, L. & J. Tooby 1994. Origins of domain specificity: the evolution of functional selection. In *Mapping the mind: domain specificity in cognition and culture* (eds) L. Hirschfeld & S. Gelman, 85-116. Cambridge: University Press.

Coy, M.W. (ed.) 1989. *Apprenticeship: from theory to method and back again*. Albany, N.Y.: SUNY Press.

Crick, M. 1982. Anthropology of knowledge. *Annual Review of Anthropology* **11**, 287-313.

D'Andrade, R. 1995. *The development of cognitive anthropology*. Cambridge: University Press.

Dilley, R. 1989. Secrets and skills: apprenticeship among Tukolor weavers. In *Apprenticeship: from theory to method and back again* (ed.) M.W. Coy, 181-98. Albany, N.Y.: SUNY Press.

Downey, G. 2005. *Learning capoeira: lessons in cunning from an Afro-Brazilian art*. Oxford: University Press.

——— 2007. Seeing with a 'sideways glance': visuomotor 'knowing' and the plasticity of perception. In *Ways of knowing: new approaches in the anthropology of experience and learning* (ed.) M. Harris, 222-41. Oxford: Berghahn.

Dyck, N. & E. Archetti 2003. Embodied identities: reshaping social life through sport and dance. In *Sport, dance and embodied identities* (eds) N. Dyck & E. Archetti, 1-19. Oxford: Berghahn.

Edelman, G.F. 1992. *Bright air, brilliant fire: on the matter of the mind*. London: Penguin.

Fodor, J. 1983. *The modularity of mind*. Cambridge, Mass.: MIT Press.

——— 2000. *The mind doesn't work that way: the scope and limits of computational psychology*. Cambridge, Mass.: MIT Press.

Goody, E. 1989. Learning, apprenticeship and the division of labour. In *Apprenticeship: from theory to method and back again* (ed.) M.W. Coy, 233-56. Albany, N.Y.: SUNY Press.

GRASSENI, C. 2007. Good looking: learning to be a cattle breeder. In *Skilled visions: between apprenticeship and standards* (ed.) C. Grasseni, 47-66. Oxford: Berghahn.

HALLAM, E. & T. INGOLD 2007. Creativity and cultural improvisation: an introduction. In *Creativity and cultural improvisation* (eds) E. Hallam & T. Ingold, 1-24. Oxford: Berg.

HANKS, W.F. 1991. Foreword. In *Situated learning: legitimate peripheral participation*, J. Lave & E. Wenger, 13-24. Cambridge: University Press.

HARRIS, M. 2007. Introduction: ways of knowing. In *Ways of knowing: new approaches in the anthropology of experience and learning* (ed.) M. Harris, 1-24. Oxford: Berghahn.

HERZFELD, M. 1995. It takes one to know one: collective resentment and mutual recognition among Greeks in local and global contexts. In *Counterworks: managing the diversity of knowledge* (ed.) R. Fardon, 127-45. London: Routledge.

——— 2004. *The body impolitic: artisans and artifice in the global hierarchy of value*. London: University of Chicago Press.

——— 2007. Deskilling, 'dumbing down' and the auditing of knowledge in the practical mastery of artisans and academics: an ethnographer's response to a global problem. In *Ways of Knowing: new approaches in the anthropology of experience and learning* (ed.) M. Harris, 91-110 Oxford: Berghahn.

HIRSCHFELD, L. 2006. *Race in the making: cognition, culture, and the child's construction of human kinds*. Chicago: University Press.

INGOLD, T. 2000. Evolving skills. In *Alas poor Darwin: arguments against evolutionary psychology* (eds) H. Rose & S. Rose, 225-46. London: Jonathan Cape.

——— 2001. From the transmission of representations to the education of attention. In *The debated mind: evolutionary psychology versus ethnography* (ed.) H. Whitehouse, 113-53. Oxford: Berg.

——— 2008. Anthropology is *not* ethnography (Radcliffe-Brown Lecture in Social Anthropology, March 14, 2007). *Proceedings of the British Academy* **154**, 69-92.

JEANNEROD, M. 1994. The representing brain: neural correlates of motor intention and imagery. *Behavioral and Brain Sciences* **17**, 187-245.

——— 2006. *Motor cognition: what actions tell the self*. Oxford: University Press.

LAKOFF, G. & M. JOHNSON 1999. *Philosophy in the flesh: the embodied mind and its challenge to Western thought*. New York: Basic Books.

LAUGHLIN, C.D., E. D'AQUILI & J. McMANUS 1990. *Brain, symbol and experience: toward a neurophenomenology of consciousness*. New York: Columbia University Press.

LAVE, J. & E. WENGER 1991. *Situated learning: legitimate peripheral participation*. Cambridge: University Press.

LEE, J. & T. INGOLD 2006. Fieldwork on foot: perceiving, routing socializing. In *Locating the field: space, place and context in anthropology* (eds) S. Coleman & P. Collins, 67-85. Oxford: Berg.

MARCHAND, T.H.J. 2001. *Minaret building and apprenticeship in Yemen*. Richmond, Surrey: Curzon.

——— 2003*a*. A possible explanation for the lack of explanation; or 'Why the master builder can't explain what he knows': introducing informational atomism against a 'definitional' definition of concepts. In *Negotiating local knowledge* (eds) J. Pottier, A. Bicker & P. Sillitoe, 30-50. London: Pluto.

——— 2003*b*. Process over product: case studies of traditional building practices in Djenné, Mali, and Sanʿa, Yemen. In *Managing change: sustainable approaches to the conservation of the built environment* (eds) J.M. Teutonico & F. Matero, 137-59. Los Angeles: Getty Conservation Institute and Trus Publications.

——— 2007*a*. Crafting knowledge: the role of 'parsing and production' in the communication of skill-based knowledge among masons. In *Ways of knowing: new approaches in the anthropology of experience and learning* (ed.) M. Harris, 181-202. Oxford: Berghahn.

——— 2007*b*. Vocational migrants and a tradition of longing. *Traditional Dwellings and Settlements Review* **XIX**, 23-40.

——— 2008. Muscles, morals and mind: craft apprenticeship and the formation of person. *British Journal of Educational Studies* **56**, 245-71.

——— 2009. *The masons of Djenné*. Bloomington: Indiana University Press.

——— in preparation. *The pursuit of pleasurable work: studies in the art of furniture making*.

MARTIN, E. 2000. AES Presidential Address: mind-body problems. *American Ethnologist* **27**, 569-90.

MASON, P. 2007. Paul Mason on neuroanthropology defined (available on-line: *http://neuroanthropology.wordpress.com/2007/12/27/paul-mason-on-neuroanthropology-defined/*, accessed 5 January 2010).

MERLEAU-PONTY, M. 1962. *Phenomenology of perception* (trans. C. Smith). London: Routledge.

O'CONNOR, E. 2005. Embodied knowledge: the experience of meaning and the struggle towards proficiency in glassblowing. *Ethnography* **6**, 183-204.

PELISSIER, C. 1991. The anthropology of teaching and learning. *Annual Review of Anthropology* **20**, 75-95.

PURVER, M. & R. KEMPSON 2004. Incrementality, alignment and shared utterance. *Proceedings of the 8th Workshop on the Semantics and Pragmatics of Dialogue* (Catalog), 85-92.

PUTNAM, H. 1988. *Representation and reality*. Cambridge, Mass.: MIT Press.

RAPPORT, N. & M. HARRIS 2007. A discussion concerning ways of knowing. In *Ways of knowing: new approaches in the anthropology of experience and learning* (ed.) M. Harris, 306-30. Oxford: Berghahn.

RETSIKAS, K. 2008. Knowledge from the body: fieldwork, power and the acquisition of a new self. In *Knowing how to know: fieldwork and the ethnographic present* (eds) N. Hollsteid, E. Hirsch & J. Okely, 110-29. Oxford: Berghahn.

RIZZOLATTI, G. & L. CRAIGHERO 2004. The mirror-neuron system. *Annual Review of Neuroscience* **27**, 169-92.

———, L. FOGASSI & V. GALLESE 2001. Neurophysiological mechanisms underlying the understanding of actions. *Nature Reviews Neuroscience* **2**, 661-70.

SACKS, O. 1996. *An anthropologist on Mars*. London: Picador.

SEARLE, J. 1998. *Mind, language and society: philosophy in the real world*. New York: Basic Books.

SINCLAIR, S. 1997. *Making doctors: an institutional apprenticeship*. Oxford: Berg.

SPERBER, D. 1994. The modularity of thought and the epidemiology of representations. In *Mapping the mind: domain specificity in cognition and culture* (eds) L. Hirschfeld & S. Gelman, 39-67. Cambridge: University Press.

——— 2001. Mental modularity and cultural diversity. In *The debated mind: evolutionary psychology versus ethnography* (ed.) H. Whitehouse, 23-56. Oxford: Berg.

STOLLER, P. 1989. *The taste of ethnographic things: the senses in anthropology*. Philadelphia: University of Pennsylvania Press.

TOREN, C. 1993. Making history: the significance of childhood cognition for a comparative anthropology of mind. *Man* (N.S.) **28**, 461-78.

TURNER, V. 1983. Body, brain and culture. *Journal of Religion and Science* **18**, 221-45.

VARELA, F.J., E. THOMPSON & E. ROSCH 1991. *The embodied mind: cognitive science and human experience*. Cambridge, Mass.: MIT Press

WACQUANT, L. 2004. *Body and soul: notebooks of an apprentice boxer*. Oxford: University Press.

WHITEHOUSE, H. 1996. Jungles and computers: neuronal group selection and the epidemiology of representations. *Journal of the Royal Anthropological Institute* (N.S.) **2**, 99-116.

——— 2001a. Introduction. In *The debated mind: evolutionary psychology versus ethnography* (ed.) H. Whitehouse, 1-20. Oxford: Berg.

——— 2001b. Conclusion: towards a reconciliation. In *The debated mind: evolutionary psychology versus ethnography* (ed.) H. Whitehouse, 203-33. Oxford: Berg.

WILSON, F.R. 1998. *The hand: how its use shapes the brain, language and human culture*. New York: Pantheon.

1

'Practice without theory': a neuroanthropological perspective on embodied learning

GREG DOWNEY *Macquarie University*

Apprentices of the Afro-Brazilian danced martial art capoeira – an art said also to develop practitioners' cunning and savvy – learn primarily through imitation, along with bodily exercises and physical experimentation. They copy the movements of veteran players, haltingly at first, but with increasing animation and integrity. Teaching is primarily mimetic rather than analytic or explicit. If a novice asks too many questions, more than an instructor believes helpful (the threshold is usually quite low), a teacher will remind the student to be silent, watch closely, and imitate. During my field research in Brazil, if we interrupted *Mestre* ('Teacher') Moraes with too much questioning, he shouted, *Embora!* ('Get on with it!'); or, if feeling generous, he might stop us: *Olhe* ('Look here'). He demonstrated more slowly for those who had failed to catch a technique, punctuating his motions for emphasis at crucial moments with meaningless syllables, *Au ... au ... au ...*

With its acrobatic kicks, sly headbutts, low-to-the-ground dodges, and flamboyant ornamental moves, or *floreios*, capoeira stands out as an especially demanding form of embodied knowledge, apprenticeship necessitating not simply the acquiring of techniques or skills but a whole body transformation in strength, flexibility, mobility, perhaps even personality. Pursued intentionally through specialized training in adolescence or adulthood, the art contrasts in many ways with the (to the practitioner, at least) unremarkable daily habits and gestures that make up the habitus, as discussed by Pierre Bourdieu. Nevertheless, the shared mimetic forms of learning in both capoeira and more mundane corporeal techniques, and the influence of bodily training on capoeiristas' perceptions, suggest that the confrontation between the style of movement taught in capoeira and the everyday habitus might highlight how embodied knowledge shapes the subject. Practitioners repeatedly asserted that learning capoeira movements affected a person's kinaesthetic style, social interactions, and perceptions outside of the game (see Downey 2005b).

This chapter specifically explores how imitative learning occurs in capoeira, and sports, dance, and bodily practice more generally, and the psychological, neurological, and physical consequences of acquiring bodily knowledge. Although capoeira may be

an extreme example, the art illustrates how enculturation entails biological development, and demonstrates the neurological complexity of imitative learning. Recent
research in psychology and neurosciences allows us to attempt a neuroanthropological account of the cultural tuning of imitative learning. This biocultural study of
corporeal mimesis helps to place anthropological accounts of enculturation on a
more certain footing, but it also demands that we modify our portrayal of habitus or
embodied knowledge (or whatever we call the product of bodily enculturation),
allowing that the habitus might not be as consistent, simple, or transferable as some
accounts, including Bourdieu's own, might suggest. A neuroanthropological account
of mimesis, however, opens up an opportunity to converse across boundaries
between anthropology and such disciplines as psychology, cognitive science, and
neurology, both to integrate new findings and to assert our interest in cultural
particularity and diversity.

Bourdieu argued that practical, bodily action instilled, and was guided by, a
socially generated habitus, a 'structuring structure' internalized through interaction
with people and the physical environment. In *The logic of practice*, Bourdieu writes:
'The conditionings associated with a particular class of conditions of existence
produce the habitus, systems of durable, transposable dispositions, structured structures predisposed to function as structuring structures, that is, as principles which
generate and organize practices and representations' (1990a: 53; see also 1977). The
habitus, in Bourdieu's model, is history made flesh, a corporeal enculturation that
assures social and symbolic continuity while underwriting an individual's sense of
autonomy.[1]

With the habitus, Bourdieu attempts to overcome the dichotomy between objectivism and subjectivism in social theory, 'the scholastic dilemma of determinism and
freedom' (2000: 131). For anthropologists struggling to reconcile a tradition of conceptualizing both society and culture as structure with a growing disciplinary interest in
individual agency, the habitus has offered an attractive way to operationalize structure,
to suggest that everyday action is both strategic and yet imprinted with the actor's past,
and thus society's history (see Ortner 1984). The habitus offers an alternative to concepts like 'culture', 'ideology', 'hegemony', or 'cognitive structure', an alternative
grounded more in corporeality and quotidian activity.

Yet, when we look more closely, the habitus concept as articulated by Bourdieu leaves
certain key questions about embodied knowledge unexplored. Whereas Bourdieu was
primarily concerned with bridging problems of scale – between the individual and
social structures, history, or culture – the close analysis of bodily enculturation requires
that we also consider the gap between biology and culture, to explore links between
experience and our organic nature. Joseph Margolis (1999: 69), for example, criticizes
Bourdieu for failing to identify the 'microstructure' of habitus. Margolis warns that
there is 'a certain slackness' in Bourdieu's discussion (1999: 68): 'But if we ask *what* the
habitus is, what the telling features of its functioning structures are, what we get from
Bourdieu is a kind of holist characterization that never comes to terms with its operative substructures' (1999: 69, original emphasis). A vague psychology at the centre of the
subject may unnecessarily undermine a practice-based account of socialization; as
Anthony King describes, '[T]he overwhelming bulk of Bourdieu's work is informed
directly by the habitus' (2000: 418).

On closer examination, everyday practices, dispositions, skills, and perceptual
systems do not behave precisely like some of the more simplistic models of the habitus,

specifically those that assume bodily activities arise from a set of structural oppositions or are coherent across a range of activities. Ironically, one obstacle to the study of embodied knowledge can be an overarching concept like the habitus, if it leads researchers to consider corporeality only as a theoretical solution to other social and political questions rather than as a site for close examination. The advantage to close biocultural study, however, is that it also tends to buttress the concept of the habitus against the criticism that it is overly deterministic, fails to explain change, or cannot account for variation.

I begin by discussing virtuoso imitation in my field research on capoeira. The example suggests that to ground the habitus psychologically and biologically, we must not just describe what the embodied knowledge *does* but seek to understand how it *comes to be* through an apprenticeship in bodily practices. Because the ethnographic case is an intercultural setting – capoeira in New York City – it highlights that imitation is a 'significant bottleneck' in cultural transmission, as Oliver Goodenough (2002: 573) argues. Imitative learning can race ahead of other forms of understanding, so we need better to understand its role in shaping perception and cognition, as the body's ability to imitate limits the type of learning that occurs in mimesis. The observed developmental trajectories of capoeira expertise clash with any deterministic concept of habitus by undermining the assumption that practice progresses uniformly, as if generated by a single structure. Capoeira apprenticeship, instead, chips away at areas of bodily movement style or *hexis*, sometimes without changing overall attitudes, but other times as part of a gradual, but ultimately profound transformation. Taken as a whole, this neuroanthropological consideration of skill-learning compellingly demonstrates that the area can be a departure point for integrative research on the consequences of enculturation.

Virtuoso imitation in New York

When I moved to New York City, I looked forward to practising capoeira in the academy of Mestre João Grande, a legendary teacher, the *mestre* of my *mestre* in Brazil. Since the 1970s, capoeira has spread from Salvador throughout Brazil and internationally, with teachers now working in nearly every major North American and European city, and in places as far flung as Finland, Israel, Japan, Australia, Argentina, Mozambique, South Korea, and Singapore. Ironically, owing to the art's globalization, moving from Salvador, my primary field site and the symbolic cradle of capoeira, to Manhattan actually brought me closer to the living embodiment of Afro-Brazilian tradition, climbing the genealogy of master-disciple transmission.

João Grande spoke little English; Brazilians reported that, on occasion, his terse, deeply accented rural dialect of Portuguese was difficult even for native speakers to understand. The taciturn *mestre* taught primarily through demonstration, gesturing and physically manipulating his students' bodies directly with delicate tugs on their trouser cuffs or wrists. Students watched closely and did their best to copy his intricate combinations, some of which he communicated only with idiosyncratic hand gestures.

Deep cultural divides complicated the transmission of embodied knowledge. João Grande had Brazilian students, but he also taught African Americans, white Americans, Europeans, recent immigrants from the Caribbean, Latin America, and Africa, and even a contingent of devoted Japanese practitioners, some of whom spoke virtually no English or Portuguese. Mimetic channels in João Grande's classes were often isolated from other modes of learning; players simply dived into the practice, following the examples offered by more experienced players, at times barely grasping even the names of movements let alone any more detailed explanation.

One young American, however, posed the paradox of mimesis most sharply. James[2] had become astonishingly proficient in a few short years, developing a subtle 'old school' style, something other practitioners labour unsuccessfully for much longer to acquire, even in Brazil. James spoke only a handful of Portuguese words, although he spent many hours with the *mestre*. In spite of the obstacles, James had not merely learned capoeira; he had adopted João Grande's odd head bobs, distinctive straight-legged steps, sudden jerky movements and shoulder wobbles, a hoarse, tight-throated singing style, even elements of the *mestre*'s dress, such as wearing leather work shoes and a fisherman's cap when he played. Whether intentionally or not, James had acquired the kinaesthetic quirks and signature gestures of his teacher.[3] All the idiosyncratic traits made James's discipleship instantly legible to a knowledgeable observer; he was a kind of motor reincarnation of his teacher. Through virtuoso mimesis, James had incorporated forms of moving, gestures, and habits across all practical, linguistic, and cultural obstacles.

Mimetic learning and imitation

Bourdieu clearly posts that the acquisition of embodied knowledge – skills, habits, and a 'sense of the game' (1977) – is a central issue in his agenda for the sociology of sports:

> The problems raised by the teaching of a bodily practice seem to me to involve a set of theoretical questions of the greatest importance, in so far as the social sciences endeavour to theorize the behaviour that occurs, in the greatest degree, outside the field of conscious awareness, that is learnt by a silent and practical communication, from body to body one might say (1990b: 166).

Bourdieu repeatedly argues that behaviour in activities like sports is learned through mimesis, that this learning is 'silent and practical', unconscious and purely mimetic, without awareness or other channels of communication.[4] He often seems to focus predominantly on the question of consciousness. In a convoluted section of *The logic of practice*, Bourdieu elaborates a distinction between 'imitation' and 'mimesis' on the basis of conscious intention:

> [T]he process of acquisition [of habitus] – a practical *mimesis* (or mimeticism) which implies an overall relation of identification and has nothing in common with an *imitation* that would presuppose a conscious effort to reproduce a gesture, an utterance or an object explicitly constituted as a model – and the process of reproduction – a practical reactivation which is opposed to both memory and knowledge – tend to take place below the level of consciousness, expression and the reflexive distance which these presuppose. The body believes in what it plays at: it weeps if it mimes grief. It does not represent what it performs, it does not memorize the past, it *enacts* the past, bringing it back to life. What is 'learned by body' is not something that one has, like knowledge that can be brandished, but something that one is (Bourdieu 1990a: 73, original emphasis).

In this passage, Bourdieu alludes to the profound transformation of bodily learning, that what is 'learned by the body' is 'something that one is'. Although he does not use biological language, this chapter argues that, in fact, embodied knowledge can involve forms of material change to the body, an avenue in which past training becomes corporeal condition. Bourdieu even rehearses non-dualistic forms of thinking about embodiment when he rejects bodily 'representation' and describes the transformative power of training, a way in which we might explore the biocultural mangle of development. But in trying to characterize the distinctiveness of corporeal learning, contrasting conscious and non-conscious forms of imitation, Bourdieu insists upon a pernicious hard division between propositional and embodied learning, one that, ironically, paints practice theorists into a corner when observing skill education.

Bourdieu repeatedly insists that habitus is necessarily non-conscious and inarticulable, in marked contrast to declarative memory, and that bodily knowledge is acquired without intention or awareness. I have elsewhere argued that many forms of physical education, like capoeira, are neither so quiet nor closed to reflection; in fact, capoeira classes can be quite raucous, and the best teachers 'scaffold' students' imitation with diverse techniques that reveal sophisticated practical awareness of how to facilitate mimesis (Downey 2008).[5] By Bourdieu's definition, if they are conscious, learned movements cannot be part of the habitus, even though they may confront, even transform, key habits, postures, or characteristics of habitus.

Bourdieu's insistence on non-consciousness is in keeping with the more widespread observation in studies of motor learning that, even with the overt intention to learn, skill *itself* cannot be rendered as explicit, declarative knowledge. As Bourdieu writes, 'There are heaps of things that we understand only with our bodies, outside conscious awareness, without being able to put our understanding into words ... Very often, all you can do is say: "Look, do what I'm doing" ' (1990b: 166). Because he represents imitative learning as a non-conscious 'silent and practical communication, from body to body', Bourdieu suggests that mimesis is related to 'practice without theory', a phrase he borrows from Émile Durkheim (in Prendergast 1986: 7). But why is he so emphatic that transmission must not be conscious when we can observe in many forms of bodily training that the body must be brought into and out of consciousness in order to focus upon a technique before it becomes automatized (see Leder 1990)?

The portrait of mimesis 'without theory' or conscious intention is a hallmark of 'practice theory'. Practice theorists, following on the example of Bourdieu (1990a: 74), assert that a kind of practical mimesis allows a set of corporeal schemes 'to pass directly from practice to practice without moving through discourse and consciousness', so that they are liable neither to mistaken transmission nor to principled or practical opposition (see, e.g., Krais 1993). The habits acquired through mimesis are essential to accounts of embodied socialization because they are typically treated as the foundation for an agent's perceptions, strategies, and 'common sense' (see also Throop & Murphy 2002: 188). So, although it is 'without theory', the habitus serves to inculcate subconscious intellectual values, systems of categorization, and perceptual schemas, all very 'theoretical'; Bourdieu 'overcomes' the dichotomy between structure and agency by insisting that the agent is non-consciously structured.

Although I single out Bourdieu's model of the habitus, models of practical mimesis serve as a channel of socialization throughout much of social thought. Stephen Turner (2002: 61-4; see also 1994: 44) highlights how Max Weber, Gabriel Tarde, James Mark Baldwin, and George Herbert Mead all employed imitation in social theory. Turner identifies a broad stream of theorists deploying 'practice' theory, including Oakeshott, Polanyi, Ryle, Gadamer, and Rorty (Turner 1994: 2-3). Imitation even figures prominently in evolutionary theories of behaviour, such as Richard

Dawkins's (1976: 206) notion of 'memes', with bits of culture treated as if self-replicating through imitation.

The turn in contemporary anthropological theory toward bodily practice, away from culture as social rules, or purely cognitive or semiotic structure, is a salutary development for those interested in apprenticeship, skill, and practical knowledge, but it has not always been accompanied by careful attention to physical education or physiological change. The under-theorization of mimesis is part of a tendency to neglect enculturation, as Robert LeVine (1999) suggests, perhaps because of aversion to psychology or person-centred theoretical models. What we find in capoeira is that bodily learning can bring to conscious light some of the movement traits, postures, and tendencies that may have once been unconscious, but become problematized in transformative apprenticeship. As the novice seeks to imitate new styles of moving, one of the central obstacles he or she must confront is unconscious patterning, unexamined inhibition, and corporeal reservations that are only apparent when challenged by new kinaesthetics. When we examine the biological consequences of training, we can recognize other forms of embodied learning that may not involve passing subconscious cognitive structures; rather, training may demonstrably affect physiological change in the brain, nervous system, bones, joints, sensory organs, even endocrine and autonomic systems. Transformation of the habitus is not simply changing an underlying 'structure' but altering the organic architecture of the subject.

Imitation without intention

One of the reasons that imitation is under-explored is that the ability is so pervasive and unproblematic for humans; as Michael Tomasello (1999: 159) describes, children are 'imitation machines', seeming to imitate without difficulty. In their studies of infants, psychologists Andrew Meltzoff and Keith Moore (1977; 1983; 1989) documented basic forms of imitation within hours of birth. Richard Byrne and Anne Russon (1998: 667) point out that imitation was long considered an intellectual 'cheap trick', characteristic of animals, children, savages, and the mentally deficient. Something so effortless needs little explanation.

Although we seem to be well suited for it, however, the ethological evidence suggests that imitation is anything but easy. More than a century ago, Edward Thorndike (1898) observed that many species learn by inductive trial-and-error processes; virtually no animals other than humans, however, do so by extensive imitation. Aside from certain birds talented in vocal mimicry (perhaps easier because one hears both the model and one's own calls), and a few limited cases with primates and social animals, over a century of research on imitation has borne out Thorndike's observations. Ethologists disagree about what constitutes imitation (or what distinguishes it from 'emulation') and to what extent other animals demonstrate some potential. All researchers agree, however, that no other species even approaches humans' ability (see, e.g., Caldwell & Whiten 2002; Galef 1988; Heyes & Galef 1996; Hurley & Chater 2005; see also Donald 1991).

Psychologists studying imitation identify the 'correspondence problem' as the challenge of matching a visual image of what someone else does with a pattern of motor control (see Brass & Heyes 2005; Bruner 1972). Any animal that copies an action must somehow figure out which muscles to use and how, translating visual perception of another into a kinaesthetic formula for acting. At the same time, the animal must recognize what another intends to do and ascertain relevant input from the environment. Judging from other species, the correspondence problem is more daunting than we realize.

In capoeira instruction, teachers are aware that imitation is a challenge and use a wide range of techniques to scaffold students' imitation. A partial list includes: slowing down the model movement; parsing the target technique into component gestures; shifting between facing-toward and facing-away models; offering verbal formulae to aid sequence recall; physically manipulating the students' bodies; artificially limiting a student's degrees of freedom; abstracting parts of a technique; creating meaningless movement drills to teach basic component gestures; making an interacting player's actions fixed in drills, and many more, some invented on the spot (see Downey 2008). The more difficulty a student has, the more resourceful a skilled instructor can be. As psychologists David Wood, Jerome Bruner, and Gail Ross (1976: 89) recognize, our species' remarkable ability to learn derives not merely from our intelligence as learners, but also from our skill as teachers.

Even so, the remarkable mimetic ability of our species demands greater explanation. How do humans learn by imitation so readily when so few other species seem to do so? Social, developmental, perceptual, and even motor factors contribute to our ability to imitate, but humans' extraordinary imitative ability also appears to be facilitated by our neural architecture, specifically the strong likelihood that one's own actions, the perceived actions of others, and imagined actions are all represented in the brain in similar fashion, using neural systems that substantially overlap. That is, we may perceive others' actions as meaningful by converting them into first-person simulations, with significant consequences for intersubjective relations among people. Mimetic learning may be 'without theory', at least in part, because we perceive using neural resources that substantially overlap with those used to act, shortening significantly the leap from seeing to doing, 'reading' other people's actions at least in part with our own sense of movement. In other words, motor perception is inherently, neuroarchitecturally, intersubjective.

The neural 'common coding' of action and perceived action was hypothesized by William James (1890), but increasingly evidence from a range of fields, including brain imaging studies, neuropathology, behavioural psychology, and child development, is converging to support his hypothesis. For example, studies of 'chameleon behavior' in psychology find that people are 'primed' to act by simply observing another act, and that they sometimes unconsciously mimic actions that they observe (see Bargh, Chen & Burrows 1996; Chartrand & Bargh 1999). Likewise, 'interference' between observed and attempted actions, the chance that seeing someone do an action will confuse a person doing another, different action, also suggests that these two functions share a common form of representation in the brain (Brass, Bekkering & Prinz 2001; see also Blakemore & Frith 2005).

Theories of common motor and perceptual coding are sometimes referred to as 'ideomotor' (James) or 'simulation' (Gallese) approaches to motor perception (see Gallese 2005; James 1890; Jeannerod 1994; Prinz 1990). The plausibility of ideomotor or simulation neural theories of imitation received a substantial boost in the 1990s with the discovery of 'mirror neurons', specific individual neurons in macaques that are active when both performing and seeing an action (see Rizzolatti & Craighero 2004). Later neuroimaging data strongly indicate that similar systems exist in humans and are involved in imitation (see Iacoboni 2005; Iacoboni *et al.* 1999). Although controversy dogs some of the more sweeping generalizations about the functions of mirror neurons, imitative learning seems to be one of the most convincingly demonstrated spheres of their activity (see, e.g., Buccino *et al.* 2004).

If the neural mechanisms underlying imitative learning involve the common coding of action with perception of action, this severely undermines the plausibility of an overarching global habitus either generating action or being engendered by practice. As Wolfgang Prinz (1990) asserts in his discussion of the common coding hypothesis, the competing, standard model of perception and action, dominant since Descartes (and opposed to the ideomotor theory), is that perception and action are fundamentally separate, with the necessity of some overarching framework – what Jerry Fodor (1975; 1987) has called a 'language of thought' – or an intervening, separate level of mental representations to translate between them.

According to Bourdieu, the habitus, although embodied and unconscious, is a constellation of 'cognitive structures which social agents implement in their practical knowledge of the social world as internalized, embodied social structures' (1984: 468, cited in King 2000: 423). In other words, they are one's social position internalized cognitively as dispositions to act in status-appropriate ways. In *Pascalian meditations*, Bourdieu explains that '[t]he specific logic of a field is established in the incorporated state in the form of a specific habitus, or, more precisely, a sense of the game, ordinarily described as a "spirit" or "sense" ... which is practically never set out or imposed in an explicit way' (2000: 11). The 'most characteristic operations' of the habitus are 'movements of the body, turning to the right or left, putting things upside down, going in, coming out, cutting, typing' (1977: 116) – simple everyday movements and actions. And yet the habitus is a system of dispositions that categorizes and divides things 'into logical classes which organiz[e] the perception of the social world' (1984: 170); or, as Bourdieu elsewhere puts it, the 'schemes of habitus' are 'very generally applicable principles of vision and division' (1990a: 139).

Although he insists it is a 'practical systematicity' (and 'without theory'), Bourdieu keeps lapsing, even if only metaphorically, into abstract terms because he seeks to describe this generative system as removed from and superordinate to the actual practices. As he writes, borrowing the linguist concept, '[H]abitus is a generative grammar' (2002: 30). In summary, although Bourdieu repeatedly asserts that the habitus is embodied and unconscious, a system of socially arranged learned instincts developed through bodily practice, the habitus behaves in many of his metaphorical discussions as an implicit cognitive structure or system of categories; this mode of description suggests a model of perception and action in which the two are not commonly coded, but rather linked by a separate, unifying cognitive structure (other than the body or nervous system itself). I would argue that the use of theory-like metaphors to talk about practices that are 'without theory' may result from the simple lack of an alternative language; incorporating more biology may simply clean up a distinction that Bourdieu clearly wants to make.

Ideomotor theories argue that imitation is achieved easily because perceptions of motor activity are accomplished by simulating the same motion with minimal intervening complexity or superordinate cognitive structure. Vittorio Gallese and George Lakoff (2005: 456) describe how, in contrast, classical models of cognition draw a sharp distinction between perceptual input and active output in the brain. Similarly, the model of the habitus suggests that some *other*, higher-order abstraction must be involved in generating action, and this structure must be inculcated through mimetic training. If motor activities are perceived directly by the same parts of the brain used to execute motor action, and in the same 'language', as ideomotor models suggest, they have no need for any sort of other unconscious ideational or cognitive structure; we have true 'practice without theory'. The only problem is that the habitus from this perspective is not nearly so globally unified or easily characterized; it may be liable to partial change; and it may be susceptible to conscious examination. The ideomotor perspective does not detract from the importance of mimetic learning, but from the assumption that there must be a simple categorization-like structure expressed in practice.

Ironically, Oliver Goodenough argues, the ease with which humans learn by imitation indicates that imitation is likely a 'significant bottleneck in what can be passed on culturally' (2002: 573). Imitation may be easy, but it is 'superficial', consisting of action itself. Psychologist Cecilia Heyes reports that recent behavioural experiments and neurological evidence suggest that 'symbolic mediation is unnecessary … for imitation learning' (2005: 172-3). Since action is perceived *as* action and reproduced without translation into some other, abstracted neural representation, imitation is likely not a good channel to transmit implicit structures, hidden premises, or shared presuppositions (see also Turner 1994). Goodenough explains: 'This action-to-action step in the transmission process creates a very narrow doorway through which human culture must pass, a true bottleneck' (2002: 575-6).[6] Heyes goes so far as to conclude that the evidence of ideomotor supports for imitation makes mimesis 'unlikely to provide a basis for cultural exchange' (1993: 999).

If practice is learned through imitation – if it is truly 'without theory' – then we likely neither incorporate an underlying cognitive structure when we perceive movement, nor do we need one to execute action. This argument takes us to the biocultural heart of the habitus, what it is, how it could come to be, and how it might help us to explain human activity.

Habitus as embodied knowledge

The 'imitation bottleneck' is a formidable ontological and developmental obstacle for any account of the habitus, but the concept is certainly worth salvaging with a more robust model of enculturation, one including other channels of communication, even the conscious ones that Bourdieu is at such great pains to deny. However, we are still confronted with the problem of systematicity, a trait that I find inconsistent with neurological evidence of how motor learning occurs and the complexity of neural perceptual-motor processes. Ironically, Bourdieu has come under criticism for asserting the homogeneity of the habitus from a range of other perspectives, even though he resolutely defended his position.

For example, Bourdieu highlights the unity and systematicity of the habitus, insisting that it is radically simpler than the behaviour and strategies it engenders, in one of his last accounts of the concept:

> [T]he habitus of a determinate person – or of a group of persons occupying a similar or neighbouring position in social space – is in a sense very systematic: all the elements of his or her behaviour have something in common, a kind of affinity of *style*, like the works of the same painter or, to take an example from Maurice Merleau-Ponty, like the handwriting of a person who keeps her style, immediately recognizable, when she writes with instruments as diverse as a pencil, a pen or a piece of chalk and on media as different as a sheet of paper and blackboard. To this example gives a concrete intuition of this systematicity. It is not a logical systematicity; it is a practical systematicity (2002: 28, original emphasis).

He goes on to offer as an example the unified 'lifestyle' of the bourgeoisie, in which speech, finances, and love all follow the same principle (2002: 29). In his ethnographic writing about Algeria, Bourdieu argues that the habitus is 'a system of durable, transposable dispositions which functions as the generative basis of *structured, objectively unified* practices' (1979: vii, emphasis added). An agent's actions are made by the habitus, which is not merely a haphazard assemblage of dispositions, but rather a coherent system. When Bourdieu uses the habitus concept to analyse sociological and ethnographic data – for example, in his discussion of the Kabyle house (e.g. 1990a: 271-83) – the simplicity of the habitus and its ability to generate an utterly systematized dualistic worldview of male and female, light and dark, east and west, closely resembles a structural analysis (as other critics have pointed out).

In my ethnographic research, capoeira practitioners described something very much like the habitus in the art, an implicit 'sense of the game' that practitioners allegedly develop through apprenticeship. Although practitioners disagreed about many things, they were relatively unanimous in arguing that the *fundamento*, or 'secret foundational matter', of capoeira is *malícia*, or 'cunning'.[7] *Malícia* is a kind of streetwise savvy, an opportunistic eye, a gift for evasion and trickery, and a playful ability to overcome dangers in everyday life (see Downey 2005b: 123-5ff.; Lewis 1992: 49). One could very easily call it a capoeira 'lifestyle', an attitude used to confront many dimensions of life. When Mestre Nestor Capoeira describes *malícia*, like Bourdieu, he claims it is practical, learned mimetically, and unified: Nestor calls *malícia* 'non-rational, lived, experiential knowledge' (2002: 24).

> Its basic theme is: within this 'valley of tears,' inside this cruel jungle that is our world, the capoeira player has an inner psychological structure and a vision of life, as well as the practical means for his economic survival ... that will permit him to take and enjoy the best that life has to offer (2002: 20).

The acquisition of *malícia* also resembles Bourdieu's account of the habitus. Over the course of apprenticeship, according to Nestor, the player 'begins to accept' *malícia* as a guiding principle, even though non-conscious,

> in the roda [ring] when playing with his colleagues, in his relationship with his teacher, and in his daily life 'outside' capoeira. He begins to feel (and I mean 'to feel' and not 'to think rationally') all of that as a part of the reality of life (which he did not see, or did not want to see or accept before) (2002: 19).

Malícia is neither explicitly taught nor learned, according to Nestor, although the movements and playing techniques themselves are intentionally acquired:

> It is realized by playing the game with different players, inside the roda to the sound of the berimbau [the principal musical instrument in capoeira], over the years. It's not something that can be rationalized. It's not something that can be understood by the mind, although it is, itself, a form of understanding. It is, yes, a living, experiencing, absorbing, digesting, incarnating (1992: 121-2).

Other Brazilian observers have also noted links between comportment, class position, and worldview in capoeira, much like the habitus, even describing the practitioners' distinctive swaying gait as a sign of an opportunistic flair for living among *malandros*, cunning 'rogues' of the lumpen-proletariat who survived on their wits (see Downey

2005*b*: 127-33). *Malícia* would seem to be an ideal analogy to the habitus, even if it is learned later in life than everyday movements: class-based, embodied, flexible, social opportunities internalized, and admittedly opaque or immune to articulation as a philosophy even if practitioners were eloquently evocative.

But, here's the rub. Was James, this prodigious mimic in New York City, becoming more *malícioso*, or cunning, as he developed into a virtuoso physical performer? Of course, an observer cannot say for certain; the best way to conceal one's *malícia* would be to feign innocence. But I did not observe heightened wariness or cunning in anything he said or did outside the capoeira *roda*. The same traits that made him such a quick study and exemplary student – his diligence, patience, dedication, humility, work ethic, and sharp-eyed attention to detail – still shone through.

Even the optimistic, spiritualist Mestre Nestor Capoeira acknowledges that some players become exemplary physical practitioners without developing a *malícioso* outlook on life. Others who have very weak physical techniques and a limited movement repertoire seem to play above their level with extraordinary cunning. During my field research in Brazil, some capoeira *mestres* lamented that their students, who played capoeira only in academies, did not develop the overall outlook on life of practitioners of old, who became savvy and streetsmart because they played in dangerous open, public *rodas* and had to survive on their wits.

As I survey my memory of practitioners, I find inconsistency across their achievement: one was good mostly at fast games, lousy at slow; another played solidly but without much flair; another was a sly composer of songs but overly nervous if pressed aggressively during a game; a novice who quickly mastered certain moves struggled with others. Capoeiristas recognize variety and inconsistency in practice. They recognize that some inhibitions give way faster than others, that practice takes hold in fits and starts. Some students simply never got that good, even though they had the same opportunities to learn and train. Proficiency was hardly uniform, nor was it gained at a single gulp, as if generated by a single schema.

In other words, Bourdieu insists that the habitus is a single, simple generative principle that creates practice; the unevenness of learning, the slow pace, inconsistency, and piecemeal acquisition of techniques in capoeira suggests a much more complex, diffuse process, even if it is only that the obstructing unconscious habitus gives way unevenly to attempts at its transformation. Expertise in capoeira was as varied as the experts, never mind the incomplete forms of bodily knowledge owned by those who gave up or stalled along the way. The 'sense of the game' in capoeira is diversified, slowly acquired. This 'sense', or, more accurately, 'senses', includes a range of abilities and tasks: learned reaction patterns to another's movements; visual attention, including during difficult tasks like acrobatic movements; joint mobility and muscular strength; heightened susceptibility to particular stimuli, such as musical rhythms, and the ability to deal with competing stimuli, such as feints or distractions; cardio-vascular endurance, including techniques for self-control, even the ability to surrender control of bodily pacing and tension to the orchestra; and a 'sense' for the dramatic or humour that takes various forms. Players learn in idiosyncratic fashions and fail to learn in equally idiosyncratic fashion. Teachers do things in diverse ways, some of them more effective for some students than others. Mestre Pastinha argued that *cada qual é cada qual*: 'each one is each one', capoeira skill was unique, peculiar to the practitioner.

In summary, the ideomotor theory of movement, neurological evidence, and the ethnographic demonstrations of uneven bodily transformation suggest that a person's habitus is likely composed of a great diversity of motor skills, in places weakly coupled, some of them characteristic of different social positions and learning experiences. 'The' habitus for capoeira is actually a concrete set of perceptual-motor skills and modifications to the organic body. Different practitioners acquire them unevenly. Moreover, many skills take a long time to acquire because they actually necessitate physiological change: stronger muscles, greater flexibility, more acute perceptual-motor ability, and slowly developed, incrementally learned patterns of behaviour. As recent research in neurosciences continues to reveal, perceptual and motor learning entail physiological change (see, e.g., Paz, Wise & Vaadia 2004).

Theories of modularity or modularization in the brain, known principally in anthropology through the work of Noam Chomsky (see 1988), also imply that a unified structure of thought is unlikely (see Fodor 1983; 2000).[8] When one studies carefully how the brain and body work, one finds organs that do not need to simplify complex processes into generative structures, or require top-down control by over-arching schemes to produce emergent consistency. As psychologist Annette Karmiloff-Smith suggests, human 'development does not seem to be a drive for economy' (1992: 23). The notion of a unified structuring structure is elegantly modernist and functional; the human brain and body, however, are baroque, cobbled together by evolution, biological processes, and individual development. The brain has redundant, conflicting structures. Rather than a single structuring structure, the brain appears to be full of what Andy Clark (1989: 69) has called 'kludges', systems that look messy and inefficient from a design perspective. Effort is changed into ability only over time and through gradually accumulating change, and it may have a very narrow range of application.

In an example I have discussed elsewhere (Downey 2007), the visual system consists of several circuits that do not share all the information that they produce, nor do they operate according to the same principles (Jacob & Jeannerod 2003). For example, the dorsal visual pathway for motor control and the ventral visual pathway, which allows for object recognition and conscious visual awareness, do not share all information; this is why a person can duck to avoid a flying object without recognizing what it was. Conversely, the dorsal pathway, although it orientates action, does not provide information for long-term memory as readily as the ventral object recognition system. Training may affect one system more than another, even parts of a system rather than the whole. Some parts of these visual systems only respond to specific sorts of stimuli: for example, mirror neurons only activate when viewing organic movements that one has learned, not when observing robotic simulations of the same actions.

Brain modularization suggests that cognitive schemas, if they do exist, likely cannot affect all motor and perceptual activity. Everyday automatic activity, perceptions, and unconscious dispositions – precisely the sort of activity that the habitus allegedly explains – are among the *poorest* candidates for a unifying treatment (consciousness, in contrast, might be a domain-general function). Therefore, to compile diverse training, skills, and perceptual abilities into a single 'structured structure predisposed to function as a structuring structure' reduces observed complexity and discontinuity. Instead of a unified, abstract habitus, we observe cultural diversity in development, affecting different biological systems in a range of ways. How training would affect our visual system, for example, with its distinct channels, is an empirical question liable to research; because we are investigating the effects of diverse forms of enculturation, ethnography and careful attention to cross-cultural variation are an essential part of that research.

'Embodied knowledge' in place of 'habitus'

Ian Hunter and David Saunders (1995) offer a fascinating discussion of Claude Lévi-Strauss's introduction to the works of Marcel Mauss. According to Hunter and Saunders, Lévi-Strauss reads Mauss's discussion of bodily techniques as incomplete because Mauss did not find the 'unconscious mental structures' which gave rise to the diversity of techniques (Lévi-Strauss 1987: 49, cited in Hunter and Saunders 1995: 67). Lévi-Strauss thinks that Mauss's work is 'merely a preliminary procedure'; in contrast, Hunter and Saunders recognize that Mauss is 'resolutely non-dialectical'. Flying in the face of later practice theory, Mauss writes that 'those human attributes we call "bodily" and "mental" have no essential relation to each other. No relation of identity or opposition, of unity or difference' (cited in Hunter & Saunders 1995: 69). Not that the 'bodily' and 'mental' have *no* relation, but just that they not no *essential* relation; depending on the bodily technique, they may have quite complex relations, but these are heterogeneous, diverse, reversible, and require empirical study.

Our path forward, if we recognize that the habitus may in fact be incompletely unified and heterogeneous like the brain, is to extend the radical restraint that Mauss exhibited, to patiently work out the connections between individual 'bodily' and 'mental' attributes in greater detail. We will find pockets of continuity, recurring systems that have their own consistency, but they will likely not be on the level of the whole body; they will be issues like the imitation bottleneck, modular systems that tend to do certain sorts of tasks, with greater and lesser degrees of plasticity.

In other words, I do not advocate that we replace the 'habitus' with a better concept; the evidence I cite suggests that embodied knowledge is crucial for all the reasons Bourdieu identified, even though it is not as unified as he sought to argue. Bourdieu overcame the theoretical dualism between subjective action and objective social structure, spanning the gap in scale between the individual's actions and social reproduction. His subtle descriptions of the role of bodily learning avoid body-mind dualism, but he fails to incorporate any evidence of organic or psychological processes, so we are still left with a bloodless, nerveless abstract 'body', a continual problem for exclusively cultural discussions of embodiment. As Tim Ingold has argued, '[S]kills are literally embodied, in the sense that their development entails specific modifications in neurology, musculature, and even in basic features of anatomy' (2000: 375). Close attention to skill acquisition holds out the promise of integrating biological and cultural approaches to enculturation, placing the discussion of habitus on a solid foundation. Far from 'biological determinism', a kind of cultural-biological dynamism prevails when we recognize that gene expression in muscles depends upon their use, that skills training modifies the body's neural systems, and that such basic traits as bone density and composition are affected by behaviour patterns.[9]

Conclusion

Instead of simply asserting that culture is 'embodied', we should engage actively with those disciplines – human biology, functional morphology, neurosciences, cognitive and neuropsychology – that specifically study the human body, its malleability, and the material dimensions of learning processes. In those fields, we can ally ourselves with scholars who recognize the complexity and dynamism of human organic development, as Marchand suggests in his introduction to this volume. The study of sports, dance, musical apprenticeship, and similar physical practices makes clear that skill is not simply the 'embodiment' of 'knowledge', but rather physical, neurological, perceptual, and behavioural change of the individual subject so that he or she can accomplish tasks that, prior to enskilment, were impossible. If anthropological discussions of 'embodied knowledge' contend with humans' organic nature, we will better integrate social and cognitive theory and may bring anthropological concerns to a much wider audience interested in the social conditioning of the brain. As research in the neurosciences yields abundant evidence of the fine tuning of the nervous system by experience, we find opportunities to enlarge concepts like the habitus to include insights from other disciplines that study the subject from a variety of perspectives. We must be open to the possibility, however, that even key concepts may require significant modification as a result of the exchange.

Unfortunately, this retrenching of theoretical ambitions, the renunciation of generalized structuring structure like 'habitus', may make the resulting analysis appear superficial, the theorizing insufficiently bold. To talk about habitual bodily tension, postural muscle and its relation to stress, looking behaviour such as visual scanning patterns, socialization and forms of social interaction, invites the criticism that the theorizing is shallow, pedestrian, disorderly. As Lévi-Strauss writes about Mauss, his careful analysis of 'miscellaneous' bodily techniques could be transcended: '[I]t was a matter of distinguishing a purely phenomenological given, on which scientific analysis has no hold, from an infrastructure simpler than that given, to which the given owes its whole reality' (Lévi-Strauss 1987: 41, cited in Hunter & Saunders 1995: 67). Relinquishing Lévi-Strauss's assertion of a single infrastructure, however, reveals an immense space of heterogeneous 'operative substructures', some of them neurological, that we might fruitfully study.

In fact, what underlies the diversity of practices is not a cognitive 'infrastructure simpler than that given' but the culturally malleable biological structure that was there all along: the human body itself, including the complicated neural systems that turn experience into physiology and perception. The 'deep structuring' of practice is a deep enculturation of specific bodily systems. For example, training in capoeira shifts the sensory channels that a person draws upon to balance, develops top-down techniques for relaxing muscles and diffusing tension, and fashions behavioural patterns that bring previously unnoticed sensory information to awareness (habits of looking around suspiciously, for instance).

Although Bourdieu's theory of the habitus focuses attention on bodily habits, skills, and non-discursive modes of knowing, it does so in service to other intellectual ends: to explain social class or dispel the dichotomy between structure and agency, for example. In contrast, the study of embodied knowledge as deep enculturation of the body can take these practices as research objects themselves, bringing together biological and cultural approaches, just as Bourdieu brought together sociological scale processes with individual subjectivity. This requires psychologically plausible accounts of skill development and engagement with those fields that take the body as their object of study (see Downey 2005a).

Anthony King has argued that the habitus is not a satisfactory account of how subjectivity arises, that Bourdieu's discussion of mimesis, as he puts it, casts 'a shroud of deadening objectivism over living interactions between virtuosic individuals' (2000: 429). If we do not seek to expand the account of enculturation beyond the brief discussions by Bourdieu, King is right; we satisfy ourselves with a cursory account of motor learning, skill acquisition, perceptual training, social interaction and other subtle forms of cultural learning. Moreover, we assume that mimesis happens – unconsciously, invariably, unproblematically, and without error. Automatic and unexamined mimesis as a social theory rules out the possibility of error, failure, idiosyncrasy, or unintentional innovation in the process of each novice's guided discovery of skills. In fact, these occur all the time in our ethnographic research.

To return to Bourdieu's discussion of mimetic learning, and to the notion of 'practice without theory', in *The logic of practice*, he writes: 'What is "learned by body" is not something that one has, like knowledge that can be brandished, but something that one is' (1990a: 73). 'Embodied knowledge' *is* the body, the organic entity modified by behaviour, training, and experience, deeply encultured. Bourdieu did not realize how revolutionary his formulation was for biocultural approaches to enculturation; his attention was focused elsewhere. Calling this transformation 'habitus' or treating it as cognitive structure only postpones this recognition. Skill learning is not the internalization of a shared 'sense' or transmission of a reified cultural structure. Rather, enskilment is the patient transformation of the novice, the change of his or her muscles, attention patterns, motor control, neurological systems, emotional reactions, interaction patterns, and top-down self-management techniques. Opening up the habitus to exploration, recognizing that it is a stand-in for the organic body, filling in some of the substructures, allows us to explore the baroque, diverse, and surprising channels through which culture in training takes hold of us all.

NOTES

This piece was prepared with support from the Richard Carley Hunt Fellowship from the Wenner-Gren Foundation for Anthropological Research, Inc. (GR 7414). I want to thank especially Trevor Marchand, Daniel Lende, Richard Fardon, Laurie Frederik, John Sutton, and a sharp-eyed anonymous reviewer for their engagement over questions of learning, coaching, and embodied knowledge.

[1] See Anthony King's (2000) discussion of the relation of the habitus concept to Bourdieu's 'practical theory'. This paper leans heavily on readings of King, as well as Crossley (2001), Margolis (1999), and Throop & Murphy (2002) for its discussion of imitation in Bourdieu's work.

[2] This student's name is a pseudonym. Masters are referred to by their public names (*apelidos*).

[3] Some of the movement traits that James adopted were also a result of changes in João Grande's body, such as ongoing problems with arthritis in his knees. Students of João Grande who worked with the *mestre* earlier often did basic techniques differently. James was so capable of imitation that he was acquiring traits of João Grande's body, such as the effects of ageing on his mobility; the communication between the two transformed João Grande's physiology into James's 'embodied culture'. This example highlights the difficulty of treating bodily development and skill training as forms of 'culture' or 'knowledge', as these are typically understood.

[4] This discussion of imitative learning has very little to do with the discussion of mimesis in the work of such theorists as Walter Benjamin (1968 [1936]; 1986 [1933]), Theodor Adorno (1984), Max Horkheimer (Horkheimer & Adorno 2002), Michael Taussig (1993), Homi Bhabha (1984), and Paul Stoller (1995). For these thinkers, the dominant archetypes for understanding mimesis are theatre, semiosis, sympathetic magic, or mass production rather than imitative learning. Although these innovative discussions of cultural mimesis have inspired significant insights, they leave unexplored the practical and perceptual capacities that lie at the core of human mimesis.

[5] Although socio-cultural learning theorists typically trace their perspective to the work of Lev Vygotsky (esp. 1978), Wood, Bruner & Ross (1976) were the first to use the term 'scaffolding'. On pedagogic scaffolding, see also Bliss, Askew & Macrae (1996), Downey (2008), and Pea (2004).

[6] In fact, Goodenough's argument is a much broader one about 'cultural replication'. He insists, ' "Ideas" as such do not replicate – there is no direct brain to brain link that allows the transmission of the internalized information structure' (2002: 574). However, he does not question whether this might undermine the notion of an 'internalized information structure'.

[7] This definition of *fundamento* is from Paul Johnson's (2002: 4) discussion of the Afro-Brazilian religion Candomblé.

[8] Part of the reason modularity is resisted in anthropology is the adoption of the term by evolutionary psychologists (for a critique, see Fodor 2000). Trevor Marchand has been especially helpful in expanding my understanding and awareness of the debate about modularity.

[9] On gene expression in muscles, see Halayko & Solway (2001) and Vogel (2001); on bone structure and composition, see Fausto-Sterling (2005).

REFERENCES

ADORNO, T.W. 1984. *Aesthetic theory* (trans. C. Lenhardt). London: Routledge & Kegan Paul.

BARGH, J.A., M. CHEN & L. BURROWS 1996. Automaticity of social behavior: direct effects of trait construct and stereotype activation on action. *Journal of Personality and Social Psychology* **71**, 230-44.

BENJAMIN, W. 1968 [1936]. The work of art in the age of mechanical reproduction. In *Illuminations: essays and reflections* (trans. H. Zohn), 217-51. New York: Schocken Books.

——— 1986 [1933]. On the mimetic faculty. In *Reflections* (trans. E. Jephcott), 333-6. New York: Schocken Books.

BHABHA, H. 1984. Of mimicry and man: the ambivalence of colonial discourse. *October* **28**, 125-33.

BLAKEMORE, S.-J. & C. FRITH 2005. The role of motor contagion in the prediction of action. *Neuropsychologia* **43**, 260-7.

BLISS, J., M. ASKEW & S. MACRAE 1996. Effective teaching and learning: scaffolding revisited. *Oxford Review of Education* **22**, 37-61.

BOURDIEU, P. 1977. *Outline of a theory of practice* (trans. R. Nice). Cambridge: University Press.

——— 1979. *Algeria 1960* (trans. R. Nice). Cambridge: University Press.

——— 1984. *Distinction: a social critique of the judgement of taste* (trans. R. Nice). London: Routledge & Kegan Paul.

——— 1990*a*. *The logic of practice* (trans. R. Nice). Stanford: University Press.

——— 1990*b*. *In other words: essays towards a reflexive sociology* (trans. M. Adamson). Stanford: University Press.

——— 2000. *Pascalian meditations* (trans. R. Nice). Stanford: University Press.

——— 2002. Habitus. In *Habitus: a sense of place* (eds) J. Hillier & E. Rooksby, 27-34. Burlington: Ashgate.

BRASS, M., H. BEKKERING & W. PRINZ 2001. Movement observation affects movement execution in a simple response task. *Acta Psychologica* **106**, 3-22.

——— & C. HEYES 2005. Imitation: is cognitive neuroscience solving the correspondence problem? *Trends in Cognitive Science* **9**, 489-95.

BRUNER, J.S. 1972. Nature and use of immaturity. *American Psychologist* **27**, 687-708.

BUCCINO, G., S. VOGT, A. RITZL, G.R. FINK, K. ZILLES, H.-J. FREUND & G. RIZZOLATTI 2004. Neural circuits underlying imitation learning of hand actions: an event-related fMRI study. *Neuron* **42**, 323-34.

BYRNE, R.W. & A. RUSSON 1998. Learning by imitation: a hierarchical approach. *Behavioral and Brain Sciences* **21**, 667-721.

CALDWELL, C.A. & A. WHITEN 2002. Evolutionary perspectives on imitation: is a comparative psychology of social learning possible? *Animal Cognition* **5**, 193-208.

CAPOEIRA, N. 1992. *Capoeira: os fundamentos da malícia*. Rio de Janeiro: Editora Record.

——— 2002. *Capoeira: roots of the dance-fight-game*. Berkeley: North Atlantic Books.

CHARTRAND, T.L. & J.A. BARGH 1999. The chameleon effect: the perception-behavior link and social interaction. *Journal of Personality and Social Psychology* **76**, 893-910.

CHOMSKY, N. 1988. *Language and problems of knowledge*. Cambridge, Mass.: MIT Press.

CLARK, A. 1989. *Microcognition*. Cambridge, Mass.: MIT Press.

CROSSLEY, N. 2001. The phenomenological habitus and its construction. *Theory and Society* **30**, 81-120.

DAWKINS, R. 1976. *The selfish gene*. Oxford: University Press.

DONALD, M. 1991. *Origins of the modern mind: three stages in the evolution of culture and cognition*. Cambridge, Mass.: Harvard University Press.

DOWNEY, G. 2005*a*. Educating the eyes: biocultural anthropology and physical education. *Anthropology in Action: Journal for Applied Anthropology in Policy and Practice* **12**: 2, 56-71.

———— 2005b. *Learning capoeira: lessons in cunning from an Afro-Brazilian art*. New York: Oxford University Press.

———— 2007. Seeing without knowing, learning with the eyes: visuomotor 'knowing' and the plasticity of perception. In *Ways of knowing: new approaches in the anthropology of knowledge and learning* (ed.) M. Harris, 222-41. New York: Berghahn Books.

———— 2008. Scaffolding imitation in capoeira training: physical education and enculturation in an Afro-Brazilian art. *American Anthropologist* **110**, 204-13.

FAUSTO-STERLING, A. 2005. The bare bones of sex: part 1 – sex and gender. *Signs: Journal of Women in Culture and Society* **30**, 1491-527.

FODOR, J. 1975. *The language of thought*. Cambridge, Mass.: Harvard University Press.

———— 1983. *The modularity of mind: an essay on faculty psychology*. Cambridge, Mass.: MIT Press.

———— 1987. *Psychosemantics: the problem of meaning in the philosophy of mind*. Cambridge, Mass.: MIT Press.

———— 2000. *The mind doesn't work that way: the scope and limits of computational psychology*. Cambridge, Mass.: MIT Press.

GALEF, B.G., Jr 1988. Imitation in animals: history, definition, and interpretation of data from the psychological laboratory. In *Social learning: psychological and biological perspectives* (eds) T.R. Zentall & B.G. Galef, Jr, 3-28. Hillsdale, N.J.: Erlbaum.

GALLESE, V. 2005. Embodied simulation: from neurons to phenomenal experience. *Phenomenology and the Cognitive Sciences* **4**, 23-48.

———— & G. LAKOFF 2005. The brain's concepts: the role of the sensory-motor system in conceptual knowledge. *Cognitive Neuropsychology* **22**, 455-79.

GOODENOUGH, O.R. 2002. Information replication in culture: three modes for the transmission of culture elements through observed action. In *Imitation in animals and artifacts* (eds) K. Dautenhahn & C.L. Nehaniv, 573-85. Cambridge, Mass.: Bradford Books (MIT Press).

HALAYKO, A.J. and J. SOLWAY 2001. Plasticity in skeletal, cardiac, and smooth muscle: invited review: molecular mechanisms of phenotypic plasticity in smooth muscle cells. *Journal of Applied Physiology* **90**, 358-68.

HEYES, C.M. 1993. Imitation, culture and cognition. *Animal Behavior* **46**, 999-1010.

———— 2005. Imitation by association. In *Perspectives on imitation: from neuroscience to social science*, vol. 1: *Mechanisms of imitation and imitation in animals* (eds) S. Hurley and N. Chater, 157-76. Cambridge, Mass.: Bradford Book (MIT Press).

———— & B.G. GALEF, Jr (eds) 1996. *Social learning in animals: the roots of culture*. San Diego: Academic Press.

HORKHEIMER, M. & T.W. ADORNO 2002. *Dialectic of enlightenment: philosophical fragments* (ed. G.S. Noerr; trans. E. Jephcott). Palo Alto, Calif.: Stanford University Press.

HUNTER, I. & D. SAUNDERS 1995. Walks of life: Mauss on the human gymnasium. *Body & Society* **1: 2**, 65-81.

HURLEY, S. & N. CHATER (eds) 2005. *Perspectives on imitation: from neuroscience to social science*, 2 vols. Cambridge, Mass.: Bradford Books (MIT Press).

IACOBONI, M. 2005. Neural mechanisms of imitation. *Current Opinion in Neurobiology* **15**, 632-7.

————, R.P. WOODS, M. BRASS, H. BEKKERING, J.C. MAZZIOTTA & G. RIZZOLATTI 1999. Cortical mechanisms of human imitation. *Science* **286**, 2526-8.

INGOLD, T. 2000. *The perception of the environment: essays in livelihood, dwelling and skill*. London: Routledge.

JACOB, P. & M. JEANNEROD 2003. *Ways of seeing: the scope and limits of visual cognition*. New York: Oxford University Press.

JAMES, W. 1890. *Principles of psychology*. New York: Holt.

JEANNEROD, M. 1994. The representing brain: neural correlates of motor intention and imagery. *Behavioral and Brain Sciences* **17**, 187-245.

JOHNSON, P.C. 2002. *Secrets, gossip, and gods: the transformation of Brazilian Candomblé*. Oxford: University Press.

KARMILOFF-SMITH, A. 1992. *Beyond modularity: a developmental perspective on cognitive science*. Cambridge, Mass.: MIT Press.

KING, A. 2000. Thinking with Bourdieu against Bourdieu: a 'practical' critique of the habitus. *Sociological Theory* **18**, 417-33.

KRAIS, B. 1993. Gender and symbolic violence: female oppression in light of Pierre Bourdieu's theory of social practice. In *Bourdieu: critical perspectives* (eds) C. Calhoun, E. LiPuma & M. Postone, 156-77. Chicago: University Press.

LEDER, D. 1990. *The absent body*. Chicago: University Press.

LÉVI-STRAUSS, C. 1987. *Introduction to the work of Marcel Mauss* (trans. F. Baker). London: Routledge & Kegan Paul.

LEVINE, R.A. 1999. An agenda for psychological anthropology. *Ethos* **27**, 15-24.

LEWIS, J.L. 1992. *Ring of liberation: deceptive discourse in Brazilian capoeira*. Chicago: University Press.

MARGOLIS, J. 1999. Pierre Bourdieu: habitus and the logic of practice. In *Bourdieu: a critical reader* (ed.) R. Shusterman, 64-83. Oxford: Blackwell.

MELTZOFF, A.N. & M.K. MOORE 1977. Imitation of facial and manual gestures by human neonates. *Science* **198**, 75-8.

———— & ———— 1983. Newborn infants imitate adult facial gestures. *Child Development* **54**, 702-9.

———— & ———— 1989. Imitation in newborn infants: exploring the range of gestures imitated and the underlying mechanisms. *Developmental Psychology* **25**, 954-62.

ORTNER, S. 1984. Theory in anthropology since the sixties. *Comparative Studies in Society and History* **26**, 126-66.

PAZ, R., S.P. WISE and E. VAADIA 2004. Viewing and doing: similar cortical mechanisms for perceptual and motor learning. *Trends in Neurosciences* **27**, 496-503.

PEA, R.D. 2004. The social and technological dimensions of scaffolding and related theoretical concepts for learning, education, and human activity. *Journal of the Learning Sciences* **13**, 423-51.

PRENDERGAST, C. 1986. *The order of mimesis: Balzac, Stendhal, Nerval, Flaubert*. Cambridge: University Press.

PRINZ, W. 1990. A common coding approach to perception and action. In *Relationships between perception and action* (eds) O. Neumann & W. Prinz, 167-201. Berlin: Springer-Verlag.

RIZZOLATTI, G. & L. CRAIGHERO 2004. The mirror-neuron system. *Annual Review of Neuroscience* **27**, 169-92.

STOLLER, P. 1995. *Embodying colonial memories: spirit possession, power, and the Hauka in West Africa*. London: Routledge.

TAUSSIG, M. 1993. *Mimesis and alterity: a particular history of the senses*. New York: Routledge.

THORNDIKE, E. 1898. Animal intelligence: an experimental study of the associative process in animals. *Psychological Review and Monograph* **2**, 551-3.

THROOP, C.J. & K.M. MURPHY 2002. Bourdieu and phenomenology: a critical assessment. *Anthropological Theory* **2**, 185-207.

TOMASELLO, M. 1999. *The cultural origins of human cognition*. Cambridge, Mass.: Harvard University Press.

TURNER, S.P. 1994. *The social theory of practices: tradition, tacit knowledge, and presuppositions*. Chicago: University Press.

———— 2002. *Brains/practices/relativism: social theory after cognitive science*. Chicago: University Press.

VOGEL, S. 2001. *Prime mover: a natural history of muscle*. New York: Norton.

VYGOTSKY, L.S. 1978. *Mind in society: the development of higher psychological processes* (eds M. Cole, V. John-Steiner, S. Scribner & E. Souberman). Cambridge, Mass.: Harvard University Press.

WOOD, D., J.S. BRUNER & G. ROSS 1976. The role of tutoring in problem solving. *Journal of Child Psychology and Psychiatry* **17**, 89-100.

2

Learning to listen: auscultation and the transmission of auditory knowledge

TOM RICE *University of Exeter*

How do we learn to listen? I became interested in this question whilst conducting ethnographic fieldwork at St Thomas' Hospital in London. The research was a continuation of a previous study that explored the acoustic dynamics of hospital life, focusing on patients' experiences of ward soundscapes at the Edinburgh Royal Infirmary (Rice 2003). Broadening the scope of that inquiry, the study at St Thomas' set out to examine the various ways in which medical professionals use and apply auditory knowledge in a modern clinical setting. I was granted Honorary Observer status by the Guy's and St Thomas' NHS Hospital Trust, and so was allowed to observe a wide variety of clinical interactions. Stethoscopic listening, however, stood out as a striking example of an acoustic technique which many medics use daily in their work.

The sounds that doctors interpret using auscultation could be understood as the acoustic traces of bodily processes. The pivoting and rotation of bones in their joints, the movement of matter through the gut and water across the kidneys, for instance, all create noises which, to a trained ear, describe the condition and functioning of the body. The muscular action of the heart, the movement of blood through its vessels and chambers, and the flow of air in and out of the lungs generate a variety of sounds that are of value in assessing the state of the cardiovascular system. Auscultation is therefore particularly useful in this area of medicine. I spent much of my fieldwork in the Cardiothoracic Unit at St Thomas' shadowing doctors and observing their interactions with patients. I became increasingly interested in learning to listen, and, by adopting an apprenticeship-style methodology (e.g. Stoller 1989; Wacquant 2004), began participating in classes in which medical students were introduced to the auscultation of the heart.

The students with whom I studied were in their third year of medical school. While the time taken to qualify as a doctor varies depending on a person's route through the education system and the structure of their particular course, the students I came to know expected their medical training to take five years. Classes during the first two years (known as the 'pre-clinical' or sometimes the 'pre-cynical' years) generally take the form of lectures and tutorials. The emphasis is on anatomy and on the necessary aspects of chemistry and biology for understanding the constitution, function, and treatment of the body within a Western medical framework. Having completed their pre-clinical training, the subjects of my study were embarking on three 'clinical years', during which the focus is on sessions of supervised contact with patients on the hospital wards. They would be introduced to the procedures and techniques necessary for their future work as doctors. Auscultation was one such technique.

The students sometimes remarked that while the 'pre-clinical' phase of their education had, broadly speaking, been orientated towards 'brain work', the 'clinical' years would be devoted to 'body work'. In making this essentially Cartesian distinction, students were drawing attention to what they perceived to be two different kinds of knowledge that were in the process of transfer in the two educational stages. The classroom/lecture theatre years generally involve the passing on of information – theoretical, factual, and schematic – while the final three years, characterized by 'situated learning' in the clinical setting (Lave & Wenger 1991), are more concerned with the transmission of practical skills. The students were also demonstrating awareness of the fact that while medical work is directed towards the patient's body, it also implicates the doctor's body, or in their case, that of the medical student. Competence in diagnosis and in the management and administration of care demands well-honed senses and practised skills. Auscultation requires a carefully trained sense of hearing and an acute sensitivity to sound. The students would have to become attentive listeners in order to be good doctors.

In his book *Making doctors*, Simon Sinclair (1997), himself a qualified doctor-turned-anthropologist, presents a study of medical training based on fieldwork conducted among students at London's University College Hospital, where he himself studied. He describes classes in which students encounter a range of different clinical techniques, including auscultation. His aim is to show how these techniques and the pedagogies which teaching doctors bring to them serve to articulate wider 'dispositions' (Bourdieu 1980: 54) – attitudes which structure the practical and ideological approach that doctors, individually and collectively, take towards reality. These dispositions are themselves constituents of an integrated medical 'habitus' (Bourdieu 1980: 60). Sinclair sees medical school as a process through which that habitus is reproduced in new generations of doctors.

My research aims to reveal the detail and complexity of a practice which might otherwise be subsumed by, or regarded as merely another technique embedded within, a more encompassing medical habitus. By focusing on the sensory complexities of auscultation, I respond to Downey's anxiety (this volume, voiced through Margolis 1999: 68) that crucial particularities of embodied knowledge may be engulfed or obscured by the 'slackness' of habitus as a conceptual structure. By challenging the sorts of presumptions about bodily uniformity which allow Sinclair, for example, to position medical students as vessels or blanks in and through whom the medical habitus is regenerated, I explore how schemes of perception are assimilated in diverse ways by those who encounter them. Perceptual abilities and aptitudes vary, meaning that creativity and resourcefulness are continually demanded of teachers and students alike.

The ethnographies of Feld (1996), Gell (1995), and Weiner (1991) focus on sound and auditory knowledge among the Kaluli, Umeda, and Foi, respectively, and their work is of particular relevance to my interest in the ways in which stethoscopic listening is learned. These anthropologists each observe and describe complex structured engagements with the sonic environment. Feld, for example, illustrates how an understanding of the ways in which Kaluli people engage with the layered soundscape of their forest habitat (produced by moving water, birdsong, and insects) is crucial for comprehending the nature of their intertwined language, topography, aesthetics, and cosmology (Feld 1990; 1991; 1996; 2003).

All three authors produce fascinating accounts concerning the importance of sound in the lives of the communities they study, and convey how informants hear their worlds. Feld produces especially evocative passages, describing how Kaluli terms such as 'lift-up-over sounding' capture the distinctive acoustic texture of the Bosavi rainforest (1996: 100). In a sense, the combination of his writings and recordings offer the reader/listener a lesson in how to hear like a Kaluli. Feld is also proactive in documenting his own processes of learning to listen as ethnographer and sound-recorder. He describes how he would play his forest soundscape recordings to his informants, allowing them to twiddle the knobs of the cassette player, creating 'an ethnoaesthetic negotiation' through which he was able to begin to understand how the Kaluli hear 'the dimensionality of forest sound, how they would balance a mix of birds, water, cicadas, voices and so forth' (Feld & Brenneis 2004: 467).

'Ethnographies of sound' tell us a great deal about how communities attach salience and meaning to particular sounds and categories of sounds (Gell 1995: 233). They show the manner in which sensory knowledge develops through ongoing interaction with the environment. Feld writes: 'One knows the time of day, season of year, and placement in space through the sensual wraparound of sound in the forest' (1996: 100). He continues: 'This way of sensing and hearing the world is internalized as bodily knowledge, part of the everyday "body hexis" (Bourdieu 1977: 8), the naturalized regime of "body techniques" (Mauss 1979 [1935]) basic to routine Kaluli encounters in their world' (1996: 100). Yet Feld's use of Bourdieu obscures a great deal that might be of value to a person interested in the teaching and learning of auditory knowledge. What particular perceptual skills does this 'body hexis' involve, and in exactly what ways is it reproduced among individuals or across generations? Feld's analysis also positions shared ways of knowing through sound as apparently unproblematic, unaffected by differences of perceptual sensitivity or interpretation. It is tempting to ask: what issues are presented at an individual and societal level for a person born deaf or hard of hearing into such an 'auditory culture' (Gell 1995: 236)?

Despite having been described as 'medicine's acoustic culture' (Sterne 2003: 191), it is clear that auscultation does not represent a system of auditory knowledge of the depth or complexity of those described in the above examples. Indeed, the technique might be said to be firmly embedded in the 'visualist' culture which some anthropologists consider the West in general (e.g. Classen 1998; Tyler 1984) and Western biomedicine in particular (e.g. Draper 2002; Foucault 1973) to represent. Medical students will not learn to auscultate in the same way that, for instance, Kaluli acquire the 'naturalized regime of "body techniques"' which constitute their way of 'sensing and hearing the world' (Feld 1996: 100). Yet perhaps because it is encountered in adulthood, and because it situates listening as a conscious act that requires reflection and necessitates attempts at articulation, auscultation might represent a practice in which the dynamics of a kind of auditory skill can be accessed and described closely, rather than being couched in vague terms as 'body techniques'. Cohen's contribution to this volume draws attention to the importance of detail in accounts of the making and re-making of knowledge. She describes the potential of ethnographic engagement in communities of practice to reveal the 'micromechanisms' and 'processes' underpinning human knowledge. The example of auscultation presents a valuable opportunity to probe the underlying organizational and operational workings of a system of auditory knowledge.

While focusing on the minutiae of a kind of listening, I do not attempt to provide an account of auditory cognition like that offered by, for example, Lerdahl and Jackendoff (1984) and Jackendoff (1992) in relation to musical listening. And although I make occasional reference to points at which my own research and studies from psycho-acoustics reinforce or complement one another, this is not an interdisciplinary study. It does aim to provide the kind of empirical data which, Cohen suggests, may be valid and useful in future attempts to engage with listening as a system of perception, but, more importantly, it centres on one of the key themes of this collection: namely examining the ways in which bodily, and, more specifically, sensory, factors enable and constrain the production and reproduction of human knowledge.

The 'lub dub'

My application to be an honorary observer obliged me to have a supervisor at St Thomas', so I approached Consultant Cardiologist Dr John Coltart, who was Head of Cardiothoracic Services at the time. Dr Coltart told me that my research interested him because he had long been conscious of the importance of listening in his everyday practice. He considered his ears to be one of his most important clinical tools, and, as he had been teaching auscultation for a long time, was interested in the qualities that made students good listeners. Agreeing to act as my supervisor, he also suggested that I attend his classes. Dr Coltart was in charge of teaching the so-called 'chest rotation' to a different group of students each academic term.

For the third-year medical students with whom I worked, the curriculum for the first clinical year was structured around three 'rotations', each being a three-month course on the abdomen, head, or chest. The 'abdomen' rotation involves an introduction to abdominal medicine and surgery; the 'head' rotation contains elements of psychiatry, neurology, and ophthalmology; and the 'chest' rotation consists of cardiovascular and respiratory medicine (including teaching on 'ear, nose, and throat' or 'upper respiratory tract' medicine). During the chest rotation, students learned to examine the cardiovascular system and became familiar with common signs and symptoms of related diseases. Cardiac auscultation was taught as part of the cardiovascular examination and was central to Dr Coltart's lessons, although he also taught special classes on other clinical topics such as heart failure and myocardial infarction or 'heart attack'.

On our first day of the chest rotation I sat with a group of eight medical students around a table in a seminar room. Dr Coltart asked, 'What sound does a heart make?' From our blank expressions it was apparent that none of us knew. This seemed at odds with the fact that most people know what a heart sounds like and, as Ackerman points out, '[w]e're used to associating the heart with sound' (1990: 190). Even though one might not actually listen to a heart very often, one is sometimes aware of one's own heart pumping and the texture of sound that it creates in the ears. The beating heart also has a high profile in popular culture and is often used in television and film soundtracks. But while recognizing the sound might be easy, describing it is evidently more difficult.

With no answer forthcoming, Dr Coltart responded to his own question:

> You might be familiar with the song by Peter Sellers and Sophia Loren in which they sing about her heart 'going boom boody-boom'. Well, this describes the heartbeat quite nicely. 'Boom boody-boom' suggests the heartbeat has four components: 'boom', then 'boo-dy', and another 'boom'. In fact the

heart does have these four sounds, but because of the way our ears are designed we can't easily separate the many components. So in medicine we say the heart has two main sounds. We say it goes 'lub dub'.

Dr Coltart went on to explain that the first heart sound, the 'lub', is caused by the closure of the mitral and tricuspid valves, and the second, the 'dub', by the closure of the aortic and pulmonary valves. Figure 1, showing the valves and their position in relation to the rest of the heart, may be helpful here.

Dr Coltart went on to explain that normally when blood flows around the heart and across the valves, it does so smoothly, meaning that the only sounds that can be heard through a stethoscope are the closing snaps of the valves, which create the 'lub' and 'dub'. Sometimes, though, a physiological event triggers the blood flow to become turbulent and this turbulence produces what are known as 'heart murmurs'. For instance, if a valve becomes stiff for some reason (e.g. through calcification) and blood is forced through a narrower opening than is normally made by a valve (this restriction of blood flow is known as 'stenosis'), turbulence will be created and a murmur produced. If the valve fails to close properly, or becomes 'floppy', then blood passing through it will flow back (a development known as 'regurgitation') and another murmur will be produced, though at a different stage in the cardiac cycle and with a different sound. Problems with valves are not the only cause of murmurs. Holes in the septum (the muscle wall separating the two sides of the heart), for instance, can cause large volumes of blood to be forced back and forth between the chambers, producing a murmur known as a 'shunt'. Some murmurs appear to have

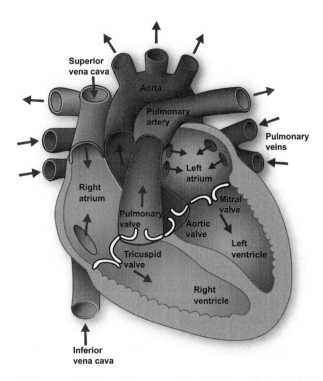

Figure 1. A simple diagram of the heart. (Image reproduced with permission of the Texas Heart Institute: *http://www.texasheart.org.*)

no physiological basis at all, being caused by unexplained turbulence in the blood flow. These are known as 'innocent' or 'flow' murmurs. In general, though, heart murmurs are linked to malfunctioning valves. Dr Coltart claimed that murmurs are the cardiologist's 'bread and butter'. Most of our rotation was therefore devoted to learning to hear and identify them.

Cardiac auscultation is an example of what Chion describes as 'causal listening', namely 'listening to a sound in order to gather information about its source' (1994: 25). Doctors attend to murmurs to learn about the valves, vessels, and haemodynamics of the heart. Having provided his students with basic oral instruction as to how auscultation of the heart works, Dr Coltart went on to offer further, more sophisticated explanations of how subtleties of pitch, rhythm, and dynamics in a murmur express particular physiological changes. In doing so, he communicated an interpretative structure through which a range of heart sounds could be given diagnostic meaning, referenced to physical events in the bodily interior. As I will go on to illustrate, instructing the students actually to recognize the sounds occurring in patients was more complicated, and required a number of pedagogic strategies.

It is important to point out that auscultation of the heart tends to be used in the context of a more general examination which normally includes the taking of a clinical history, a series of careful observations from the foot of the bed, and the taking of pulses as well as many other small checks and procedures, all of which shape the listener's expectations of what will be heard. *The Oxford handbook of clinical medicine* makes this point plain. Its authors claim that auscultation is

> generally, but wrongly, held to be the essence of cardiovascular medicine at the bedside. A caricature of cardiology ward rounds is of the anxious junior gabbling through the history, while noting his chief's fingers twisting his stethoscope, impatient to 'get down to the main business' of listening to the heart – thereby blotting out all talk in favour of a few blissful minutes communing with the 'lub' and the 'dub'. This is absurd ... if you spend time listening to the history, and feeling pulses, auscultation should hold few surprises: you will often already know the diagnosis (Longmore, Wilkinson & Torok 2001: 39).

Auscultation belongs, then, within a web of interconnected techniques used in examining patients and is regularly used to confirm diagnoses formulated on the basis of other observations. None the less, medical practitioners regard it as an important skill in its own right, and for the purposes of this chapter I focus on cardiac auscultation itself as an 'apprenticeship in hearing' (Downey 2002: 504).

Before listening

With the exception of the initial class, in which we were introduced to the theoretical principles of auscultation, sessions for the chest rotation took place on the cardio-thoracic wards. Dressed in white coats and clutching notebooks and stethoscopes, we followed Dr Coltart to the bedsides of patients whose conditions, he judged, were appropriate to our instruction. This almost invariably meant that the patients had a heart murmur of some kind. We formed a semi-circle around the bed with Dr Coltart at the head on the patient's immediate left, spatially indexing his status and authority in relation both to his students and to the patient. One of us then pulled the privacy curtain closed.

Dr Coltart emphasized the importance of maintaining good relationships with patients, and in a polite and good-humoured way he introduced us as 'young doctors' to those he had chosen as models or exemplars. He then asked for our observations. Was the patient sitting up? Were they speaking comfortably; breathing evenly and regularly; speaking and behaving compliantly? Was the patient over- or underweight? Were there scars from previous operations? Were there bandages, tubes, cylinders, at the bedside? After gathering answers to his questions, Dr Coltart demonstrated the cardio-vascular examination, drawing attention to particular signs of the patient. Among the checks involved were the inspection of the patient's hands and fingers, feeling of pulses in the wrist and neck, noting the colouration of the cornea and health of the teeth, and feeling for any abnormal vibrations through chest palpation.

Having demonstrated these examination stages, Dr Coltart proceeded next to the auscultation of the heart. He emphasized that the stethoscope's diaphragm (the part pressed to the patient's chest) should be cleaned with alcohol and warmed against the back of the hand so it would not feel too cold against the patient's skin. He then showed us how to move our hands over the chest in order to find the 'apex beat', the lowest and outermost point at which the beat of the heart can be felt. This is the point at which cardiac auscultation should begin. Inserting the earpieces of his stethoscope and taking the diaphragm carefully in his hand, Dr Coltart requested that we remain quiet in order to optimize conditions for listening in an often noisy ward. Doctors, like Ituri pygmies (Turnbull 1961) and Umeda (Gell 1995), preserve a degree of discipline around noise, recognizing the importance of quiet at times when careful listening is necessary. Drawing our attention to the need to push down with the diaphragm so as to make a firm connection with the flesh, Dr Coltart quickly listened at the apex beat, and then indicated how we should move the stethoscope to other 'key points' (see Fig. 2) where

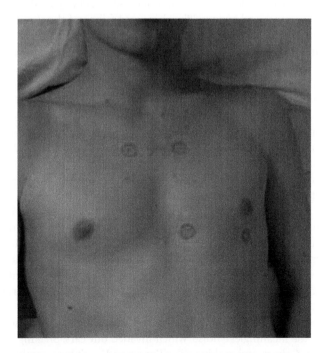

Figure 2. Key listening points for cardiac auscultation. (Image reproduced with permission of the Queen's University Belfast Clinical Skills Education Centre.)

sounds produced by the heart valves can be most easily discerned. In doing so, he effectively marked out a map of listening points on the patient's chest. After the demonstration, Dr Coltart instructed his students to auscultate the patient's heart in turn. The students tried hard to imitate Dr Coltart's listening postures and to reproduce the assured air with which he handled the stethoscope. They found themselves struggling, however, not only with the more overt bodily actions, but also with the subtler perceptual processes of listening.

Non-sense

Using a stethoscope for the first time can be a slightly disconcerting experience. On inserting the earpieces, the sounds to which one is accustomed disappear. The outside world is sealed off; it becomes muted, distant. Scientists working in psychoacoustics have observed that during experiments carried out using headphones, 'physiological noise of vascular origin' (i.e. noise created by the heartbeat and the circulation of blood, also known as 'self-generated noise') becomes trapped inside the ear (Anderson & Whittle 1971; Soderquist & Lindsey 1972). This effect is also produced by the earpieces of the stethoscope so that, paradoxically, the first heart sounds one hears upon inserting them are often one's own. One also quickly learns that the diaphragm of the stethoscope is highly sensitive. The tiniest knock or scrape transmits sudden and painfully loud sounds down the tubes into the ears. After experiencing a few of these unpleasant sonic shocks, one begins to handle the stethoscope with great care.

Placing the stethoscope on the patient's chest can also be perturbing at first because it involves entering the cocoon of warm air that surrounds his or her body. This air is charged with the patient's smell, pleasant or otherwise. Touching the skin, one becomes aware of its temperature and texture. The rising and falling of the chest can be felt, as can the patient's breath on one's face. It becomes easy to notice certain details of the skin, its colour, the presence of pigmentation, scars, and moles. Pressing down the diaphragm of the stethoscope also creates a sense of the skin's resistance, indicating its age and condition, the presence of muscle, bone, and fat.

Just as the physics of the stethoscope suggest that the vibrations of the chest wall are conducted through tubes directly to the ears of the physician, the sensation for the auscultator is one of a sudden rush of body sounds up the tubes, suffusing the ears. Instead of the doctor penetrating the patient's body with a kind of 'auditory gaze', the sensation is more one of the patient's body penetrating that of the listener. Yost writes that sounds presented over earphones are generally perceived by experimental subjects as being 'inside the head' rather than 'out in space' where actual sound sources usually appear (1994: 178). The same is true for the sound conveyed to the earpieces of the stethoscope. Making sense of the cacophony is almost impossible at first. There is only the feeling of something like a sonic draught reaching the head and one becomes overwhelmed, or, as Ellman writes, 'stuffed with sound' (1993: 101). This is not to say that the other senses are negated or somehow deleted from experience, but the sense of hearing is given a definite immediacy and priority in the sensory present.

In the earlier lessons of the rotation, few of us could make any sense of what we perceived to be the meaningless 'noise' which invaded our ears. Shaking our heads we apologized to Dr Coltart, saying things like 'I'm sorry, I can't hear anything. I honestly can't hear anything'. As a student named Tom explained,

> When you first come in you don't know what you're listening for. You're just listening. You've got your ears open and everything's coming in and you're like 'Arrrgh!' The first time I came in I didn't know anything. I didn't know what were the heart sounds, I was just listening and thinking 'Oh my God'.

Mary agreed: 'You try to convince yourself that you're hearing something but actually you have no idea'. Like Tom and Mary, many students initially despaired of their inability to control the stethoscope and the sounds produced with it.

Focusing

Dr Coltart encouraged his students to focus and 'listen into' the sounds the stethoscope produced. The type of listening shifted from being directly 'causative' towards what Chion, citing Schaeffer (1967), refers to as 'reduced listening'. The focus was 'on the traits of the sound itself, independent of its cause and of its meaning' (Chion 1994: 29). Many students shut their eyes, screwing them up tight as if attempting forcibly to channel or divert their attention away from their eyes and into their ears. They seemed to be trying to create a sealed perceptual space in which auditory information could be purified and optimized by shutting out potential sensory distractions. Harjit was an eye-closer. 'If you close your eyes you can hear better. You have to suspend all your other senses and put all your energy into your ears', she said, later referring to this state as 'murmur mode'. Other students kept their eyes open to listen, but stared blankly ahead or into the middle distance as they did so. 'Your eyes may be open but you lose your vision. You stare into space but you don't see anything because your concentration is in your ears', said Dave. Here the gaze is disengaged. It has been vacated or shut off in order to allow sounds to become the focus of attention. Auscultation, then, requires an unusual acoustic effort, a special kind of concentration. 'A will', as Dave put it, 'to think yourself into your ears'.

In much the same way that experienced concertgoers might close their eyes and let their heads drop back, abandoning themselves to the music, the students' efforts to listen also constituted a kind of 'performance of listening'. This was perhaps helpful for convincing themselves that they were listening as attentively as possible, but it also served to demonstrate to their teacher that they were trying hard and that even if they were not actually able to detect anything meaningful, at least their self-application was good and they were making an effort. Students were later advised that a clear demonstration of listening communicates to the patient that conversation should be suspended and it is time for the doctor to concentrate. This 'performance of listening' therefore served as a technique for both shutting out extraneous sound and distracting presences, and, if necessary, shutting up the patient.

After finding their auditory focus, Dr Coltart told the students to listen for what he called the 'landmark' sounds, the 'lub' and 'dub', that compose the heartbeat. He suggested that if these were soft, then we should nod our heads with each beat, or tap out the rhythm with one foot, thus marking and reinforcing the sounds with bodily movements. He also encouraged us to listen whilst feeling the patient's pulse, as this would enable us to anchor or link the sounds of the heart to tactile sensations. It would also help us to discern whether there were delays between the heartbeat and the rise of the pulse. Such signs could be of potential clinical significance. Listening, then, could involve a kind of sensory cross-referencing, whereby tactile information is used to reinforce that in the auditory mode. After a few lessons most of us were able to recognize the 'lub' and 'dub' with some degree of certainty, although we periodically encountered patients whose heart sounds were indiscernible to us.

Next, Dr Coltart asked us to listen for heart murmurs and other abnormal heart sounds. He used both a temporal and a visual-spatial framework in order to describe the auditory focus that is necessary. To start with, he suggested that we try devoting units of time to the elements of what we were hearing:

> There's no way that you can hear all of the information that's there in one go. You've got to have points that you're listening for and that you can work from. You've got to listen for five seconds to everything, then for five seconds you've got to find the heart sounds, then you've got to listen for five seconds for any murmurs before or after those sounds.

He also suggested that we mark the first and second heart sounds using imaginary lines, and then, if additional sounds could be detected, draw or shade in the spaces on either side of the first or second heart sounds in which they occurred (Fig. 3). He depicted murmurs in this way on notepads and blackboards. This diagrammatic formulation of sounds was helpful to students who were not accustomed to working in sound alone and found it easier to visualize them. Dr Coltart claimed, however, that as one becomes familiarized with heart sounds and more confident at recognizing the different kinds of murmurs, one ceases to rely on mental images.

Evidence from psychoacoustics suggests that people are able to separate specific 'acoustic objects' from their background, isolating particular elements for focused attention. Indeed, the ear works by attending to *parts* of complex sounds, rather than all aspects at once. As Moore explains:

> It seems that we are not generally capable of attending to every aspect of the auditory input ... rather, certain points are selected for conscious analysis ... it appears that the complex sound signal is analysed into streams, and we attend primarily to one stream at a time. This attended stream then stands out perceptually, while the rest of the sound is less prominent (2003: 294-5).

It may be that Dr Coltart's system for spatially and temporally demarcating the different parts of a sound facilitates this process of 'streaming'. Moore also identifies distinct 'analytic' or 'synthetic' modes of hearing. The 'analytic' mode allows the listener to attend to individual components of a sound, thus effectively muting other parts, while

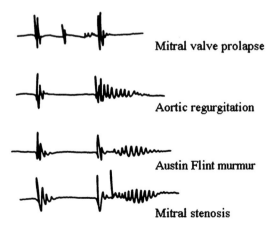

Mitral valve prolapse

Aortic regurgitation

Austin Flint murmur

Mitral stenosis

Figure 3. Heart murmur sketches.

the 'synthetic' mode fuses elements into a single percept (2003: 282). Warren suggests that an element of training may be necessary in order for listeners to shift effectively between the 'analytic' and 'synthetic' modes (1982: 63). Following an experiment in which a series of tones were played to doctors through a stethoscope, Welsby, Parry, and Smith (2003) noted that practised auscultators were effective at filtering out extraneous or misleading sounds. This suggests that they had become adept at shifting between the analytic and synthetic modes of hearing.

Listening alone together

Daniel Shindler (2004) remarks upon students' 'enthusiasm for the stethoscope' when introduced to auscultation. Indeed, my fellow students were surprisingly keen to practise listening to murmurs. They visited the cardiothoracic wards after class, asking nurses on duty if there were any murmur patients to whom they might listen. They returned repeatedly to see patients whose murmurs were challenging. The consequences of this repeated listening for the patients is a subject I discuss elsewhere (Rice 2008). But despite their general enthusiasm, students nevertheless experienced difficulties with learning to listen.

In the contexts described in this volume by Marchand and Makovicky, the physical substance of materials with which teachers and pupils are working (wood and thread, respectively) is shown to be integral to the teaching process. Participants in the teaching interactions appear to have a strong visual, tactile, and even olfactory engagement with their materials. At the same time, a student's work with and upon that material indicates how well particular actions and techniques are being performed, and hence how well the student is progressing. Wood and thread bear the physical traces of a practitioner's skills (or lack of them), and hence can easily be made the subject of comparison and discussion. The medical students, on the other hand, found it difficult to establish common points of reference for the sounds they were hearing and it was difficult to gauge or have confidence in their own progress as listeners.

Auscultation is considered a solitary, isolating perceptual experience. This is partly because the sounds of the body are not publicly shared in the way that music played over a stereo, for instance, might be. Students were obliged to listen in sequence, one after the other, making it difficult to ascertain that everyone was experiencing exactly the same sound. Teaching stethoscopes have been developed to tackle this problem. As shown in Figure 4, these instruments have one large central diaphragm connected to two sets of earpieces, and as many as ten, enabling a teaching doctor and students to listen simultaneously. These instruments are rare, however, and I never saw one used during my time at St Thomas'. Auscultation was always a solitary endeavour, the doctor or student listening to sounds that he or she alone could hear. The listener was isolated in a particular perceptual moment.

One way in which Dr Coltart, and teaching doctors more generally, sought to get around the problem of the subjective isolation of listening was to provide students with CD recordings of various murmur examples with voiceovers describing their distinguishing features. The recordings allowed students to listen collectively to the very same sound and ensured that they were hearing the intended sound. Students found the CDs helpful, boosting confidence that they were hearing what they were *meant* to hear and not sounds produced by their own mishandling or misplacement of the stethoscope.

Dr Coltart also wanted students to be capable of instantly recognizing some of the most common heart murmurs, 'as one knows a dog's bark'. The ejection systolic

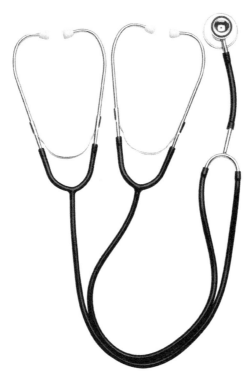

Figure 4. A teaching stethoscope. (Image reproduced with permission of St John Ambulance Supplies.)

murmur of aortic stenosis, for example, occurs when the aortic valve becomes stiffened and no longer opens fully enough to allow easy blood flow. As a consequence, the blood is forced through the narrowed valve, resulting in a distinctive, harsh, sometimes squeaky murmur. The CD familiarized students with such archetypal examples, and with other common heart sounds. They were then able to compare murmurs heard on the wards with these memorized sounds or sonic templates.

CD recordings detach heart murmurs from patients, effectively turning them into portable sonic objects. Practice listening was therefore no longer restricted to the hospital, freeing students to auscultate in their own bedrooms or while travelling to and from class. This also released them from the pressure they felt when listening in Dr Coltart's presence. Some listened to the CD while reading, which they claimed allowed the murmurs gradually to seep into the memory rather than being forcibly memorized. A few students visited websites where they could listen to heart murmur recordings and view phonocardiograms (digitally produced diagrams of heart sounds). These effectively served the same purpose as the classroom sketches drawn by Dr Coltart, though they tended to be more detailed, colourful, and aesthetically pleasing for the students (Fig. 5).

Though considered to be helpful, the recorded sounds are much 'bigger' and 'cleaner' than those procured through a stethoscope. When listening to a patient, sounds can be muddled and obscured by subcutaneous fat, vascular noise, and breath

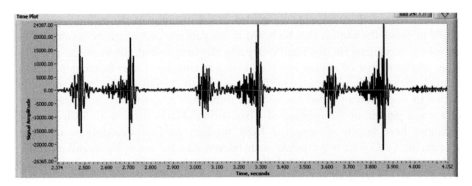

Figure 5. A phonocardiogram of the murmur of mitral regurgitation. (Image reproduced with permission of Bsignetics.)

sounds from inside the body. Recordings and sound files lack the background noises of the wider ward/patient context as well as the realism of the stethoscope-user interface. After several days of listening students could reliably complete the 'heart sound quiz' at the end of the CD, but finding and recognizing the same murmurs through a stethoscope when faced with a live patient proved more challenging and required many weeks of practice. Even by the end of the rotation no student was consistently successful in this task.

Speaking sound

The teaching of auscultation also presents a linguistic problem, or a problem of vocabulary. While the previously mentioned ethnographies by Feld, Gell, and Weiner point to the highly sophisticated acoustic vocabularies exhibited by members of the Papuan societies they study, sonic terminology is generally held to be comparatively under-developed in Western societies. It is not simply that there is a 'Spartan economy of words' for engaging with auditory phenomena, but that, as Walter Murch argues, Western cultures have never developed the concepts or language to describe or cope with sound (Marchand, introduction, this volume; Murch 1994: xvi-xvii).

While standing at the bedside of patients, Dr Coltart often tried to produce evocative descriptions of particular heart sounds for his students, saying things like: 'It's that long, low, rumbling sound I want you to be getting', or 'Can you hear that harsh, rasping, almost squeaking sound?' While terms like 'lub dub', and even 'murmur', are clearly onomatopoeic, Dr Coltart also resorted to more conspicuous forms of mimicry. 'It's the "ush, ush, ush" I want you to listen to', he might say, or the 'lup dup shh, lub dup shh'. On several occasions Dr Coltart acted out the murmur of aortic stenosis by saying 'eek, eek, eek', accenting the noise with an upward gesture of his fist to indicate the effort required to pump blood through the narrowed valve. Students also used onomatopoeia in describing what they heard to one another. The performance of sounds and use of nonsense words and syllables often had a comic effect, partly because of their perceived contrast with the serious manner and formal terminology that supposedly characterized clinical discussions. I would suggest, however, that these vocalizations were yet another attempt to break down the subjective isolation of listening, and make the stethoscopic auditory experience a shared and communal one through public language and gesture.

René Laennec, the man widely regarded as the inventor of the stethoscope, used simile to evoke the sounds that he heard in his patients and which he wanted other doctors to recognize. He described one particular lung sound, for instance, as 'a tinkling similar to that of a small bell just ceasing to ring, or of a fly buzzing in a china vase' (1846: 320). Elsewhere he described how the thickening of the bronchial tubes caused by pneumonia yielded a sound that sometimes resembled snoring, the cooing of a wood pigeon, or the rubbing of a bass string (Marks 1972: 71-2). Such acoustic analogies have largely disappeared from modern medical descriptions of heart sounds, but Dr Coltart nevertheless made reference to, for example, 'seagull murmur' and 'a gallop rhythm'. He suggested that the gallop rhythm, which is produced when a third heart sound is audible in addition to the expected two, should have the same cadence as the word 'Kentucky', the first heart sound forming the 'Ken', the second heart sound the 'tuc', and the third sound the 'ky'. The rhythm produced when a fourth heart sound is present was likened to the word 'Tennessee'. While a third heart sound comes after the two expected ones, the fourth heart sound precedes them. Interestingly, a third heart sound is not required for a fourth to be present, so in the three syllables of 'Tennessee' the fourth heart sound makes the 'Tenn', the first the 'ess', and the second the 'ee'. By invoking more familiar acoustic patterns, these metaphors make otherwise inchoate sounds more immediately comprehensible (Fernandez 1974: 120).

Those new to auscultation have difficulty communicating what they hear, but doctors have developed a formula for defining heart murmurs using a set of four parameters. They might refer, for instance, to 'a soft, grade II ejection-systolic murmur at the left sternal edge'. The murmur is thereby classified in terms of its tone, volume (on a scale of I to VI), place in the cardiac cycle, and location on the chest. This method greatly reduces the scope for possible confusion arising from attempts to evoke the actual sound of the murmur. It should be pointed out, however, that the ability to frame sounds through a set of reference-points has not entirely resolved the problem of establishing consensus on what has been heard. Murmurs can be very subtle. Also, like other kinds of diagnostic work, auscultation is interpretative or hermeneutic. Doctors form independent judgements and develop their own opinions. The knowledge which auscultation produces is always contestable. Despite efforts to 'fix' murmurs objectively through careful description, it is still common for doctors to disagree on the nature of what can be heard. In an excerpt on 'the heart sounds', *The Oxford handbook of clinical medicine* states that '[t]he first and second sounds are usually clear'; however, '[c]onfident pronouncements about the other sounds and soft murmurs may be difficult. Even senior colleagues disagree with one another about the more difficult murmurs' (Longmore *et al.* 2001: 80). In auscultation, sounds cannot be reliably or unproblematically codified.

Simon Sinclair observes that heart murmurs 'are notoriously hard for novices to identify' (1997: 202). But despite the complexities involved in learning to listen, the students gradually increased their proficiency at detecting and interpreting heart sounds. This came with applying the pedagogic techniques invented by doctors, but, above all, with practice. Progression was not uniform, and as Downey points out, expertise arises 'in diverse fashion and unevenly' (this volume). But as one student, Alistair, put it, 'When we started we could hear a sound and that was about it. Then we could hear the two heartbeats and a load of muffle. Now we can listen to that muffle and usually understand what it means'.

Harder hearing

A few months into fieldwork my right ear became itchy and painful, and my hearing a trifle impaired. It seemed likely that I had caught something from a stethoscope. The earpieces are known to be a site at which pathogens accumulate, and people who share stethoscopes often develop ear infections. I had used a spare ward stethoscope on a number of occasions and so now was obliged to return to the hospital as an outpatient.

When I walked into the waiting room of the ENT (Ear, Nose and Throat) Department, I was surprised to see one of the students I had met on the chest rotation. Rhydd was equally surprised to see me. He explained that his ears felt continually blocked and he was finding it increasingly difficult to hear, so he came to have them syringed. I explained my own reason for attending the clinic, and he proceeded to tell me all about the doctor I would be seeing. The doctor, it turned out, had been one of his teachers. While talking together, Rhydd nodded and smiled at a girl walking past.

'Who's that?' I asked.
'Her name is Nirit. She's a third-year medic as well. She's going into the audiology clinic which is not surprising – she's deaf'.

This was interesting, and I wondered how she coped with the auditory practices that I understood to be so important to medicine. I asked Rhydd if he could arrange a meeting.

Nirit and I met a few days later in the café at St Thomas'. In speaking to her, I was in no way aware of her deafness and did not have to make any concessions in terms of altering my speech. She described herself as 'hearing-impaired' and explained that few people are totally deaf. She considers herself representative of that grey zone within the population who live between deafness and a totally hearing world. Nirit's hearing impediment is congenital. She has 70 per cent hearing loss in each ear, but explained: 'It isn't that I don't hear. I have found strategies to hear in spite of my impediment'. She wears hearing aids and lip-reads. Nirit went on to describe how she made the choice to live as a hearing person in a hearing world. This decision met with disapproval from some members of a group with which she worked. They expected her to assume a 'Deaf' identity and maintain solidarity with other Deaf people by refusing to adapt to the hearing world. Oliver Sacks (1989) observes the strength of this ideology among some deaf people in his book *Seeing voices*.

Nirit acknowledged that there are certain features of medical practice that make the path difficult for the hearing-impaired. Medics spend considerable time attending to weak or elderly people who often speak in a soft, unclear manner. Nirit is also aware that she is easily thrown by accents and unusual words, and hospital background noise further impedes concentrated listening. In the operating theatre, much of the face, including the mouth, is covered, thereby concealing lips, facial expression, and normal self-evidence of the speaker and making comprehension especially challenging. Though strategies may be employed (in the operating theatre, for example, surgeons can be asked to wear small radio microphones which relay their voices to a hearing aid), the numerous existing hurdles suggest that medicine is likely to remain a testing career for the hard-of-hearing.

For Nirit, four areas of medicine stood out as highly 'auditory' in nature, or, rather, as being specializations in which listening is especially important. These are general practice, paediatrics, respiratory medicine, and cardiology. Nirit's hearing impairment made her reluctant to go into any of these areas, and cardiology in particular. She would find it hard to cope with the responsibility were she unable to detect a sound that was an important diagnostic clue and jeopardize a patient's health as a consequence. 'I don't want to spend all my life wondering if a patient's well-being has been compromised by my hearing', she said.

The 'chest rotation' included instruction in the rudiments of two of the areas identified by Nirit, namely respiratory medicine and cardiology. A great deal of auscultation practice was demanded in these elements of the training, and the technique presented obvious challenges to Nirit. She acquired an amplified stethoscope (see Fig. 6) manufactured in such a way that the main tube extending from the diaphragm plugs into a small amplifier which, in turn, is connected to the earpieces. The sound picked up by the diaphragm travels up the tube, is amplified half-way, and continues in normal fashion to the earpieces. In addition to making the sounds from patients louder, the device can also be tuned to amplify high or low frequencies.

Nirit had been anxious about auscultation. She pointed out that she was used to listening because the fact that her *hearing* is impaired makes *listening* all the more important. She must actively seek out the sounds most people hear easily and take for granted. In day-to-day life, Nirit used lip-reading and other cues to fill in for missing sounds. In auscultation, however, supporting information was not immediately available, leaving her sense of hearing uncomfortably exposed. She explained that her amplified stethoscope also worried her because she did not know whether it was distorting sounds. She thought she might be hearing things that were not there. This feeling is reported by almost all students learning auscultation, but Nirit believed the problem to be more acute in her case, undermining her confidence in judging what she heard.

One teaching doctor offered Nirit extra one-to-one supervision in auscultation. He took her around the wards to practise listening on patients with exemplary heart murmurs and gave her more time to listen than she received during normal classes. Nirit found the technique of tapping or acting out elements of the sounds with gestures particularly helpful. She believed that doing this, even if only in her head, was a good way of confirming to herself the acoustic dynamics of the sounds she was detecting. She also appreciated the care taken by the teaching doctor to describe and mimic sounds accurately. She felt that this process of verbalization provided a way of moving the

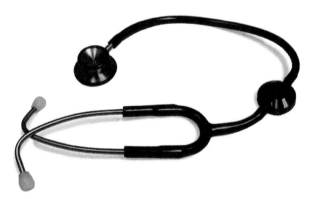

Figure 6. An amplified stethoscope. (Image provided with permission of Harris Communications, Inc.: *http://www.harriscomm.com*.)

sounds out of her perceptual uncertainty into a space in which their features and characteristics could be shared and thereby verified.

By taking turns at listening and afterwards comparing thoughts, the teaching doctor and Nirit were together able to analyse and monitor her hearing. The teaching doctor directed Nirit's attention to areas of relative perceptual strength and weakness. He advised her to pay particular attention to certain parts of sounds and to trust her judgement on others. Gradually, Nirit's ear for heart murmurs became more reliable. The perceptual isolation she experienced, 'amplified' by the amplified stethoscope, was slowly dispelled, giving way to relative confidence. Her faith in both the technology and her own sense of hearing grew. By the end of the chest rotation, Nirit recognized that although some fellow students were better skilled, some were less competent than her. This was in fact the case for every rotation, not just those which drew heavily on auditory skills.

To use her amplified stethoscope, Nirit had first to remove her hearing aids and insert the earpieces of the instrument, listen, and then take them out and reinsert her hearing aids. While this would be fine for her medical exams, she felt that in a normal medical setting the same procedure might undermine patients' confidence in her diagnostic abilities. Patients might be suspicious of a doctor dependent on hearing aids, questioning his or her capacity for detecting the necessary clinical signs. A report produced by members of the Health and Sciences Department at Staffordshire University entitled *Enabling disabled doctors* suggests that doctors with visible disabilities of all kinds occasionally encounter assumptions of incompetence made by patients (Morgan & Chambers 2004). Nirit was concerned that patients might not realise that, in fact, her hearing is sufficient for carrying out her duties. While becoming confident with her use of the stethoscope, she nevertheless recognized that she would need to be creative in managing patient reactions to her methods and securing their trust.

The amplified stethoscope allows Nirit to use auscultation in the same way as other medical students. But the technique continues to hold greater challenges for her than for most of her peers. Nirit's example demonstrates that bodies, and the perceptual capacities they support, are not uniform or homogeneous, but are sites for the production of difference. Nirit's hearing problems do not prevent her from participating in what might be described as the 'common schemes of perception' which characterize the medical habitus (Bourdieu 1980: 60). But plainly, thinking in these terms could lead us to dismiss what is important and interesting in Nirit's example, namely that certain tasks are more problematic and fraught with doubt and uncertainty for her than for other students. Her sense of hearing requires that she be singularly inventive and resourceful in her approaches to her medical training.

Conclusion

On a number of occasions I heard senior doctors remark that the stethoscope is 'a dying technology' and auscultation 'a dying art'. When asked to elaborate, they pointed to the increasing use of cardiac ultrasound or echocardiography in heart examinations and consequent diagnoses of heart disease. In echocardiography, ultra-high-frequency sound is used to produce detailed, real-time images of the functioning heart, its interior and haemodynamics. Echocardiography machines are presently expensive, cumbersome, and complicated to operate, and they require the services of a qualified technician. But new technology is rapidly making them more portable and user-friendly. In time, I was told, medical practitioners will walk onto wards carrying cardiac ultrasound devices in their pockets. Echocardiography will replace auscultation as the primary method for bedside heart examination, rendering the stethoscope obsolete. A number of written sources also make reference to the 'death of the stethoscope', again pointing to the impact of new technologies on diagnostic practice (e.g. Babu 1999; Kirsch 1998).

Daniel Shindler (2004) points out that the demise of the stethoscope 'has been wrongly but repeatedly foretold over the years'. He refers to 'the old tale of an early twentieth-century radiologist who placed a stethoscope prominently for all to see in a coffin-shaped display case. It was his mistaken belief that X-ray of the heart would shortly render the stethoscope obsolete'. There was certainly no evidence of stethoscopes being consigned to drawers or dustbins at St Thomas'. Indeed, auscultation was of considerable importance in the teaching curriculum. Given that the students with whom I worked would qualify in three years, it seems unlikely that they, as doctors, will certify the stethoscope dead. On the contrary, their practice would appear to ensure its continued use. Furthermore, the fact that auscultation is a low-tech, cost-effective method of making quick health assessments of the heart valves means that the technique is likely to retain its use value, notably in countries where health care is underresourced. None the less, the notion that the art of auscultation is endangered is of clear interest to discussions of this knowledge-making practice.

Writing on echocardiography, Draper points out a paradox in the technology, namely that 'sound is used to give light to the bodily interior' (2002: 777). It might be argued that auscultation does the same. In *The birth of the clinic*, Foucault imagines Laennec (the inventor of the stethoscope) listening to a patient's heart. Foucault suggests that Laennec is listening in order to visualize a heart he cannot see, thereby using his interpretation of its sounds to extend and augment his gaze (1973: 165). But in echocardiography, sonic information is transduced in such a way as to produce images that are visually legible. The heart is made materially accessible to the eyes, rather than the mind's eye. Sounds are no longer used to anticipate a visual gaze, but bring about its direct fulfilment.

While auscultation could be said to represent a means of visualizing the bodily interior, cardiac ultrasound belongs more immediately to what Duden calls medicine's 'visual command performance'. It epitomizes a drive for visual knowledge of the body which, she suggests, pervades medical culture (1993: 21). It could be argued that it is because echocardiography satisfies medicine's overarching project of visualization that many doctors consider that it is destined to bring about the end of auscultation. My research, however, offers a different set of perspectives on this speculated fate, grounded in observations about the teaching and learning of auscultation.

On one hand, doctors are inventive, resourceful, and ultimately quite successful at imparting the auditory knowledge which stethoscopic listening demands. They have developed a combination of techniques which productively direct the novice's attention, memory, and recognition skills. By practising in the learning environment of a hospital ward, the listening skills of most medical students progress and continue to develop throughout their careers. But, on the other hand, my research also reinforces the point that auscultation is 'a difficult skill to acquire' (Roy 2009: 4). The amount of practice and repetition required make the skill costly in terms of both time and energy for teachers and students alike. The inherent subjectivity of auditory experience and judgement, as well as the difficulty of fluent and confident communication about sounds, has made auscultation problematic for doctors since its inception. The challenges and constraints of listening as a way of knowing are made apparent in its transmission. While new diagnostic technologies like echocardiography will present their own set of problems and complexities as ways of knowing, doctors may find them more acceptable or manageable than those implicated in stethoscopic listening. At the very least, doctors may resist using and teaching auscultation in clinical practice as less-demanding and training-intensive diagnostic technologies emerge.

In his contribution to this volume, Downey writes that 'our remarkable ability to learn derives not merely from our intelligence as learners, but also from our skill as teachers'. This remark is optimistic, even congratulatory. Such a tone is almost irresistible when contemplating the wide and varied range of skills humans are able to acquire and pass on to others. The doctors with whom I worked did indeed demonstrate impressive practical intelligence in enacting pedagogic strategies for the teaching of stethoscopic listening. The doctor who took responsibility for coaching Nirit also showed admirable personal dedication and patience. But perhaps it could be argued that the medical profession has been unable decisively to overcome the challenges of auscultation and the difficulties presented by the transmission of this kind of auditory knowledge. A consequence may be that, in technologically advanced clinical settings like the cardiothoracic unit at St Thomas', cardiac auscultation will gradually disappear from the daily skill set of doctors and students.

NOTE

The research upon which this chapter is based was made possible by an ESRC Ph.D. Studentship. The writing-up was supported by an ESRC Postdoctoral Research Fellowship held at the Department of Sociology, University of Cambridge, and was supervised by Georgina Born. I want to thank Trevor Marchand and Sophie Day for their input at various points in the development of this chapter. Thanks also to Dr John Coltart and the students with whom I worked during my Observership at St Thomas' Hospital.

REFERENCES

ACKERMAN, D. 1990. *A natural history of the senses.* New York: Vintage.

ANDERSON, C.M.B. & L.S. WHITTLE 1971. Physiological noise and the missing 6dB. *Acustica* **24**, 261-72.

BABU, A.N. 1999. Death of the stethoscope (available on-line: *http://www.acpinternist.org/archives/1999/03/letters.htm*, accessed 11 January 2010).

BOURDIEU, P. 1977. *Outline of a theory of practice* (trans. R. Nice). Cambridge: University Press.

——— 1980. *The logic of practice* (trans. R. Nice). Cambridge: Polity.

CHION, M. 1994. *Audiovision: sound on screen.* New York: University of Columbia Press.

CLASSEN, C. 1998. *The color of angels: cosmology, gender and the aesthetic imagination.* London: Routledge.

DOWNEY, G. 2002. Listening to capoeira: phenomenology, embodiment, and the materiality of music. *Ethnomusicology* **46**, 487-509.

DRAPER, J. 2002. 'It was a real good show': the ultrasound scan, fathers and the power of visual knowledge. *Sociology of Health and Illness* **24**, 771-95.

DUDEN, B. 1993. *Disembodying women: perspectives on pregnancy and the unborn.* Cambridge, Mass.: Harvard University Press.

ELLMAN, M. 1993. *The hunger artists: starving, writing and imprisonment.* London: Virago.

FELD, S. 1990. *Sound and sentiment: birds, weeping, poetics, and song in Kaluli expression.* Philadelphia: University of Pennsylvania Press.

——— 1991. Sound as a symbolic system: the Kaluli drum. In *The varieties of sensory experience: a sourcebook in the anthropology of the senses* (ed.) D. Howes, 79-99. Toronto: University Press.

——— 1996. Waterfalls of song: an acoustemology of place resounding in Bosavi, Papua New Guinea. In *Senses of place* (eds) S. Feld & K.H. Basso, 91-135. Santa Fe: School of American Research Press.

——— 2003. A rainforest acoustemology. In *The auditory culture reader* (eds) M. Bull & L. Back, 223-39. Oxford: Berg.

——— & D. BRENNEIS 2004. Doing anthropology in sound. *American Ethnologist* **31**, 461-74.

FERNANDEZ, J. 1974. The mission of metaphor in expressive culture. *Current Anthropology* **15**, 119-45.

FOUCAULT, M. 1973. *The birth of the clinic: an archaeology of medical perception* (trans. A.M. Sheridan Smith). New York: Vintage.

Gell, A. 1995. The language of the forest: landscape and phonological iconism in Umeda. In *The anthropology of landscape: perspectives on place and space* (eds) E. Hirsch & M. O'Hanlon, 232-54. Oxford: University Press.

Jackendoff, R. 1992. *Languages of the mind: essays on mental representation*. Cambridge, Mass.: MIT Press.

Kirsch, M. 1998. The death of the stethoscope: murmurs of discontent (available on-line: *http://www.acpinternist.org/archives/1998/12/stetho.htm*, accessed 11 January 2010).

Laennec, R.T.H. 1846. *A treatise on mediate auscultation and on diseases of the lungs and heart* [trans. A member of the Royal College of Physicians]. London: H. Baillière.

Lave, J. & E. Wenger 1991. *Situated learning: legitimate peripheral participation*. Cambridge: University Press.

Lerdahl, F. & R. Jackendoff 1984. An overview of hierarchical structure in Music. *Music Perception* **1**, 229-52.

Longmore, M., I. Wilkinson & E. Torok 2001. *The Oxford handbook of clinical medicine*. Oxford: University Press.

Margolis, J. 1999. Pierre Bourdieu: habitus and the logic of practice. In *Bourdieu: a critical reader* (ed.) R. Shusterman, 64-83. Oxford: Blackwell.

Marks, G. 1972. *The story of the stethoscope*. Folkestone: Bailey Brothers and Swinfen.

Mauss, M. 1979 [1935]. Body techniques. In *Sociology and psychology: essays by Marcel Mauss*, 95-123. London: Routledge & Kegan Paul.

Moore, B.C.J. 2003. *An introduction to the psychology of hearing*. London: Academic Press.

Morgan, L. & R. Chambers 2004. *Enabling disabled doctors: a scoping exercise*. Staffordshire University: Disabled Doctors Action Group.

Murch, W. 1994. Foreword. In *Audiovision: sound on screen*, M. Chion, vii-xxiv. New York: University of Columbia Press.

Rice, T. 2003. Soundselves: an acoustemology of sound and self in the Edinburgh Royal Infirmary. *Anthropology Today* **19**: 4, 4-9.

——— 2008. ' "Beautiful murmurs": stethoscopic listening and acoustic objectification'. *The Senses and Society* **3**, 293-306.

Roy, D.L. 2009. The pediatrician and cardiac auscultation. Unpublished manuscript.

Sacks, O. 1989. *Seeing voices: a journey into the world of the deaf*. Berkeley: University of California Press.

Schaeffer, P. 1967. *Traité des objets musicaux*. Paris: Seuil.

Shindler, D.M. 2004. Hand-held ultrasound and the stethoscope. *US Cardiology* (available on-line: *http://www.touchcardiology.com/articles/hand-held-ultrasound-and-stethoscope*, accessed 11 January 2010).

Sinclair, S. 1997. *Making doctors: an institutional apprenticeship*. Oxford: Berg.

Soderquist, D.R. & J.W. Lindsey 1972. Physiological noise as a masker of low frequencies: the cardiac cycle. *Journal of the Acoustic Society of America* **52**, 1216-20.

Sterne, J. 2003. Medicine's acoustic culture: mediate auscultation, the stethoscope and the autopsy of the living. In *The auditory culture reader* (eds) M. Bull & L. Back, 191-217. Oxford: Berg.

Stoller, P. 1989. *The taste of ethnographic things: the senses in anthropology*. Philadelphia: University of Pennsylvania Press.

Turnbull, C. 1961. *The forest people*. London: The Reprint Society.

Tyler, S. 1984. The vision quest in the West, or what the mind's eye sees. *Journal of Anthropological Research* **40**, 23-40.

Wacquant, L. 2004. *Body and soul: notebooks of an apprentice boxer*. Oxford: University Press.

Warren, R.M. 1982. *Auditory perception: a new synthesis*. New York: Pergamon.

Weiner, J. 1991. *The empty place: poetry, space and being among the Foi of Papua New Guinea*. Bloomington: Indiana University Press.

Welsby, P.D., G. Parry & D. Smith 2003. The stethoscope: some preliminary investigations. *Postgraduate Medical Journal* **79**, 695-8.

Yost, W.A. 1994. *Fundamentals of hearing: an introduction*. San Diego: Academic Press.

3

The craft of skilful learning: Kazakh women's everyday craft practices in western Mongolia

ANNA ODLAND PORTISCH *School of Oriental and African Studies*

On a cold winter's day, two Kazakh friends and I went to a dumpling shop for lunch in Ölgii, a town of 30,000 mainly Kazakh inhabitants in the western-most province of Mongolia, Bayan-Ölgii. The small eatery was full. Steaming bowls of salty milk tea served with butter and bowls of freshly steamed mutton-filled dumplings busily changed hands over the counter. We secured a table and went to the counter to order. As we stood waiting our turn, we overheard two women discussing my sweater in audible terms. It was a bright green cashmere sweater which my aunt had given to me after she had washed and shrunk it. It was already a few years old and was beginning to show signs of wear. About this rather unimpressive sweater one of the ladies asserted, 'It's cashmere, yes ... She bought it in Ulaanbaatar [Mongolia's capital] ... She paid 500,000 tögrög for it! [an extortionate amount]'. 'Really?!' said the other, with a mixture of outrage and interest. We did not know these women and left them to their conversation. But I did find it striking when, later that month, another lady, in the course of our conversation, stretched out her hand to feel my sweater and assess the quality of the material. 'That's a nice sweater ...' Then after a pause, 'Do you need it? I could use it. I need green thread for a wall hanging'.

The incident in the dumpling shop prompted my Kazakh friend Bulbul to recount a childhood experience. When she was little, her uncle worked in Russia, having completed his university degree there. He would come back to his family in Bayan-Ölgii once a year, bringing presents. One year he brought his little niece a knitted, rainbow-coloured set of clothing. Bulbul loved this outfit and wore it almost every day. One of her aunts began to show interest in the outfit and would say things like, 'Those clothes doesn't suit you'; and while trying to pry them from Bulbul she would ask, 'Are they so precious to you? More precious than your aunt?' Bulbul got a season's wear out of the clothes, keeping them safe under her mattress when not worn. But her aunt eventually got her hands on them, and the outfit was unravelled and the yarn used in an embroidered wall hanging.

Peter Dormer notes how craftspeople tend to have an enriched experience of the world: 'To possess [craft knowledge] ... in any form is to see the world in an enriched way compared with someone who does not possess it' (1994: 68). There is nothing magical about this, he continues: 'If you are a dentist ... you cannot help noticing the shape of people's mouths and cheeks and making inferences about the state and number of their teeth' (1994: 68). Most Kazakh women in Bayan-Ölgii, particularly in rural areas, make a range of domestic textiles, and in their everyday lives may be said to engage in a 'creative dialogue' with their environment more broadly. Through having learned to make different types of textiles, and through often being engaged in several craft projects at any one time, these women not only approach an isolated and distinctive area of their daily tasks with specialized expertise, but they often engage with their wider social, material, and natural environment with a view to 'appropriating' or 'recycling' ideas and materials in their own practices.

This chapter focuses on Kazakh women's everyday craft practices. I discuss how this craft is learned by younger generations and how women continue developing their craft skills throughout their lives (cf. Rice's view of auscultation as a continuous learning process, this volume). Domestic textile production in Bayan-Ölgii is highly innovative, partly due to difficulties in getting adequate tools and good-quality prefabricated materials, threads, and dyes. It is also a craft that remains relevant in the everyday lives of the Kazakh living in this remote part of Mongolia. Carpets, wall hangings, and other textiles are used in the home as soft furnishings, and are exchanged at weddings between clans. The craft is thus characterized by changing fashions and shifting ideas about good practices.

I discuss the sense in which ideas of good practice are conveyed to learners, and how women are inspired by and learn in dialogue with their material and social environment. I focus on the detail of producing a felt carpet (*syrmaq*) in order to consider the types of orientations and reflections that are involved both in learning and in more expert craft practices.

Conscious reflection is often associated with the design aspect of making an artefact. In this vein, reflection involved in routine and expert cultural practices is seen as a mental process of 'stepping back' from the more unthinking, 'mechanical' execution of a task; it is considered a separate 'purely mental' activity which lends itself well to articulation. On the other hand, the execution of a practice is often seen to be 'purely bodily', and therefore 'tacitly' or 'unconsciously' undertaken and regenerated. This assumption about the relation between 'conscious thought' and 'manual execution' recurs in different guises in practice theory and phenomenological approaches to learning and practice.

Practice theory claims that learning processes occur through the assimilation of master patterns (*topoi*) which serve to reproduce the habitus through the bodily *hexis*. Thus learning results in 'an incorporated state' which, much like a toolbox, contains the 'instruments' for ordering the world. In such a view, the habitus becomes a domain of implicit knowledge (see Downey's and Retsikas's critical discussions, this volume). Its practitioners are instrumental in its reproduction and in changes to the habitus, yet their routine practices are 'unconscious' or unreflective in nature. They do not require reflection in the way that they are learned, nor in the way that they are executed (e.g. Bourdieu 1977: 72). Learning routine practices becomes a process whereby these *topoi* are interiorized and become 'second nature' (Bourdieu 1971). Practices are thus only *apprehended* through a reflective turning-back to practices *already* carried out: master-patterns 'govern and regulate mental processes *without being consciously apprehended and controlled*' (Bourdieu 1971: 193, emphasis added).

A similar relationship between 'reflection' and 'practice' is implied in certain instances in anthropology's use of phenomenology. Here Husserl's notion of *Lebenswelt*, or life-world (1931), a world of immediate, shared experience and the 'common-sense', is prioritized. Phenomenological approaches usefully focus on this 'lived immediacy' of experience and argue against the persistent 'occlusion of the somatic, ... of the physical aspects of Being, a denial of the grounds of our natural humanity' (Jackson 1996: 18). By instead basing our understandings in an immediacy of experience, it is thought that we may come closer to understanding the 'world of sensible experience' (Jackson 1996: 15; see also Csordas 1990; cf. Ingold 2000: 289-420; Wacquant 2004: 97).

Yet in emphasizing the bodily and material aspects of experience over intellectual capabilities, rationalization in language, and abstract theory, one might say that there is an implicit reversal of the Cartesian dualism: the body, not the mind, is elevated to a status worthy of investigation.

While I would agree with the phenomenological insight that 'practical knowledge lies in what is accomplished through it, not in what conceptual order may be said to underlie or precede it' (Jackson 1996: 34), what I seek to do in this context is to begin formulating a more inclusive notion of reflection as *part* of practice itself, based on the ethnographic examples of Kazakh craftswomen's practices. Like many of the authors in this volume, my focus is on the kinds of knowledge evidenced in practice, on the ways such knowledge is communicated, and the means by which learners improve. In this sense, I am concerned with the processes involved in 'intelligent action' (Marchand, introduction, this volume), as part of both early learning stages and more expert executions.

I argue that the details of Kazakh women's daily craft practices and learning processes suggest that these are reflective, focused, and aware in nature. I discuss the sense in which assessment is an integral part of the process of learning and improving one's craft. I consider the nature of assessment and the role that rules or principles of 'good craft practice' play in increasingly 'fluent' and complex expert practices. I do so in order to reconsider the relationship between reflection and practice. This is relevant to how anthropologists approach the study of learning everyday and expert types of knowledge; and, by implication, how the continuation of cultural practices across generations is understood.

Methods, data and theory

The understandings presented here are based on a year's fieldwork and apprenticeship with a Kazakh family in western Mongolia. My 'live-in' apprenticeship enabled me to form an understanding of the learning environment, the role of craftswomen within the household and the community, the place of craft production in daily life, and the social uses of these crafts. Moreover, it helped me to understand the teacher-learner relationship from both an observational and a personal perspective; to observe others' reactions to my own activities and their assessments of my progress and of the artefacts I made (see Coy 1989). It also allowed me to understand the means by which techniques were demonstrated; and to work alongside other learners, observing how they dealt with the different aspects of production.

By learning the craft myself, I was gradually able to engage other women in more meaningful conversations and exchanges by virtue of sharing a set of abilities and activities with them. Moreover, I was able to reflect on my own learning process as a means to 'learning about learning' (see Goody 1989: 254-5). From this perspective, my approach was one that echoes Ewing's comments that one can use one's own reactions as an observational tool to understand a subject or situation (1992: 264).

It would be difficult, therefore, to posit a neat division between description and interpretation, as indicated by Cohen (this volume). My role in undertaking this learning process was not simply to gather data, but rather to expose myself to situations with which I had no familiarity, in order to learn something new, not just about the production of domestic textiles, but about human learning and skill. The ideas presented here are therefore founded in a set of personal experiences that were neither disinterested nor objectively lived (see Jackson 1996: 27; Merleau-Ponty 1992: 362).

This kind of tentative participation and observation allows us to embark on learning processes *in situ*, to subject ourselves to the kinds of bodily routines and motor-sensory experiences that we are investigating: to develop calluses or aching shoulders, to aspire to the fluid dexterity of an expert practitioner, and to scrutinize the learning process towards that level of dexterity from a personal perspective. Thus, like Bloch (1991), I would contend that anthropology has a methodological advantage over other disciplines, and this may be particularly true in our studies of learning and knowledge.

It is exactly this kind of experience and engagement that allows us to bring new perspectives and interpretations to studies of learning and knowledge carried out in other disciplines and to work constructively in dialogue with those disciplines. It is also this methodological foundation that allows us to question assumptions in philosophy, cognitive science, and psychology that often present us with significant 'lacunae' in our understandings of learning and knowledge (see Marchand, introduction, this volume).

The domestic setting for everyday learning

Some 100,000 Kazakhs live in Mongolia and are concentrated mainly in the two western-most provinces (*aimag*) of Bayan-Ölgii and Khovd (Finke 2004; NSO 2001: 50). The Kazakh form the largest minority in Mongolia and are also the most recent minority to have settled in the country (*c.*1860s-1940s). Responding to Russian and later Soviet interventions and unrest in the area that today is Kazakhstan and the Chinese province of Xinjiang, Kazakhs settled in what became in 1940 the 'Kazakh province of Mongolia', Bayan-Ölgii *aimag* (see Akiner 1995; Baabar 1999; Finke 2004; Kinayatuly 2001; Mendikulova 1997; Svanberg 1999).

Today, most Kazakhs in this remote, mountainous region are dependent on domestic animals for their livelihood, either directly or indirectly through family networks. Many move several times a year with their herds between distant seasonal settlements. Some families with smaller herds stay close to their winter house during the summer but nevertheless set up a yurt (*kiiz yi*, lit. 'felt house') as a reception room, to accommodate guests, or simply because they consider it a more comfortable living space after being confined to the house throughout the long, cold winter months (see Kaemaelashuly 2005).

The summertime yurt (and to a lesser extent the winter house) is richly furnished with textiles. In the large, round living space of the yurt, the lattice walls are clad with densely embroidered wall-hangings. Embroidered panels are attached with woven ribbons that 'cordon off' each bed, and brightly coloured satin curtains enclose beds. Embroidered geometric patterns decorate piles of pillows sitting on top of decorative chests. Embroidered panels decorate neatly arranged stacks of suitcases and other furnishings and the grassy floor is covered with sturdy, colourful felt carpets (Fig. 1).

Figure 1. Interior of the yurt, furnished with embroidered and felt crafts, summer settlement in Dayan, near Chinese border, summer 2005.

These soft furnishings are made by women and girls in daily life. Many are made from local raw materials such as sheep's wool and camel's hair, often combined with prefabricated materials and dyes that can be purchased in town. These domestic crafts sit side by side with bought furnishings such as factory-made 'mock-Persian' carpets. In the seat of honour (*tör*) situated directly opposite the door, televisions and DVD players[1] are displayed on top of decorated chests. Clocks, imported plastic-framed mirrors from China, and other household items are arranged amongst photographs of family members along the lattice walls of the yurt.

Summer settlements are typically small. Three or four related households may move to summer pasture locations (*jailauw*) and form a settlement (*auyl*), setting up their yurts in close proximity. Living so closely together means that much of household work is distributed among all members of the settlement. Other people's activities are easily heard, and there is constant awareness of what others are doing and where they are. Many daily tasks such as milking the sheep, goats, and cattle and churning butter are performed by several girls and women working together or taking turns.

Many of the tasks involved in crafts production are similarly collaborative. Beating sheep's wool in preparation for rolling it to produce felt is done by five or six women and girls working together. The rhythmic beating can often be heard several miles away. It is easily recognized by someone who has participated in the task, and can prompt more distant neighbours to come and help.

Learning the skills involved in herding animals and processing their products thus usually involves working with, and contributing to, the activities of one's family members and neighbours. In tasks such as rolling felt (Fig. 2), girls begin to participate by working alongside parents and older siblings. Five or six people kneel in a line in front of a rolled-up reed mat with sheep's wool distributed inside it, and rolling usually takes at least an hour (see Batchuluun 2003: 55-109). Less experienced participants learn to adjust the rhythm of their movements to others so that they do not stop, slow, or accelerate the task to hand, or make mistakes that will disrupt the flow of work (see Gatewood 1985; Palsson 1994: 912). While engaged in the task, the more experienced help learners by instructing them how

Figure 2. Girls rolling felt, summer settlement near Ulaankhus district (*sum*), summer 2004.

to comport themselves or how to do a particular task: 'Don't lean here', 'Pull up your sleeves', and suchlike (see Argenti 2002: 507-8). Of course mistakes are sometimes made, and the unfortunate person at fault is often made fun of long after the event. A memorable incident may even result in a lasting nickname.

As children get better at certain tasks, they become more involved and gain increasing responsibility (see also Bunn 1999: 77; Empson 2003: 219-20). The notion that apprentices to a craft learn through 'unobtrusive observation' (Singleton 1989: 26) rings true in certain contexts in Bayan-Ölgii, particularly where young people work with elders.[2] In such situations, learners are usually busy with other household tasks, while discretely observing an elder's activities. But an equally important means of learning is by obtrusive participation: young children follow their older siblings or parents around and want to be part of their activities, but they get in the way and slow things down. Often a young child is left behind crying loudly as his older siblings walk off with buckets to fetch water or push him aside as they get on with cutting pasta for the evening meal (see High 2008: 49-50). Learning is tied to a willingness to be part of others' daily activities.

Unlike professional trades described in a number of works on apprenticeship (e.g. Kondo 1990; Marchand 2001; Philip 1989; Simpson 2006; Singleton 1998), craft production in Bayan-Ölgii is part of a daily routine, the main aim of which is the running of the household, and not necessarily craft production. Those aspects of craft production which involve an individual focusing on a particular task, such as working on an embroidery or quilting a carpet, are nevertheless part of a wider routine involving other household members. Working in this context involves an awareness of others' activities and the priority of different household tasks at different times of the day (see Venkatesan, this volume). The members of small communities formed of relatives work in collaboration on many related tasks, and each individual activity has its place in terms of the shifting priorities of the household and settlement.

Learning in collaborative situations is, then, a means of developing a sense of the social relations that inform households and small communities. Who does what when, who oversees the work, the extent to which people participate and the manner in which they do so, are all reflections of a dynamic and situational social hierarchy. As one Kazakh friend commented, 'On entering the yurt you immediately assess the composition of the group of people present and situate yourself in relation to them' (S. Daukeyeva, pers. comm., September 2006). Situating oneself is done in terms of one's spatial positioning (e.g. where one sits or works), the types of activities engaged in, forms of address and joking behaviour, and many other behavioural and discursive adjustments. Age, status, gender, and degree and kind of relatedness all inform people's actions and interactions (see Bruck 1997; Humphrey 1993; Portisch 2007: chap. 2).

Learning to make soft furnishings is one way in which girls learn to situate themselves within dynamic and situational hierarchies. The production of soft furnishings falls within women's area of responsibility and is part of a gender-specific role.[3] Marriage is virilocal, and a young bride is usually expected to be the hardest-working member in her husband's household. She is the first to rise in the morning and endures the longest working day (see Hamayon & Bassanoff 1973). Sitting about idly is considered ill mannered. Women often commented that working on an embroidery or carpet was a way of keeping busy, and a welcome diversion from other, more physically demanding household chores. A woman who creates and maintains a beautifully decorated home is admired as hard-working and gifted. Moreover, she provides a role model to her children and other household members in and through her daily actions, including her craft practices. She in turn passes on her skills by going about her daily work and involving others in that work. Teaching and learning in this domestic context thus involve communicating and understanding a socially recognized identity that is implicated in notions of women's social responsibility and moral integrity.

Mastering a craft, such as textile production, is not merely a question of being able to execute certain techniques or achieve a 'fluency' of working with particular tools and materials. It is part of a 'formative' process in a wider sense that involves situating oneself within a particular group of relatives and community in a socially recognized manner, and developing a certain status in virtue of one's skills (see also Coy 1989; Dilley 1989; Lave & Wenger 1991; Marchand 2001; Simpson 2006).

Learning and assessment
In the small village of Soghaq, our neighbour's 11-year-old daughter, Duska, began making crafts with a simple embroidery project for her father (Fig. 3). Later that year,

Figure 3. Duska working on her first embroidered panel for her father, Soghaq village, winter 2005.

she began helping her mother with more complex projects. Duska was in the fifth grade at the local school, and in the mornings after milking the cows she helped chase them to pasture. She was a skinny girl, much smaller than the family's large, humped, hairy cows. On icy mornings she could be seen encouraging the cows along by hurling large rocks after them, her pigtails, tied with large pink bows for school, swinging energetically around her head. After school, Duska helped out with most household tasks. She collected water from the well, and cooked and cleaned the house. In the afternoons and evenings she did her homework, and occasionally she sat down to embroider, watching her mother out of the corner of her eye as the older woman worked on a carpet.

Duska's mother showed her how to do certain tasks by demonstrating them, but, for the most part, this involved no direct didactic instruction (see Venkatesan, this volume). Duska learned specialized techniques in craft production by watching her mother, by trying to execute similar steps or achieve a similar material outcome, and by developing her own ways of dealing with difficult aspects. In this way she learned techniques, ways of handling tools and materials, and ways of comporting herself. Watching and practising were instrumental in developing specific 'techniques of the body' (Mauss 1973 [1950]) and particular motor-kinaesthetic understandings and abilities. Moreover, in watching her elders, Duska also importantly developed an ability to assess and improve her own skilled actions.

In drawing a pattern (oyu) on a piece of felt for a carpet, Apiza, Duska's aunt and neighbour, stood over the material and considered its qualities and dimensions. The piece was laid out on the low table where the family ate all meals. Duska, Bota (Apiza's daughter), and I stood by the warm stove and watched her with anticipation. Apiza felt the material with her hand and made a decisive move as if to start drawing with the charcoaled twig that Bota had prepared for her, but hesitated and again ran her hand over the uneven material. She then began to trace a light outline across the centre of the felt, dividing it into four equal parts, and proceeded to draw the light, rounded outline of a pattern in one corner. Having reached halfway across one quarter, she stopped and rubbed out part of the line with her hand. She measured the whole piece by placing her hand across it. She drew a ghost line across the material with her index finger and proceeded to draw with the twig, tracing thin rounded patterns in each of the four corners.

Apiza assessed the pattern outline, reflected on the whole piece, adjusted and altered her actions, and finally arrived at a pattern that she judged adequate. Throughout the process, Apiza never turned to us to articulate her thoughts about having drawn the pattern off-balance. Rather, we learned as much in a more direct manner, namely by watching the ways in which she communicated a certain assessment of her own work in progress through bodily actions (see Marchand, 'Embodied cognition and communication', this volume). Apiza's demonstration did not simply communicate a technique for producing a certain type of pattern which we might later copy. Importantly, it communicated the practice of continually assessing one's work in progress and consequently adjusting one's actions to achieve an intended outcome, and ultimately make improvements.

Learning through practice is in important ways implicated in learning to assess one's own actions in relation to others' work. When Duska started embroidery, she began with a piece upon which her mother had already completed a few stitches. She inspected these demonstration stitches and tried to copy their style, length, tightness, and density. Her mother's stitches served as a 'stitch goal-type', which Duska tried to approximate. She was able to make progress in her own practices partly because she was able to assess her own work in relation to standards set by others' techniques and crafts. This skill-based type of assessment is an integral part of the learning process. As Dormer argues, it is an important way in which one is able to make purposeful improvements (1994: 57).

Duska's increasing ability to assess the standard of her own work in relation to her mother's was not very different from more experienced craftswomen's experiments with new techniques, tools, and materials. Certainly, as a woman becomes more experienced, she is likely to have a fuller understanding of executing a wider vocabulary of stitches, and it may be easier for her to copy others' practices, to learn new techniques, and to invent different ways of achieving a particular outcome. Nevertheless, learning a technique involves working in relation to others' work, as do more experienced modes of improving and innovating.

Kazakh women visit neighbours and relatives, sit in their yurt or winter house, and, while having tea and discussing daily matters, they take inspiration from the carpets and wall hangings around them. They assess each other's work, and are often able to identify the craftswomen behind certain pieces. Occasionally they judge a pattern to be badly drawn or felt to be poorly rolled, and they mock the crafts of others in scathing terms. Like Dormer's dentist, who has learned to assess the state of people's dental health by peering into their open mouths and scraping and drilling at their teeth, so Kazakh girls learn to assess the quality of others' work through a long and often tedious process of sewing and quilting. Their assessment of other women's work comes out of a direct engagement with making similar artefacts.

One might also argue that craftspeople learn from the materials and tools with which they work. West (2007) has made this point in relation to cheese-makers in France, who learn their craft partly 'from the cheese' itself (Ingold makes a similar point in 2000: 294-311). As much as they learn from teachers or co-learners, apprentices learn from the materials and tools as these respond in particular ways to actions and have certain outcomes. Yet the learning process, even when narrowly focused on an artefact, is always orientated towards others' previous actions with those same or similar artefacts. Even when working alone, apprentices to a craft are situated within a tradition peopled and defined by other practitioners.

In Ingold's words, learning is an unfolding process of 'guided rediscovery', informed by other skilled practitioners, in which one follows in the footsteps of existing 'trails' of activity within human 'taskscapes' (2001; see Makovicky, this volume). Other craftspeople's actions may be improved upon or may be executed in a less successful or useful manner, or of course may fall into disuse altogether. Nevertheless, we stand on the shoulders of others who have gone before us, as Gombrich (2002) argued, and this is an important characteristic of learning a technique as well as learning to make skill-based assessments.

Making skill-based assessments with one's fingertips

While visiting a craftswoman in Ölgii, I was shown a carpet which was considered particularly poor quality. I inspected the carpet and could not see anything awry with the pattern, colours, or stitching. The woman insisted, however, that the carpet was 'bad quality'. She held the carpet between her hands, one hand feeling the surface and the other feeling the back of the carpet, and repeated her judgement. In response to my continued perplexed expression, she took my hand and instructed me to feel the stitches on the back of the carpet for myself. The stitches were large woolly strands, and some had worn and broken. 'You see?' She looked keenly at me. In order for a 'mosaic-style' carpet to hold together, the stitches on the back (facing the floor) have to form small, pin-prick sized dots, tightly sewn so that they become 'embedded' in the thick felt. In this way, they do not wear so quickly when people sit, sleep on, or walk over the finished carpet. The craftswoman who had made this carpet had achieved a beautifully balanced pattern, but had not had the time, inclination, or skill to sew small stitches on the reverse.

Rather than rehearse a list of 'principles of good carpet-making' to me, or launch into a generalized explanation of stitching, the woman in Ölgii found it more immediately precise to draw my attention to the stitches by letting me feel the back of the woolly carpet. She herself had assessed the carpet, not merely by taking it in visually, but through such motor-kinaesthetic actions and sensory engagement (see Retsikas, this volume).

Assessment is often understood as a form of 'mental reading', or a retrospective way of discerning and evaluating actions, techniques, or their material outcome. In her discussion about learning to blow glass, O'Connor links such a form of reflection to the novice stage of learning, arguing that this element is 'never an operative mechanism of proficiency' (2005: 189). With proficiency, she argues, one attains a type of synergy between intention and performance, a 'bodily intentionality' (2005: 190). The reflective aspect of creation is understood as a semantic barrier to lived experience. It is a meaningful interruption and self-evaluation of one's own actions that stands in the way of a fluent practice that would otherwise be uninhibited.

O'Connor's observations recall Ingold's notion that early learning stages may be guided by rules and representations, whereas skill is only truly present from the point where the craftsperson may dispense with these (2000: 415). The achievement of fluency occurs at the point where skill becomes 'practical knowledge' or 'knowledgeable practice' (2000: 316; cf. Dormer 1994: 20). I agree with O'Connor and Ingold that an unfolding learning process involves a development over time, and results in an increasingly 'fluent' practice that makes it less and less necessary to stop in one's tracks and consider progress (see Makovicky, this volume).

Moreover, there are evidently important differences between the practices of a novice and a master. In other apprenticeship contexts, the various learning stages are described as being characterized by different practical tasks paired with different skill-levels (e.g. Kondo 1990; Simpson 2006; Singleton 1989: 18). Similarly, carpet-making in Bayan-Ölgii is a step-by-step learning process that begins with simple tasks and moves on to more complex ones as girls grow older. This does not, however, imply that there is a qualitative difference between the types of learning characterizing different stages, or that the learner moves from mental 'readings' and 'graduates' into a bodily based performative intentionality. The implication of such an understanding is that a novice relies on 'rules and representations' in order to learn a task. Once learned, these 'rules' would then somehow be 'forgotten' or melt into the background of a skilled practice that is mainly unreflective.

That is not to say that novices do not work more slowly, or compare their efforts more frequently to those of others in trying to judge the tasks they execute within a social field for which the parameters are set by peers and co-learners. On the other hand, it is through repeated practice that one achieves a level of fluency; and that fluency does not constitute a break or a separate kind of knowledge from the practice it builds upon. Rather than understand the initial stages of learning as being predominantly guided by rules and representations, and more expert stages as being marked by unreflective execution, in the case of carpet-making I would argue that the learning trajectory of novices and the practices of more experienced craftswomen are part of the same continuum.

Carpet-making involves a tactile and motor-kinaesthetic engagement with the arte-fact. Assessment is one aspect of this engagement. As illustrated above, Apiza experi-mented with the carpet design, adjusted it to the quality of the material, assessed the material by feeling the surface, and thereby developed her design. In this sense one might say that assessment is premised in sensory, somatic, and mental understandings that work together to make the execution a purposeful exercise.

Thus, rather than understanding the process as a set of skills that have been inte-grated into a bodily routine and are 'guided' by mentally held ideas, rules, or represen-tations, and which with experience become 'less guided' by these, I would suggest that reflection is a constitutive aspect of all levels of practice. The notion of 'the man who thought with his fingers' (Mauss 1973 [1950]; Warnier 1999) is perhaps the best approxi-mate description of the complex of mental, somatic, sensory, and kinaesthetic under-standing that is involved in reflective and purposeful action.

As Dormer suggests, constitutive rules reside in the craft activity itself (1994: 60). That is to say, one incorporates the 'internal logic' of a craft into 'the fabric of the body and the texture of the mind' (1994: 60). In this respect, Dormer echoes Ryle's notion that knowing rules is an ability to *perform* intelligent operations, rather than knowing an *extra* fact or truth: 'Knowing a rule is knowing how. It is realised in performances which conform to the rule, not in theoretical citations of it' (Ryle 1990: 217; see Marc-hand, 'Embodied cognition and communication', this volume).

Incremental complexity

Returning to Apiza's actions described above, drawing a pattern for a felt carpet involves several aspects which have to be held in mind simultaneously. In terms of creating a pattern, no space should be left 'blank' or 'outside' of the visual dynamic created by the pattern. Qajghaliuly, an author of a recent work on patterns used in Kazakh crafts, likens the colour symmetry and figure-ground reversal patterns to M.C. Escher's drawings (2004: 395). He argues that Escher's work is similar to Kazakh patterns in that foreground and background are equivalent and in the use of two contrasting colours that are equally visually dominant. I would add that in Escher's work, one (or both) of the contrasting colours tends gradually to emerge as predominant in one part of the image. In Kazakh patterns there is no such dynamic. The two contrasting components of the design are equivalent and balanced throughout the design.

Thus Kazakh designs contradict Dormer's sensible observation on visual composi-tion that '[b]ecause the eye is generally searching for a coherent pattern (because we are trying to make sense of what we see) ... a conflict in the overall strategy of a compo-sition will be uncomfortable because the brain cannot resolve the two opposing pat-terns' (1994: 55). Dormer is here discussing learning the craft of lettering, and further notes that '[y]ou have to keep an eye on the particular, the local and the overall aspects of your design to check what white or black patterns have appeared' (1994: 55). While Dormer's aim is to achieve just one single pattern, in carpet-making the process is much the same, but the aim is to achieve two patterns of equal weighting. Kazakh carpet patterns are 'irresolvable' visual compositions (Fig. 4).

Kazakh patterns, particularly those used in carpets and wall hangings, are rounded, symmetrical, and made up of mirror images and inversions. As Bunn has pointed out in the context of Kyrgyz felt carpets, being able to draw patterns involves 'an ability ...

Figure 4. Drawing of *syrmaq* by Biqumar, a tenth-grade student at the Ten Year School in Ulaankhus district (*sum*) centre.

to draw symmetrically the inside and the outside of each traditional pattern. This ... skill is most important because it requires the capacity to hold in one's mind the relationship of the part to the whole at all times' (1995-6: 78, emphasis added). This pertains likewise to Kazakh carpets in Bayan-Ölgii. In terms of execution, the only other task I can compare drawing a Kazakh pattern with is drawing two mirroring patterns using two pens simultaneously with the right and the left hand. Drawing a Kazakh pattern gives the same sense of two aspects of one design being created simultaneously.

A craftswoman also has to consider the type of carpet being made. If it is one with several sections (Fig. 4), the size and type of patterns in the individual sections have to be in proportion with one another. Drawing the pattern therefore requires one to keep in mind the size and style of the patterns in each section of the resulting carpet, which has to be imagined as a whole.

Moreover, patterns should be a certain dimension. While variation exists, it is generally thought that if a pattern is too small and too detailed it will not make for a durable carpet. A highly detailed pattern will be difficult to cut out, it will require an inordinate amount of stitching along the seams, and sewing on of a decorative 'embossing yarn' (*jiek*) to cover the join between the pieces. All this detail is time-consuming and will wear easily when the carpet is put to everyday use on the floor. Some women commented that small patterns are indicative of an overly ambitious craftswoman, and her strategy is bound to back-fire when, after she has diligently sat for months stitching and quilting her detailed carpet, it comes apart after only one season's use. Conversely, very large patterns are seen as an expression of laziness, and are not considered to be aesthetically pleasing. 'Clearly she was in a rush to complete her carpet ... It's dreadful', Apiza remarked about a neighbour who had just completed a carpet featuring an excessively large pattern. A well-made carpet has a pattern of a certain middle-range size, which will prove more durable, and which will also serve to express just the right balance of modesty and diligence.

In addition, a craftswoman must be mindful of the quality of the felt. A particularly thin or fluffy section which has not been thoroughly rolled may not lend itself well to being cut, and should probably be quilted. The pattern should therefore be drawn in such a way as to make the most of the felt. Felt is rarely rolled in a completely even fashion, and, ideally, the resulting thin, thick, or fluffy parts should be compensated for in the design of the pattern.

Drawing a pattern is the first step in constructing a piece that is composed of several layers and has to be conceptualized in three dimensions. A mosaic-style carpet is made up of a base layer of felt and a top layer which is in turn made of two pieces of felt of contrasting colours that are stitched together 'mosaic-style'. As described above, Apiza was preparing to draw the top-layer pattern. Two pieces of felt of contrasting colours (e.g. dark brown and light beige) were laid on top of one another, stitched together, and a design was drawn on the top piece. A sharp knife was subsequently used to cut through both pieces at the same time along the line of the pattern, thus achieving two more or less identical pieces. The pieces were disentangled and the opposing pieces were matched up and stitched together. The top layer was thus made of a combination of dark brown and beige felt, and was later sewn onto a base layer of felt. The leftover set of contrasting pieces would be used in a second carpet.

It can be difficult to cut out two pieces simultaneously (one on top of the other) and achieve smooth edges along both. As a result, the bottom of the two layers might have jagged edges. These jagged edges nevertheless need to match up with the smoother, opposing edges of the top piece. The two are stitched together, and when the decorative 'embossing yarn' is sewn over the join, it can sometimes be difficult to cover the mismatched sections.

At each stage in the process, a craftswoman builds upon her own previous steps, and often also those of others who may have participated in rolling the felt, and she tries to accommodate imperfections. She must also keep in mind the steps to come. In order to make a good-quality carpet, each action has to have several orientations at once: part and whole, top and bottom layer, parts that are seen and parts that are not, past and current actions, and an imagined and evolving goal-type. Fluency in this craft therefore is not simply achieved by mastering certain isolated techniques, such as drawing a balanced pattern or cutting a smooth line through thick felt, and combining them in linear fashion. Fluency is achieved when one is able simultaneously to assess one's own and other's previous actions and their material outcome, and to build upon these and integrate them into the piece-in-the-making. It also involves an ability to direct the execution towards an intended type of artefact, while knowing in advance the possible material outcome of one's current actions. Fluency, in this sense, is an ability to hold several orientations in mind at once.

Reflective practice

Different stages of the process involve positioning one's body in appropriate ways, holding the materials in a manageable fashion, and adjusting movements to the tools. The sharpness of the knife or the length of the needle influences the physical movements required to achieve a certain outcome (Warnier 2001). One's engagement with the piece as it develops relies on minute and continual bodily and cognitive corrections and an intelligent attention to the qualities and responsiveness of the materials and tools.

What seems on the surface to be a relatively simple task (i.e. that of drawing the pattern) is in fact reliant on a complex understanding of a series of conditions that must be co-ordinated to work together. A pre-existing design can never simply be applied to the material (see Makovicky, this volume). The size and qualities of the materials vary, and this affects the possibilities for the design. The goal-type is therefore not fixed, but emerges in this engagement.[4]

At the level of learning motor skills, Downey's comments (2005) are relevant. Drawing on the work of Bernstein, a Russian scientist who worked in physiology and biomechanics, Downey warns that it would be erroneous to consider a motor skill as a mere 'imprint' or a 'trace' somewhere in the brain, as if it were a motor formula or cliché (2005: 27). Bernstein argued that '[r]epetitions of a movement or action are necessary in order to *solve a motor problem* many times (better and better) and to *find the best ways* of solving it' (1996: 176, emphasis in original). In other words, we learn motor skills by rehearsing possible solutions to a problem, since 'in material conditions, external conditions never repeat themselves and the course of the movement is never ideally reproduced' (1996: 176).

The gist of the argument is simple: one never steps into the same river twice. Not only are materials, tools, and conditions in the wider environment not exactly replicated from one instance to another, but the individual also changes, and her or his actions and techniques are not reproduced according to an ideal. Problems have to be solved through intelligent attention to shifting conditions, by building on previous experiences with similar tasks or circumstances. Moreover, similar problems do not always comprise the same set of composite aspects.

The details of our practices are never perfect reproductions of the actions of others, nor of our own. In Bernstein's words, '[P]ractice ... does not consist in repeating the means of solution of a motor problem time after time, but in the process of solving this problem again and again by techniques which we change ... and perfect ... from repetition to repetition' (1967: 134). Learning motor skills involved in everyday and expert types of knowledge involves practice that is never precisely repetitive in a mimetic sense; rather, '[p]ractice is a particular type of repetition without repetition' (1967: 134; see also Ingold 2000: 353). Mastering a craft such as carpet-making is a problem-solving ability whereby one adjusts one's actions and interactions in relation to shifting conditions.

As we become better at executing certain skills, these may come to form what Bernstein termed 'background corrections' (1996: 188). For instance, as we become better at keeping our balance on a bicycle, our field of attention becomes more encompassing: initially we focus on staying upright and moving forwards while making appropriate kinds of bodily movements; later we may include steering and moving through traffic at a certain speed within our field of awareness. Similarly, in my own case of learning to quilt a carpet, I initially focused on executing a type of stitch to a certain regular specification, stitches that would form a continuous and smooth line across the surface of the felt. In time my concerns became more encompassing: I strived to stitch pin-prick-sized dots on the reverse side of the woolly fabric, which would not be seen but only be felt with the fingertips as one works. As I progressed, I became better at directing this regular and smooth line of quilting across the relevant section of the carpet, and I became better at keeping in mind these different aspects of the execution at the same time.

It is perhaps not so much a question of certain 'mastered' abilities 'receding from consciousness', but rather a question of becoming better at simultaneously keeping several aspects of an execution in one's awareness, and continually weighing up different aspects against one another. Background corrections are not 'waiting in a background level library, ready, like a toy hidden in a firecracker. They must be developed and exercised' (Bernstein 1996: 188). The ability to become more 'fluent' does not involve 'forgetting' certain tasks, or letting them 'slip from consciousness', as is often implied. 'Mastery' involves the development and expansion of one's field of awareness while at the same time weighing up all components involved. This may particularly become clear when something goes wrong: when the line of quilting goes astray, when one's foot slips off the pedal. The action that has not had the intended outcome does not suddenly emerge from the recesses of the unconscious in such situations; instead it assumes more importance in one's overall field of awareness.

In the minutiae of our practices we evaluate our surroundings and the materials and tools with which we work; we adjust actions and dispositions; we assess progress, rhythm, timing, and positioning; we take conscious steps towards improving our practices, and towards developing and adjusting a goal-type in the process. These are constituents of reflective and intelligent practices.

Conclusion

Their penchant for scandalous gossip (*ösek*) aside, the women in the dumpling shop were assessing the quality of my green sweater and evaluating its potential for use in an embroidered piece. Dormer's notion that craftspeople live their craft and have an enriched experience of the world is not something that applies merely in the isolated circumstances of a 'workshop setting', as his own work amply suggests. Learning a skill often comes to inform the craftsperson's experience of the world more generally. Such an enriched experience is not a passive understanding or appreciation of others' work, but is, rather, implicated in continuing to learn and expand one's own craft practices.

Learning techniques, improving one's craft, and integrating new materials and sources of inspiration involves making skill-based assessments of one's own work and that of others, and of pieces in the making and finished artefacts. Making such skill-based assessments, I argue, is not guided by a 'separate' mental process composed of rules and representations which 'melt away' once a certain level of expertise is achieved. Instead, reflection and assessment are integral to the practices of both novices and accomplished craftswomen. Rather than being imposed according to a separate set of mentally held principles, assessments are based in somatic-sensory interactions with practical tasks, with tools and materials. Learning to make such assessments involves developing an increasingly detailed and complex understanding of the whole production process.

In passing on the craft of carpet-making to future generations, craftswomen do not engage in 'unconscious' or 'tacit' knowledge production. Rather, they communicate specific and unambiguous lessons concerning craft practices and material artefacts through bodily expressions and actions (see Marchand, 'Embodied cognition and communication', and Retsikas, this volume), and they teach learners explicit lessons about quality and craft practice through encouraging learners' own sensory-somatic engagement with the textures and qualities of the materials with which they work.

Learning this craft is far from a 'finite' process whereby existing 'cultural templates' or generative 'master-patterns' are assimilated with motor abilities that can thenceforth be mechanically and unthinkingly executed. Nor is mastery a matter of memorizing a sequence of techniques to be replicated in different contexts. Rather, the learning process is a responsive and dynamic one in which learners develop increasingly complex understandings. Fluency is not achieved by all women in exactly the same way; instead individuals emphasize, take pleasure in, and excel at different aspects of the craft. Learning to master this craft is thus more akin to entering into a continued skill-based creative and evaluative dialogue with one's environment in the widest sense.

NOTES

The research on which this chapter is based was generously supported by the School of Oriental and African Studies with a Research Student Fellowship, the Committee for Central and Inner Asia (Cambridge) with a travel grant, and the ASA/Radcliffe-Brown Trust Fund with a thesis-writing grant. Further work has been made possible by an ESRC post-doctoral fellowship (PTA-026-27-1959). The research is based on a year's fieldwork and apprenticeship with Ustav and Apiza's family in the village of Soghaq, Bayan-Ölgii *aimag*. I would like to remember, with this chapter, Apiza's older brother, Dr Biqumar Kaemaelashuly, Bayan-Ölgii's most formidable ethnographer, who died an early death in 2007; and I would like to thank Apiza, the family, and Biqumar's niece, Bulbul, whose clothes were recycled by her aunt and whose friendship made my research possible.

[1] In remote settlements, large electrical appliances are often run with the use of generators or solar panels, and 'packages' comprising TV, DVD player, and solar panel with relevant cables can be bought at the market in Bayan-Ölgii *aimag*.

[2] I use the term 'elder' simply to indicate someone who is older than a said person. At the same time, age is probably the most significant delineator of social hierarchy, and behavioural and discursive practices are most clearly defined in terms of people's relative age (see Portisch 2007: chap. 2).

[3] Anyone interested in craft production is able to participate and learn. Men might be derided for their 'feminine skills' but are not excluded by any taboos or restrictions (cf. Messick 1987). When men participate in craft production they usually assist their wives, who keep overall responsibility for the work.

[4] That is not to suggest that in other crafts, such as making bricks to a certain specification (Marchand 2001) or producing Japanese sweets (Kondo 1990), individual executions do not correspond more precisely to the goal-type, because precision is more instrumental in these cases.

REFERENCES

AKINER, S. 1995. *The formation of Kazakh identity: from tribe to nation-state*. London: Royal Institute of International Affairs.

ARGENTI, N. 2002. People of the chisel: apprenticeship, youth, and elites in Oku (Cameroon). *American Ethnologist* **29**, 497-533.

BAABAR, B.-E.B. 1999. *Twentieth-century Mongolia*. Cambridge: The White Horse Press.

BATCHULUUN, L. 2003. *Felt art of the Mongols* (trans. E. Thrift). Ulaanbaatar: Institute for the Study of Arts and Culture, Mongolian University of Arts and Culture.

BERNSTEIN, N.A. 1967. *The co-ordination and regulation of movement*. Oxford: Pergamon.

——— 1996. On dexterity and its development. In *Dexterity and its development* (eds) M.L. Latash & M.T. Turvey, 1-244. Mahwah, N.J.: Lawrence Erlbaum Associates.

BLOCH, M. 1991. Language, anthropology and cognitive science. *Man* (N.S.) **26**, 183-98.

BOURDIEU, P. 1971. Systems of education and systems of thought. In *Knowledge and control: new directions for the sociology of education* (ed.) F.D. Young, 189-207. London: Collier-Macmillan.

——— 1977. *Outline of a theory of practice* (trans. R. Nice). Cambridge: University Press.

BRUCK, G. VOM 1997. A house turned inside out: inhabiting space in a Yemeni city. *Journal of Material Culture* **2**, 139-72.

BUNN, S. 1995-6. Kyrgyz *shyrdak*. *Textile Museum Journal* **34-35**, 74-91.

——— 1999. The nomad's apprentice. In *Apprenticeship: towards a new paradigm of learning* (eds) P. Ainley & H. Rainbird, 74-85. London: Kogan Page.

COY, M. (ed.) 1989. *Apprenticeship: from theory to method and back again*. Albany, N.Y.: SUNY Press.

CSORDAS, T.J. 1990. Embodiment as a paradigm for anthropology. *Ethos* **18**, 5-47.

DILLEY, R.M. 1989. Secrets and skills: apprenticeship among Tukolor weavers. In *Apprenticeship: from theory to method and back again* (ed.) M. Coy, 181-98. Albany, N.Y.: SUNY Press.

DORMER, P. 1994. *The art of the maker*. London: Thames & Hudson.

DOWNEY, G. 2005. *Learning capoeira: lessons in cunning from an Afro-Brazilian art*. Oxford: University Press.

EMPSON, R. 2003. Integrating transformations: a study on children and daughters-in-law in a new approach to Mongolian kinship. Ph.D. thesis, King's College, University of Cambridge.

EWING, K. 1992. Is psychoanalysis relevant for anthropology? In *New directions in psychological anthropology* (eds) T. Schwartz, G.M. White & C.A. Lutz, 251-68. Cambridge: University Press.

FINKE, P. 2004. *Nomaden im Transformationsprozess: Kasachen in der post-sozialistischen Mongolei*. Münster: LIT Verlag.

GATEWOOD, J.B. 1985. Actions speak louder than words. In *Directions in cognitive anthropology* (ed.) J.W. Dougherty, 199-219. Urbana: University of Illinois Press.

GOMBRICH, E. 2002. *The sense of order: a study in the psychology of decorative art*. London: Phaidon.

GOODY, E. 1989. Learning, apprenticeship and the division of labour. In *Apprenticeship: from theory to method and back again* (ed.) M. Coy, 233-58. Albany, N.Y.: SUNY Press.

HAMAYON, R. & N. BASSANOFF 1973. De la difficulté d'être une belle-fille. In *Études Mongoles*, Cahier 4, 7-74. Nanterre: Université de Paris.

HIGH, M. 2008. Dangerous fortunes: wealth and patriarchy in the Mongolian informal gold mining economy. Ph.D. thesis, King's College, University of Cambridge.

HUMPHREY, C. 1993. Women, taboo and the suppression of attention. In *Defining females: the nature of women in society* (ed.) S. Ardener, 73-92. Oxford: Berg.

HUSSERL, E. 1931. *Ideas: general introduction to pure phenomenology* (trans. W.R. Boyce Gibson). London: Allen & Unwin.

INGOLD, T. 2000. *The perception of the environment: essays in livelihood, dwelling and skill*. London: Routledge.

————— 2001. From the transmission of representations to the education of attention. In *The debated mind: evolutionary psychology versus ethnography* (ed.) H. Whitehouse, 113-53. Oxford: Berg.

JACKSON, M. 1996. Introduction: phenomenology, radical empiricism, and anthropological critique. In *Things as they are: new directions in phenomenological anthropology* (ed.) M. Jackson, 1-50. Bloomington: Indiana University Press.

KAEMAELASHULY, B. 2005. *Kazakhtyng baiyrghy baspanalary, yi-jihazdary, ulttyq kiim-keshek, ydys-ayaq, as-susyn, tamaq-taghamdaryna qatysty salt-daestyrler* (Traditions and customs relating to indigenous Kazakh dwellings, interior, national costume, utensils, food, drink and dishes). Ölgii, Mongolia.

KINAYATULY, Z. 2001. *Mongholiyadaghy Qazaqtar* (Mongolia's Kazakhs). Almaty, Kazakhstan: Dyniejyzi Qazaqtarynyng Qauwymdastyghy.

KONDO, D.R. 1990. *Crafting selves: power, gender, and discourses of identity in a Japanese workplace*. Chicago: University Press.

LAVE, J. & E. WENGER 1991. *Situated learning: legitimate peripheral participation*. Cambridge: University Press.

MARCHAND, T.H.J. 2001. *Minaret building and apprenticeship in Yemen*. Richmond, Surrey: Curzon.

MAUSS, M. 1973 [1950]. Les techniques du corps (sixième partie). In *Sociologie et anthropologie*, 365-86. Paris: Presses Universitaires de France.

MENDIKULOVA, G.M. 1997. *Istoricheskie sud'by Kazakhskoi Diaspory: proiskhojdenie i razvitie* (The historical fate of the Kazakh Diaspora: origins and development). Almaty, Kazakhstan: Ghylym.

MERLEAU-PONTY, M. 1992. *Phenomenology of perception* (trans. C. Smith). London: Routledge & Kegan Paul.

MESSICK, B. 1987. Subordinate discourse: women, weaving, and gender relations in North Africa. *American Ethnologist* **14**, 210-25.

NSO (NATIONAL STATISTICAL OFFICE OF MONGOLIA) 2001. *2000 Population and housing survey*. Ulaanbaatar, Mongolia.

O'CONNOR, E. 2005. Embodied knowledge: the experience of meaning and the struggle towards proficiency in glassblowing. *Ethnography* **6**, 183-204.

PALSSON, G. 1994. Enskilment at sea. *Man* (N.S.) **29**, 901-27.

PHILIP, L. 1989. *The road through Miyama*. New York: Random House.

PORTISCH, A.O. 2007. Kazakh *syrmaq*-production in western Mongolia: learning and skill in a domestic craft tradition. Ph.D. thesis, School of Oriental and African Studies, University of London.

QAJGHALIULY, A. 2004. *Oyu i oi* (Design and idea). Almaty, Kazakhstan.

RYLE, G. 1990. Knowing how and knowing that. In *Gilbert Ryle: collected papers*, vol. 2: *Collected essays 1929-68*, 212-25. Bristol: Thoemmes Antiquarian Books.

SIMPSON, E. 2006. Apprenticeship in western India. *Journal of the Royal Anthropological Institute* (N.S.) **12**, 151-71.

SINGLETON, J. 1989. Japanese folkcraft pottery apprenticeship: cultural patterns of an educational institution. In *Apprenticeship: from theory to method and back again* (ed.) M. Coy, 13-30. Albany, N.Y.: SUNY Press.

————— (ed.) 1998. *Learning in likely places: varieties of apprenticeship in Japan*. Cambridge: University Press.

SVANBERG, I. (ed.) 1999. *Contemporary Kazaks: cultural and social perspectives*. Richmond, Surrey: Curzon.

WACQUANT, L. 2004. *Body and soul: notebooks of an apprentice boxer*. Oxford: University Press.

WARNIER, J.-P. 1999. *Construire la culture materielle: l'homme qui pensait avec ses doigts*. Paris: Presses Universitaires de France.

————— 2001. A praxiological approach to subjectivation in a material world. *Journal of Material Culture* **6**, 5-24.

WEST, H. 2007. Patrimony and apprenticeship in the making of an artisan cheese. Paper given at the SOAS Anthropology Seminar Series on *The transmission of knowledge*, 31 January.

4

'Something to talk about': notation and knowledge-making among Central Slovak lace-makers

Nicolette Makovicky *Wolfson College, Oxford*

In the volume Preface, Marchand asks how anthropologists might 'chronicle manifestations of human knowledge that "exceed language" ' (p. Siii). This chapter addresses the consequences of codifying and circulating such knowledge. Having worked amongst lace-makers in Central Slovakia since 2003, I often witnessed their struggle to articulate craft knowledge in a manner that is helpful to colleagues and pupils. With skilled movement deeply ingrained in bodily practice, words seemed inadequate for describing technique. Instead, many craftswomen made use of a simple system of notation to make themselves understood. These drawings are the lace-maker's equivalent to 'knitting recipes', conveying the necessary information for a lace-maker to reproduce a design. As an objectified form of bodily practice, drawings facilitate the communication and exchange of knowledge across generations and communities. Notation, however, is not simply a neutral tool for the recording, exchange, and dissemination of information. Indeed, precisely because notation affords procedure to be separated from practice and disembeds craft knowledge from its geographical, social, and historical context, its use has concrete consequences for lace-makers' understandings of skill, proficiency and design composition. The construction of diagrams and drawings creates an ongoing dialogue about the relative merits of manual dexterity, mental representations, drawings, improvisation, and creativity. In turn, these discussions and disagreements become central to divergent concepts of style, tradition, and heritage.

The link between the codification of 'folk' culture and nation-building has been amply documented (e.g. Gellner 1983; Hobsbawm & Ranger 1983; Kaneff 2004), yet the term 'codification' has generally glossed over a complex and multi-layered process of collection, classification, and reproduction of artistic traditions and lifeways. My aim is to show how in the case of lace-making the instrument of its codification, namely notation, has affected the epistemology of craft knowledge itself, rather than merely ideas of nationhood and identity. Indeed, some lace-makers themselves have taken up not only notation, but also the ethos of conservation that has historically characterized both Slovak ethnology (Podoba 2005: 245-7) and the work of the state-sponsored

Centre for Folk Art Production (Makovicky 2009). For these women, the diagrams produced through notation appear to 'store' or 'carry' not just procedural knowledge, but entire traditions. In some ways, then, everyday craft practice and nation-building have become intimately related as processes of knowledge-making, practices of codification having influenced not only lace-makers' sense of identity or the social value conferred upon their *métier*, but even their relationship to their tools and their bodies. The implications of codification are nevertheless resisted by other craftswomen who refuse to acknowledge the use of notation for the purposes of preservation and who treat diagrams merely as disposable tools. Knowledge – whether it pertains to process of production or the intricacies of a local style – is highly contested and constantly re-negotiated, and nowhere more so than in the classroom.

It is in the classroom that I begin my examination of these many, complex issues. By comparing and contrasting two different pedagogical approaches to the teaching of the craft – namely apprenticeship and classroom-based learning – I explore the epistemological conundrums faced by lace-makers who wish to understand how best to teach and share their specialist knowledge. Their search runs parallel to that in recent anthropological scholarship on 'ways of knowing' (e.g. Grasseni 2007; Hallam & Ingold 2007; Harris 2007), as well as studies on craft (e.g. Adamson 2007; Alfoldy 2007; Risatti 2007, Sennett 2008). Lace-makers ponder the significance of the learning environment for the experience of the novice and the role of the body and senses for understanding and creating knowledge, and they openly discuss the virtues and dangers of recording designs on paper. Behind these issues lies the unresolved question of whether craft knowledge is best understood as context-dependent and performative or whether it is based on rules and laws which can be abstracted from practice. While my findings correlate with anthropology's recent critique of the absolute distinction between 'tacit' and propositional forms of knowledge, and they favour a holistic approach to body and mind (Downey 2007; Marchand 2007) and an ecological approach to situated learning (Ingold 2000a; 2000b; 2001; Lave & Wenger 1991), the struggles of lace-makers to define and integrate various forms of knowledge challenge anthropologists to inquire not only into the role of cognitive, motor, and social mechanisms in the making of knowledge, but also into the ways in which people's individual models of knowledge shape their action and agency. As demonstrated below, disparate teaching methods as well as the creation of patterns and designs are implicated in contests for pedagogical, artistic, and social authority. Before turning to the issue of notation, however, I provide a short introduction to lace-making, highlighting the intimate relationship between the body, movement, and the creation of form in craft practice.

'Choreography' of the hands: how rhythm creates form

Špania Dolina is a scenic mountain village of small stone cottages perched on steep hillsides in Central Slovakia. If one takes a walk through the village on a warm summer day, one is likely to encounter elderly lace-makers sitting on low stools on their verandas or in their front gardens with pillows placed in front of them. Eager to leave the dark, cramped interiors of their cottages, the lace-makers take their work outside into the sunshine. Balancing their pillows on a low stool and equipped with various boxes containing pins and needles, spools of linen thread, cardboard and scissors, they gossip with passing friends and neighbours, and hope that a tourist might stop by to take a look and buy a piece.

Before they can demonstrate their craft, lace-makers must set up their materials on the large, heavy bolster pillow on which lace is made in Central Slovakia. Firstly, the thread (either linen or cotton for crocheting) is wound onto bobbins at each end to form a *pair* (*par* in Slovak) (Fig. 1). Once the required number of pairs has been wound, they are hung from pins stuck into the pillow through the *furma* (a pre-punched cardboard template) (Fig. 2). A seasoned lace-maker does not necessarily need to know how many pairs she will need to execute a particular pattern. Rather, she starts at a single point and keeps adding pairs as necessary to produce a certain combination of design elements. While the majority of the pairs hang down vertically from the pins, a small number of 'travelling' or 'working pairs' are intertwined with this majority in order to form the decorative elements. The working pairs may be wound with thread of a different colour or type in order to contrast with the 'ground' that is formed by the continuous presence of the neutral threads of the passive pairs.

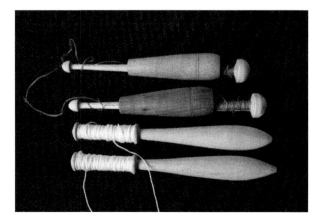

Figure 1. Bobbins from Staré Hory (top) and Špania Dolina (bottom).

Figure 2. Špania Dolina-style lace started on a diagonal and woven using a universal *furma*. One of the *working pairs* is threaded with brown linen thread, the other is threaded with white linen and has been used to create the 'fan' and the rectangular block of weave at the left of the sample. The arrows indicate the pair's starting position and its current position in the unfinished sample.

To construct the 'stitches', the lace-maker always works with two pairs – a working pair and a non-travelling pair – and, holding the bobbins in her hands, she passes one over another in the various sequences. The simplest stitch, a 'cloth stitch' or *platenko* (from *platno* – cloth), is identical to the plain (tabby) weave of a loom-woven cloth and its name is derived therefrom (Figs 3-6). Seasoned craftswomen, like those in Špania Dolina, are to some extent oblivious to the rhythmic, serial movements they produce in weaving lace. While chatting to friends, neighbours, and tourists, a lace-maker will manipulate the bobbins close to her chest and keeps an eye on the weave she is creating at the top of the pillow nearest to the pins. With her eyes on the pillow, she watches the intertwining of threads below the pins that results from her manual manipulation of the bobbins. Hence a lace-maker becomes aware of mistakes made by her hands only when a problem appears to her in the weave. In short, a lace-maker monitors the effect – the weave – rather than her movements used in creating it.

With the advantage of hindsight, this now seems a fairly obvious observation. As an apprenticing lace-maker in the villages of Špania Dolina and Staré Hory (Central Slovakia's second historical centre of lace-making), however, my own routine and

Figure 3. The starting position for the cloth stitch.

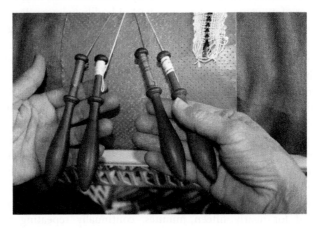

Figure 4. The central bobbin of the left pair is crossed over the central bobbin of the right pair.

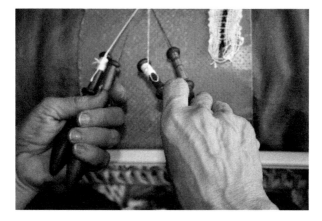

Figure 5. The (now) peripheral bobbins from each pair are crossed over the central bobbins.

Figure 6. The central bobbin from the left pair is crossed over the central bobbin from the right pair. The pairs have now changed hands and the cloth stitch is complete.

intimate relation with the technique obscured my realization that, with experience, the correct sequences of movement had become part of bodily memory. It was only when I was invited to teach lace-making to a group of school children in the regional capital, Banská Bystrica, that I was forced to reflect consciously upon my own movements. When the lesson began, I sat at a pillow and asked the pupils to stand behind me and look over my shoulder while I demonstrated with the bobbins and explained what I was doing: for example, 'Take the outer right bobbin and pass it under the right middle bobbin ...'. Initially, I found it surprisingly difficult to articulate my own actions in a manner that my pupils would understand. Some grew faint-hearted and exclaimed that it was 'too complicated', while others were eager to have a go. One by one, the motivated pupils sat down at the pillow and I either stood or sat beside them, watching their hands as they worked, and offered verbal instructions or, at times, tapped the bobbin which they were supposed to work with next. I was struck by how some pupils needed to be shown the movements only once or twice before they could reproduce them precisely. Others struggled for nearly fifteen minutes, continually repeating the four-part sequence of movements for making a simple stitch without being able to remember it.

I came to realize through giving these lessons that, in lace-making, rhythm creates form. Like a stylized dance, the movements of the hands are rhythmically repeated in order to produce a material expression.

While living and working with lace-makers, I played many roles, including apprentice, teacher, colleague and friend, fellow club member and visiting researcher. Fieldwork has often been likened to a form of apprenticeship (Coy 1989), and indeed my own fieldwork was an induction into not just one, but three communities of practice: those in the villages of Staré Hory and Špania Dolina, as well as individuals and lace-making clubs in Banská Bystrica. The technique of bobbin lace-making came to these villages in the sixteenth century with the arrival of German, Bohemian, and Croatian immigrants (Marková 1962). The men who settled in the villages worked in the local copper mines and their wives and children supplemented the family income by making lace for the urban bourgeoisie and for peasant costumes. Bobbin lace-making eventually developed into a cottage industry in Staré Hory and Špania Dolina and became increasingly important to the economic survival of these communities after the end of the nineteenth century when commercial mining became unprofitable. By the 1970s, however, urbanites began to take up lace-making alongside knitting, crocheting, and embroidery as a form of needlecraft. Lace-making courses were arranged by the Slovenský Zväz Žien (the Slovak Union of Women) and ROH (the socialist state Worker's Union) in the early to mid-1980s, and this is where most women without genealogical ties to the villages learned their skills (Sedalová 1989). Today, a number of lace-making clubs exist in Banská Bystrica where craftswomen swap tips, tricks, techniques, and designs.

Not only do all these communities have their own habits, histories, and heroines, but, as I aim to convey here, their individual members also possess quite different knowledge-making practices based on divergent conceptions of what constitutes legitimate craft knowledge, how this knowledge is related to practice, and how it is best put to use. Although everyone can identify competent work, they disagree on the definition of competency itself. Similarly, the question of how best to develop such competency in a pupil is one that occupies the minds of lace-makers from all communities.

Becoming 'skilled': pedagogies of the village and the classroom

While conducting fieldwork in 2003, I apprenticed to Ana Paličková, an octogenarian living in Špania Dolina who has made bobbin lace since childhood. Early each morning I took a bus to the picturesque mountaintop village, scrambling up the steep road to the neatly renovated miners' cottage that she shared with her son Miroslav and his wife Dagmar. Although I often arrived before Miroslav and Dagmar left for the city, Ana was already hard at work making lace either in her room or in the family kitchen, where I would join her. Hunched over a pillow and straining her eyes through a pair of large, thick glasses to see her work, Ana frequently sighed and stretched in an attempt to alleviate the pain that develops in the neck, shoulders, and lower back after a few hours of lace-making. Like many of the elderly lace-makers with whom I worked, Ana's sight was failing and her eyes became tear-filled from the exertion caused by constantly monitoring the weave in dim light. When Ana once offered me a cup of coffee, it occurred to me that her glasses were only for show: after filling the kettle with water, she placed it on the stove, then took her glasses off and bent down to turn on the stove top using one of the knobs. I realized that she could not see the numbers indicating the temperature unless she moved so close to the knob that her nose touched it. I concluded that, equally, Ana could not see her lacework very well and must have worked largely from bodily memory.

Ana's ability to make lace almost 'in the blind' suggests that decades of practice had turned the necessary sequences of movements into 'second nature'. As her apprentice, I was expected to learn and perfect the same movements, as was Zuzana, Ana's great-granddaughter and second pupil. Zuzana, a lively 6-year-old girl, often spent the weekend in the village and begged her great-grandmother for lessons until Ana relented. Before Zuzana's first lesson, Ana Paličková made a few centimetres of lace in a simple design. She then seated Zuzana on her lap and showed her the correct way to hold the bobbins, which were still too large for her small hands. She then instructed Zuzana how to perform selected movements to create a stitch, placing her own hands over Zuzana's and guiding them into the correct positions. In the beginning, Zuzana performed only the actual movement and possibly placed a pin in the correct indentation in the cardboard underlying the weave. She was allowed to perform more than one operation at a time once she learned how to handle the bobbins and could confidently perform the required movements. After each stitch, Ana asked Zuzana to tell her which pairs of bobbins she was going to pick up and move, and which she intended to leave behind, thus making sure that she understood the principle of what she was doing before proceeding to perform the actual movements. This questioning gradually ceased as Zuzana's confidence grew. Most importantly, Ana Paličková did not use marked boards, illustrations, or drawings to explain movements or their outcome. In fact, she rarely talked about patterns or designs, and she only let Zuzana use the finished lace as a guide for how to proceed once a few centimetres of the lace were completed (this took three or four lessons).

Ingold (2000b) has noted that skills are passed on not through the learning of rules or pre-formed representations, but rather by placing novices in situations where they can train their perception, action, and attention to become skilled. Learning must take the form of 'guided rediscovery' (Ingold 2000b: 356) in which novices are placed in situations where they can practise, hone their skills, and gain experience by themselves. On this point, Ingold and Ana Paličková would most certainly agree. But it would be erroneous to conclude that Ana would be satisfied if her pupils remembered to manipulate the bobbins correctly and in the right sequence. Taking into consideration that Ana taught Zuzana through constant questioning, as well as with verbal and hands-on instruction, it is apparent that getting pupils to reproduce their own movements was only a minor component in the training. Ana wanted her pupils not only to memorize specific movements, but also to understand how to respond to the visual and sensual clues generated by the thread, tools, and pillow. A pupil had to learn to count out her stitches, to remember whether to work towards the left or the right, and to bring the correct bobbins into position before she could begin making a motif. Zuzana, sitting on the lap of her great-grandmother, was taught to see the lace she made as a result of her physical activity, of which calculations, decisions, and assessments were an integral part.

In her contribution to this volume, Portisch compels us to regard conscious reflection and sensory-somatic engagement with materials and tools as 'a constitutive aspect of practice', arguing that proficiency in craft should not simply be regarded as the outcome of the assimilation of a priori or theoretical rules and representations into unreflective bodily practice. Indeed, if one observes the manner in which Ana Paličková taught lace-making to Zuzana, it becomes clear that although she eventually stopped questioning Zuzana about her every move, she did not assume that Zuzana herself had stopped deliberating over what to do next. Portisch makes an effective critique of practice theory (Bourdieu 1977; 1990), as well as claims that skilled practice relies on 'tacit' knowledge (Dormer 1997) and embodiment (e.g. Gatewood 1985; Gosselain 1992; Keller & Keller 1991; MacKenzie 1991; Reichard 1934; Urton 1997). As in other crafts, learning how to make lace undoubtedly relies, at least in part, on the novice's ability to commit a sequence of movements to bodily memory. And in the same way that, for instance, an experienced cyclist has difficulty explaining how to ride a bicycle, lace-makers often find it challenging adequately to verbalize instructions to their novices. Nevertheless, I am reluctant to conclude that a lack of overt verbal instruction demonstrates the 'low discursive saturation' (Dowling 1998) of the craft. Rather than focusing on the areas in which lace-makers remain relatively mute, my study examines how they do talk about their practice and, more importantly, what they talk about.

In discussing the problems that the inarticulate nature of many traditional crafts pose, Malcolm McCullough (2004) comments that they lack a form of notation. In this respect, lace-making is an exception. There exists a particular genre of schematic diagrams or 'recipes' for the production of a piece of lace of a certain design which enable lace-makers to create new laces without the need for detailed verbal instruction each time (Fig. 7). Photocopied or traced, and then pinned onto the pillow, such schematic drawings contained information regarding procedure, structure, and size (width, number of

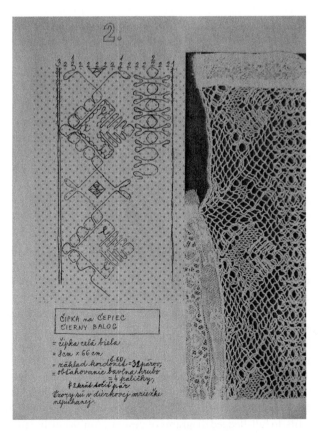

Figure 7. An example of schematic drawings used by lace-makers. (Diagram by Zlatica Frajtova.)

bobbins, and thread thickness). They are neither a mirror image of the design, nor do they list explicit stitch-by-stitch instructions (such as in the case of knitting recipes). Instead, they are drawn as a rough representation of the threaded bobbins onto an imagined cardboard template. A limited number of conventions make most patterns decipherable to all practitioners: certain symbols, such as the hash sign (#) for the 'cloth stitch', are universal, and only those bobbins that travel across the width of the lace to form the motifs are drawn into the scheme. Thus, such drawings are essentially a linear representation of the working pair(s) of threaded bobbins, charting their course across the width of the pattern and enabling a lace-maker to understand the sequence of stitches that make up a design. What the drawing shows, then, is movement.

By objectifying difficult-to-articulate bodily practice, these diagrams literally give lace-makers 'something to talk about'. They act as rhetorical devices, in that they often become a point of discussion for lace-makers even as work on a particular design is in progress. By pointing to various points of the drawings, lace-makers can discuss the best way to go from one point to the next, to turn a corner, or to avoid the pitfalls of a difficult transition from one design element to another. As recipes for the creation of a particular pattern, diagrams enable lace-makers to create, collect, and share designs between them. They are also used by the Centre for Folk Art Production (Ústredie lùdovej umeleckej výroby – ÚĽUV), an educational, research, and commercial organization under the aegis of the Ministry of Culture, to verify that the orders of lace edgings, table covers, and pictures for their shops are uniform in size and execution. Magazines specializing in needlecraft publish schematic drawings for the production of various forms of decorative edgings, furniture covers, pictures, and items such as Christmas decorations. Additional sources of ready-to-make designs are found in popular ethnographic publications and in books and pamphlets published by enthusiasts, as well as on the Internet websites of professional Czech and Slovak lace-makers who sell their designs in the form of packs of diagrams to amateurs. In fact, most of the lace-makers I came to know in Banská Bystrica collected drawings for more designs than they would ever be able to make and kept them neatly catalogued in binders, boxes, or filing cabinets marked by geographical area or the designer's name. These collections were the result of a considerable investment of time, money, and effort, and they were extremely valuable to their owners. One lace-maker humorously referred to her collection as her 'gold mine'.

The majority of the lace-makers who taught evening courses in Banská Bystrica regarded diagrams as an ideal pedagogical tool. While Zuzana had the privilege of commanding her great-grandmother's entire attention, the resources of an instructor on an evening course are divided between up to a dozen beginners, making sketches and diagrams a necessary 'surrogate' in place of an overstretched teacher. Jana Horvathová, a retired teacher of mathematics and member of the Vtačik ('Little Bird') lace-making club in Banská Bystrica, regarded such diagrams as not only a necessary teaching tool, but also a means for providing novice lace-makers with the basic stock or supply (zásoba) of motifs and grounds from which to work. Founded nearly a decade ago, and hosted by a regionally funded cultural and educational establishment, the club runs a ten-week course for beginners which competent members, like Jana, teach on a one-to-one basis. The course is offered twice a year. Jana put together a course study-pack of detailed sketches and drawings that demonstrate everything from how to wind thread on bobbins and how to make simple motifs, to full-fledged diagrams of designs. Ambitiously, Jana's programme aimed to familiarize students with a dozen or so of the most common motifs and grounds used by craftswomen in Špania Dolina before allowing them to graduate into the club, where they could benefit from the experience of others.

What struck me about Jana's description of her teaching goals was the manner in which she treated pattern as disembodied information. She regarded motifs and grounds as clearly definable entities constructed according to specific parameters (which could be illustrated using a diagram), and as separate from their actual manifestations and the bodily practices that create them. Her job, it seemed, was to give the students a 'tool-box' of rules and representations that they could apply when turning a hand to their new hobby. Jana maintains that there is a separation between the theoretical knowledge associated with producing a motif and a craftsperson's ability to execute it. This is not surprising when one carefully observes the way in which information is encoded in the sorts of diagrams Jana employs in teaching. Ana Paličková made her great-granddaughter count out her stitches, thereby giving the impression that pattern is created by the mathematical relationship between the stitches that make up the motifs. In a diagram, however, the relation between motifs appears to be one of positions in space or on a grid. The movement indicated in the drawings is that of bobbins and thread travelling across the particular two-dimensional 'space' of the grid, rather than the movement of hands that manipulate the bobbins to create the weave. Thus, despite the fact that lace is created through a highly co-ordinated, rhythmic movement of the hands, both hands and movement are invisible in these diagrams.

When comparing Ana Paličková's teaching methods with those used by club Vtačik members, the effects of using notation to record, teach, and share knowledge about motifs and designs become increasingly evident. As a tangible record of procedure, notation establishes a conceptual divide between craft knowledge as theory and as practice. As a discursive device, a diagram constitutes the abstraction of the principles of construction of stitches, motifs, and grounds not only from their original historical and social context, but also from their physical seat – namely the body. Thus, while a pupil learning 'by recipe' will not develop practice in a more rule-bound manner than one learning without the use of diagrams, she will nevertheless be presented with the principles as a set of predetermined, ahistorical and universal rules. This effect, I argue, has far-reaching consequences for the manner in which some lace-makers conceive of craft knowledge, skill, and, by extension, local style and cultural heritage.

I first voiced my thoughts on the effect of notation on practice to Hana Majerová, a professional illustrator and lace-maker based in Banská Bystrica. She responded by telling me about her own experience with diagrams as a pedagogical tool. A native of the village Staré Hory, Hana had been taught to make lace by her grandmother. After taking a degree in fine art, she moved to Banská Bystrica and worked as an illustrator. Hana's employer did not survive the privatization process that followed the demise of state socialism, but Hana spiritedly viewed her redundancy as a chance to pursue her dream of becoming a professional craftswoman. After several unsuccessful collaborations with local fashion designers, she has found considerable commercial success selling small pictures of motifs adapted from antique laces from the collections of the National Ethnographic Museum.

In spring 2007, Hana was employed to teach a beginners' evening course at the Banská Bystrica workshops of the ÚĽUV. The prospect of teaching initially pleased her, but she now described her work as a tutor as being filled with tension and mutual suspicion. Upon accepting the job, she learned that the institution offered three levels of courses (beginner, intermediate, advanced) designed to be taken consecutively, such that each built upon skills taught at the previous level. Hana was given a defined list of weaves and motifs that pupils were expected to master at the rate of one skill per week. The organization also encouraged her to assemble a study-pack of photocopied sketches that illustrate the correct sequences of moves, as well as schematic diagrams of simple designs that could act as a template for the novices as they worked. Hana deemed that this was too much material for pupils to become familiar with in a six-week course. Hence, rather than following the pre-planned syllabus supplied, she abandoned the study-pack and taught her students only the most basic cloth stitch. By using this one weave, she taught them correctly to turn corners and to make lace in the round and in a serpentine fashion (each requires different handling of the pillow and bobbins). According to Hana, acquiring basic skills lay not in simply learning to make one weave after another, but rather in mastering the process of making itself. She wanted her pupils to feel completely at ease not only with the cloth stitch, but with the tools of the trade and their own body as the guiding instrument.

Above and beyond her expression of doubt about the value of diagrams as a peda-gogical tool, Hana seemingly wanted to make a point about the nature of enskilment. The pedagogies of the village and the classroom met and clashed during her time at the ÚĽUV. Her approach to teaching was similar to that of Ana Paličková in that it not only prioritized the inculcation of sets of movements, but also emphasized familiarity with the materials and tools of the trade. In other words, Hana aimed to teach her pupils *workmanship*. While the course was originally designed to introduce students to a range of motifs and grounds without any expectation for these to be mastered to perfection, Hana's method sought to teach the principles of quality execution as the starting-point for creative expression. Her efforts to encourage proficiency above procedure were countered, however, by an institutionally defined hierarchy of tasks that the novice had to achieve in order to be acknowledged as advancing towards competence. The study-packs constituted a curriculum and thereby a set of expectations about what students were going to learn. This encouraged students to think of learning in terms of goals and landmarks to be reached.

The impact of institutionalized teaching parameters on the enskilment of lace-makers gives rise to interesting questions concerning the boundary between appren-ticeship as 'situated peripheral learning' (Lave & Wenger 1991) and apprenticeship as professional training undertaken in educational institutions away from both work-places and the everyday life of the domestic sphere. Despite a growing body of literature on apprenticeship as a form of learning, socialization, and ethnographic tool (e.g. Coy 1989; Dilley 1999; Herzfeld 2003; Marchand 2001; 2006; O'Connor 2005; Prentice 2008; Simpson 2006), anthropology has only recently begun to engage in critical ethnogra-phies of professional apprenticeships and formal training (e.g. Marchand 2008). Yet, according to design historian Glenn Adamson (2007: 125-34), craft education was a contested terrain throughout the twentieth century. He notes that competing under-standings of skill figured widely in these debates, with some parties seeking to equip young people with marketable competences while others advocated the enlightening, creative, and morally stimulating nature of manual training with little concern for its commercial application. In both cases, the notion of craftsmanship suffered. With industrialization, design and manufacture took place increasingly in separate spheres and were undertaken by separately trained workforces. As 'creativity' became increas-ingly disassociated with the 'skill' of realization, craftsmanship was relegated to the status of 'manual virtuosity'. This understanding of 'skill' as a matter of dexterity is shared by the institutionalized teaching of lace-making. With the exception of Hana, the conviction of the other teaching staff at the Banská Bystrica ÚĽUV workshops, like that of teachers at the lace-making club Vtáčik, is that students can be provided with a 'tool-box' of theoretical knowledge supplied by drawings and diagrams which can be taken home and perfected in practice. By teaching their students to make lace using a study-pack, they are also teaching them a particular political economy of knowledge that not only separates mind and body, but hierarchically ranks one way of knowing above the other. Hana's conviction that quality execution was a prerequisite for informed practice therefore challenged not only the authority of her colleagues, but also the very epistemological grounds upon which their practice is based.

Hana's experience of teaching lace-making at the ÚĽUV workshops gave both of us an opportunity to reflect upon the differences between the ways the craft is taught in the city and amongst family members in the village setting. Hana's concerns revolved around the question of what the use of diagrams as pedagogical tools meant for students' perceptions of skilled practice. My own interest was spurred on by the observation that while notation and diagrams act as rhetorical devices which help lace-makers articulate procedures and commands which are otherwise deeply embedded into bodily memory, they also render craft knowledge abstract by objectifying bodily practice. Indeed, what I hope the examples above demonstrate is that diagrams constitute much more than an innocent tool for the transfer of information from one lace-maker to another, but rather, by virtue of notation, this information and its reception begin to change. It is precisely because lace-makers are exchanging a diagrammatic representation of the procedure by which such a design is made, and not merely a sketch of a design, that these exchanges have a tangible impact on craft practice. By making procedure a matter of discourse and discussion, schematic diagrams involve instances of practice in a much larger political economy of knowledge on craft. As I shall describe below, the codification of notation has deeply influenced the manner in which craft as occupation, as heritage, and as tradition are viewed by lace-makers in Špania Dolina, Staré Hory, and Banská Bystrica alike. Indeed, schematic diagrams play a large part in the formation of these communities' opinions of each other, as well as the friendships and conflicts between them.

'Generative' vs 'imitative' craft

In late 2003, I began my second apprenticeship with Mária Jablková, an elderly lace-maker from Staré Hory. She lived in a small house set back from the road behind a neatly maintained vegetable garden. Her property was cut off from her neighbours by a small, bubbling river which I loved to listen to and which Mária regarded as handy for the quick disposal of garbage. Hana Majerová told me that Mária Jablková 'is still that old, classical lace-maker as they used to be', and Hana made no secret of the fact that Mária was her role model. Like most families in the village, Mária's mother and grandmother were lace-makers and, as a child, she had learned the basics of the craft from them. She was a long-time employee of the Centre for Folk Art Production (ÚĽUV) and had been bestowed with the title of Mistress of the Folk Arts (*majsterka ľudovej umeleckej výroby*), which she lightly dismissed as a 'prize for sticking with them for so long'.

As I sat one morning working in Mária's kitchen, she received an order for a number of furniture covers to be made for the commercial arm of the ÚĽUV. Examining the drawing and diagram that had been sent with the order, she saw that the entire design was formed by a simple s-shaped serpentine pattern executed in just one basic weave. The pattern was too simple for her liking and she therefore developed it further by tracing the design onto a piece of card and placing a glass at the apex of the 'S', thereby creating a lollipop-like shape. In the centre of this circular form, she constructed a few leaf-shaped motifs. In addition to fulfilling the order, Mária made a furniture cover with the new design and sent it to the ÚĽUV as an entry to a competition they had arranged. The pattern was later accepted into the repertoire of ÚĽUV designs and named 'Dandelion' by the organization (Fig. 8). Yet when I asked Mária what she had called this particular design, she replied that she had not given it a name. She saw it simply as a combination of elements (an s-shape, a circle, and different decorative motifs).

Mária treated the diagram sent by the ÚĽUV as a tool for producing not only the ordered lace, but also an entirely new design. She was decidedly slovenly, however, about storing designs and diagrams or keeping them in good shape, and this stood in contrast to the reverent attitude of many Banská Bystrica lace-makers, who carefully filed, photocopied, and swapped them with friends. If Mária liked a design, she kept the cardboard templates in a box under her bed, otherwise she threw them into the river behind the house or into her wood-burning kitchen stove when she no longer needed them. Her attitude was mirrored by Ana Paličková in Špania Dolina, who – much to my chagrin – had saved almost none of the diagrams, drawings, or templates of the lace she had made over more than six decades of craftwork. In Ana's case, the lack of a 'paper record' was due in part to the fact that the Torchon-style laces made in Špania Dolina are

Figure 8. The 'Dandelion' pattern.

traditionally worked entirely without sketches or indications marked on the cardboard template. The template is simply pre-punched according to grids of different dimensions. Ana and her village colleagues therefore rarely recorded the patterns they constructed but instead started the design process anew each time they made a piece of lace.

I was filled with horror while watching Mária throw diagrams and templates into the fire. This feeling was shared by many women in Banská Bystrica, who regarded the apparently lax attitude of village craftswomen towards their heritage as irresponsible. The members of Vtačik were particularly vocal. They spoke with urgency about the dangers of the craft 'dying out' together with the elderly population of the village and implemented a programme of conservation, considering it nothing less than their civic duty to salvage remnants of craft knowledge by recording the 'old designs'. If the club group could find a sympathetic lace-maker from Špania Dolina, then they made a field trip to the village in order to view and copy her work. 'Copying' generally implied borrowing a piece of lace from the original designer, studying it, reproducing it, and making a schematic diagram. The diagram was stored in a large folder kept in the office of the club's head, and a photocopied version was distributed amongst interested members. In this way, Jana Horvathová and other club lace-makers endeavoured to document the richness of the local tradition, believing that by using notation it could be preserved for posterity. Thus, while Mária and Ana regarded diagrams as tools for producing a desired product for employers, to members of Vtačik they were a 'store' or 'carrier' of knowledge of both procedure and local heritage. By recording the designs, Jana and her colleagues were attempting to extract the knowledge from the frail, elderly bodies of the village lace-makers, thereby giving permanency to the 'Špania Dolina style' and its methods of production. In other words, notation could be used as a tool for codification. Indeed, by learning to make the designs, they saw themselves as giving new life to this knowledge.

The codification of localized styles of lace was not the invention of Jana and her Vtačik colleagues. As I have documented elsewhere (Makovicky 2009), the first systematic field-based study of Slovak lace-making traditions was undertaken by researchers from the ÚĽUV in the early 1950s, resulting in the categorization of lace from different localities into defined local 'styles' that are now regarded by ethnologists and lace-makers as traditional. For example, members of Vtačik subject their collected designs to rigorous formal analysis based on information contained in a number of popular socialist-era publications from the 1980s (e.g. Géciová-Komorovská 1988; Mišik 1988) that list eighteen stylistically distinct regional 'types' of lace as codified by the ÚĽUV researchers. The ÚĽUV fieldwork formed part of a much larger project of identity creation which Deema Kaneff (2004) calls 'recontextualization'. Socialist state governments extracted folklore and folk craft traditions from their local contexts and inserted them into the state-controlled frameworks of education and culture in an attempt to control the discourse on identity. The ÚĽUV hired professionally trained artists to design simplified versions of the artefacts collected in the field, and these products were manufactured by employees like Mária Jablková and Ana Paličková, and marketed as being 'typical' or 'traditional' examples of their respective villages. As a major employer in Špania Dolina and Staré Hory, the organization played an important role in supporting the craft and village communities from the time of its founding as a loose association of 'folk art' co-operatives in 1954 until the end of state socialism in 1989. During the socialist era, the ÚĽUV had an ideological as well as a fiscal agenda that constructed the nation's rural past as the source of its new working-class culture. The

ĽUV continues to market its products as representative of local culture despite the fact that fewer village lace-makers now work for the organization and regardless of contention among some lace-makers as to whether these designs are truly representative of local traditions (Makovicky 2009).

As an instrument of 'recontextualization', I would argue that the ĽUV was responsible for a particular kind of knowledge-making which not only spoke to craftswomen's sense of national identity, but also reinforced the practices and knowledge economy of modernity, as outlined by Adamson (2007) in his history of craft. Although the ĽUV did not invent the notational form used by lace-makers to construct diagrams, it did author the criteria by which Vtačik members and many others judge the stylistic integrity of a piece. As a category of formal analysis, style and pattern were not only made easily visible in the form of a diagram, but this form of documentation meant that they came to exist in a temporal vacuum that precluded the notion of historical change or of autochthonous innovation. The notion that traditional styles were bound by local, normative aesthetics which secured their continued reproduction over time was supported by the Bratislava-based ethnologist Juraj Zajonc. He writes that while laces from historical collections are marked with 'the "signature" of the lace-maker who wove it, their attention to detail and ability to innovate', change was possible only to the extent that the lace retained its 'typical appearance' (Zajonc 1999: 23). In this way, 'recontextualization' presented the population with a timeless 'folk culture' which was at once spatio-temporally bounded and everywhere; rare and endangered, but equally a consumer good available at the nearest ĽUV outlet. By using notation as a form of preservation, the members of Vtačik believe that they are amassing a material archive of a 'folk heritage' that is carried by the elderly ladies of Špania Dolina as an unarticulated form of 'collective memory' (Halbwachs 1992).

The members of Vtačik were apparently untroubled by the question of how craft knowledge could be shared between the minds and bodies of craftswomen across generations in Špania Dolina, and, in their own case, across communities. Yet during their occasional visits to the village, they were starkly reminded of the potential problems associated with this issue. Not only were local lace-makers unwilling to share their craft knowledge, but the majority would not lend any examples of lace for copying or even talk to the Vtačik members. For me as both an apprentice of Ana Paličková's and a member of Vtačik, this sometimes required a delicate balancing act to stay neutral. One such instance was a snowy day in early December 2003 when I joined members of the Vtačik lace-making club on a visit to the village of Špania Dolina for an afternoon event of organized folk dance performances, Christmas decoration and cookies sales, and a lace-making demonstration by two club members from Banská Bystrica. Tables and walls were covered in Špania Dolina-style lace that was made by these women. Few village lace-makers came because of the snow and because the event was poorly advertised. However, those who did come curiously observed the two club members and inspected their displayed work. While fingering the lace, their only comments were 'Oh, that's not one of ours. Neither is that. No, none of this is made in Špania Dolina'. The club leader, who was standing behind a box of Christmas ornaments, issued an audible cough and, addressing the village craftswomen, she said loudly, 'But they are all Špania Dolina lace'. My impression as a bystander was that the village lace-maker was searching for evidence in the quality, patterns, and colour combinations that these laces were the work of a local craftswoman. She was not examining the design components of the lace to see whether or not it was (stylistically speaking) Špania Dolina lace. As she could not attribute the work to a fellow villager, she simply dismissed the lace as not belonging to that place. Her assertion that 'None of this is made in Špania Dolina' was not a comment on their ethnographic value, but a statement of fact.

Two disparate notions of authenticity are at play here: one based on the purity of 'ethnographically' established 'styles', and the other based on the criteria of community membership. As I shall show in the remainder of this chapter, these involve not only two different kinds of knowledge about the craft as local tradition, but also different kinds of 'knowledge-making'. Continuing my account above, the lace-makers from Vtáčik packed up in the evening and left for the city, disappointed by yet another cold reception and shaking their heads in disbelief at the ignorance of their village colleagues. And, while the lace-makers from Špania Dolina later admitted to me that they had once made designs like those being made by club members, they merely shrugged their shoulders, saying that they no longer made them. They noted that the pieces were obviously made 'by recipe' (i.e. using a diagram or template of some kind). Though the designs were authentic according to the abstract criteria of ethnographic purity, the villagers viewed the 'Špania Dolina-style' lace of the Banská Bystrica makers as an imitation product. This was partly because they were convinced that, as members of the village lace-making community, they were the rightful inheritors of the tradition, but also because they themselves did not make use of diagrams or templates. While the work of city-dwellers was 'imitative', their own was 'generative' in that it created a new product each time.

The imitation products made by Vtáčik members and other city craftswomen nevertheless worried the village lace-makers. The latter's characteristic Torchon-style lace was popular with urban makers and clients alike, and was an important source of income for villagers. They viewed the craft practices of Banská Bystrica women as an opportunistic commercial activity benefiting parasitically from the legacy that once supported their community. Indeed, because of lace-making's historical importance as a cottage industry, the right to (re)produce certain designs had always been linked to a capacity to generate income. Most importantly, this right was accorded by virtue of membership to the collective. If a lace-maker was suspected of teaching or supplying outsiders with designs, she was criticized for 'selling out' her specialist knowledge. Therefore, while in the urban sphere a large collection of schematic drawings was seen as the mark of a 'knowledgeable' lace-maker (i.e. one adept at recognizing and identifying many 'styles'; with a knowledge of the craft history, and an ability to unearth rare publication through contacts, etc.), the villagers viewed the use of schematic drawings for the recording and transmission of designs as a threat to their own commercial interests. Village lace-makers were quite anxious about imitation products flooding their market, and saw the recording of their designs as an attempt by their urban colleagues to steal the commercial enterprise for themselves.

In addition, constructing a pattern (and an accompanying diagram) requires experience and a flair for design, as well as intimate practical knowledge of how to make a given pattern. Hana Majerová would often show me the new designs and motifs she was working on. She commenced a design by drawing its outline onto a piece of cardboard. If after several hours of work she was dissatisfied with the way the lace was turning out, she then discarded it and redrew certain parts of the design before starting anew. As Hana told me one evening, making designs takes a long time because 'I never know how it will turn out until I have actually made it'. Hana's insistence that good craftsmanship involves more than manual dexterity, and lies at the heart of craft knowledge, begins to make perfect sense. Marchand (2001), writing about traditional minaret construction in Yemen, describes the mastery of an experienced builder as being reliant upon an ability to balance his creative imagination with reasoned judgement, and this is developed through experience. In similar manner, Hana made a series of educated guesses about how best to execute a design idea, but she did not expect straightforwardly to predetermine the relation between idea, materials, and method. She knew that, in the end, the process of making would determine the final outcome. Hana's own description of creating new designs clearly reveals that a sketch or drawing is developed in conjunction with the completed prototype. In other words, drawings and diagrams are not created at the beginning of the design process, but emerge at the end of the production process. In short, they are as much part of the material outcome of the lace-maker's practice as the lace.

Hana's description of the creative process highlights the essence of the epistemological distinction between the lace-makers' practice and that of city-based craftswomen, as well as the role that notation and diagrammatic representation play in the formation of concepts of knowledge. In travelling to the village to collect designs for their archive, lace-makers from Vtačik imagine that they will have access to designs that are sourced from a collectively held and historically stable repertoire of motifs. Neither Jana nor her colleagues dispute the fact that Špania Dolina lace-makers start from a blank cardboard template each time they weave a new piece. But since the components of the design are imagined to be part of a collectively held cultural heritage, they are effectively construed as belonging to no one and everyone at once. In teaching her pupils, Jana used a 'study-pack' of motifs and grounds abstracted from their original historical, social, and practical context. She had no concerns about this because she regarded the motifs and patterns found in Špania Dolina laces to be part of an ahistorical, unchanging tradition, the material components of which were separable from practitioners and their practices. By contrast, craft knowledge for lace-makers like Hana Majerová is inseparable from the instance of its practical application. Hana regarded the ability to generate designs as fundamental to everyday craft practice. Therefore the generative principles behind making and designing lace are inseparable from the agency of the craftswoman who puts them into practice. So, as much as notation gives lace-makers 'something to talk about', it also gives them something upon which to disagree.

Conclusion

Like my own experience of learning and teaching to make lace, this chapter began by examining a problem familiar to both anthropologists studying craft and craftspeople themselves: namely the difficulty encountered in verbally articulating craft knowledge that has become 'second nature' to the practitioner. Much scholarship has sought to understand the constitution of such knowledge as 'tacit' or 'embodied', or attempted a closer understanding of how it is communicated, passed on, and understood by fellow practitioners. This chapter, by contrast, has examined how notation is used by lace-makers to bypass these problems, thereby instituting real changes in the ways craftswomen understand the nature and value of craft knowledge. By focusing on the use of notation both as a pedagogical tool and as a means of codifying local styles for conservation purposes, I have sought to illuminate how notions of enskilment, tradi-tion, and authenticity have become marked by a conceptual separation of practice from procedure, and of bodily movement and memory from ostensibly universal and ahis-torical rules and representations. I have argued that these changes are not simply the consequence of a collecting-and-labelling programme instituted by the state-socialist authorities in the 1950s, and perpetuated today by such lace-makers as the club Vtačik members, but they are also, to some extent, conditioned by the objectifying nature of this notation itself, as it makes the working body invisible within its symbolic system. Effectively, notation makes it seem that the activities of making and designing lace are independent of the physical nature of situated practice, and bodily practice merely appears to have the function of materializing a pre-existing tradition.

Maurice Bloch (1998) has claimed that rendering things the object of explicit discourse changes the character of knowledge in the process. Although I am reluctant to classify craft as a specific 'kind' of knowledge, it is clear from my findings that once lace-making has been made the subject of discourse, it becomes implicated in a political economy of knowledge, thereby changing the social values that are accorded to craft practice. In this case, lace-making has become implicated in a discourse of cultural heritage and nationalism deeply marked by the practices of socialist-era ethnology and state-sponsored folk art production. Indeed, I hope to have demonstrated that the very idea that one can aggregate lace-making into different 'kinds' of knowledge (e.g. 'tacit' versus propositional knowledge) is an outcome of the notation and codification process itself. There is a striking contrast between the urban lace-makers' positive valuation of schematic diagrams as 'carriers' of knowledge with the potential to revive and conserve a dying craft, and the village craftswomen's more pragmatic view that diagrams are tools for producing an income-generating commodity. This is but one example of how an apparently 'neutral' device for recording and storing information can profoundly influence the ways in which this information is understood and manipulated. Indeed, it shows how diagrams themselves become the instrument through which boundaries between craft communities are created, contested, and negotiated. As such, the training of each Central Slovakian lace-maker socializes that individual as a member of a particular community of like-minded craftswomen. This secures the reproduction of group identity, but often leaves lace-makers unable or unwilling to accept the point of view of craftswomen from other communities.

NOTE

I would like to thank Trevor Marchand for his comments and contributions, as well as the other participants in the *Transmission of knowledge* Seminar Series at SOAS. I also thank the anonymous reviewers for their many useful insights. In addition, I would like to thank Mr Gen Fujii and Dr Laurence Douny for their comments on earlier drafts of this chapter. Lastly, I thank my teachers and friends in Central Slovakia for letting me share in their skills and their world of craft production. Names and certain details have been changed in order to protect the privacy and identity of the respondents. This research was enabled by generous funding from the Danish Research Agency (ref. no. 41347).

REFERENCES

ADAMSON, G. 2007. *Thinking through craft*. Oxford: Berg; London: Victoria and Albert Museum.
ALFOLDY, S. (ed.) 2007. *NeoCraft: modernity and the crafts*. Halifax: The Press of the Nova Scotia College of Art and Design.
BLOCH, M. 1998. *How we think they think*. Boulder, Colo.: Westview.
BOURDIEU, P. 1977. *An outline of a theory of practice* (trans. R. Nice). Cambridge: University Press.
——— 1990. *The logic of practice*. Cambridge: Polity.
COY, M.W. (ed.) 1989. *Apprenticeship: from theory to method and back again*. Albany, N.Y.: SUNY Press.
DILLEY, R. 1999. Ways of knowing, forms of power. *Cultural Dynamics* 11, 33-55.
DORMER, P. 1997. *The culture of craft: status and future*. Manchester: University Press.
DOWLING, P. 1998. *The sociology of mathematics education: mathematical myth/pedagogical texts*. London: Falmer Press.
DOWNEY, G. 2007. Seeing with a 'sideways' glance. In *Ways of knowledge: new approaches in the anthropology of knowledge* (ed.) M. Harris, 222-41. Oxford: Berghahn.

GATEWOOD, J. 1985. Actions speak louder than words. In *Directions in cognitive anthropology* (ed.) J. Dougherty, 199-220. Urbana: University of Illinois Press.

GÉCIOVÁ-KOMOROVSKÁ, V. 1988. *Slovenská ľudová paličkovaná čipka* (Slovak folk bobbin lace). Bratislava: Alfa.

GELLNER, E. 1983. *Nations and nationalism*. Ithaca, N.Y.: Cornell University Press.

GOSSELAIN, O.P. 1992. Technology and style: potters and pottery among the Bafia of Cameroon. *Man* (N.S.) **27**, 559-86.

GRASSENI, C. (ed.) 2007. *Skilled visions: between apprenticeship and standards*. Oxford: Berghahn.

HALBWACHS, M. 1992. *On collective memory* (trans. L.A. Coser). Chicago: University Press.

HALLAM, E. & T. INGOLD (eds) 2007. *Creativity and cultural improvisation*. Oxford: Berg.

HARRIS, M. (ed.) 2007. *Ways of knowing: new approaches in the anthropology of knowledge*. Oxford: Berghahn.

HERZFELD, M. 2003. *The body impolitic: artisans and artifice in the global hierarchy of value*. Chicago: University Press.

HOBSBAWM, E. & T. RANGER (eds) 1983. *The invention of tradition*. Cambridge: University Press.

INGOLD, T. 2000a. Making culture and weaving the world. In *Matter, materiality and modern culture* (ed.) P.M. Graves-Brown, 50-71. New York: Routledge.

——— 2000b. *The perception of the environment: essays on livelihood, dwelling and skill*. London: Routledge.

——— 2001. Beyond art and technology: the anthropology of skill. In *Anthropological perspectives on technology* (ed.) M.B. Schiffer, 17-31. Albuquerque: University of New Mexico Press.

KANEFF, D. 2004. *Who owns the past? The politics of time in a 'model' Bulgarian village*. Oxford: Berghahn.

KELLER, J. & C. KELLER 1991. Thinking and acting with iron. In *Understanding practice: perspectives on activity and context* (eds) S. Chaiklin & J. Lave, 124-43. Cambridge: University Press.

LAVE, J. & E. WENGER 1991. *Situated learning: legitimate peripheral participation*. Cambridge: University Press.

McCULLOUGH, M. 2004. *Digital ground: architecture, pervasive computing, and environmental knowledge*. Cambridge, Mass.: MIT Press.

MACKENZIE, M. 1991. *Androgynous objects: stringbags and gender in central New Guinea*. Chur, Switzerland: Harwood Academic Press.

MAKOVICKY, N. 2009. 'Traditional – with contemporary form': craft and discourses of modernity in Slovakia today. *Journal of Modern Craft* **2**, 43-58.

MARCHAND, T. 2001. *Minaret building and apprenticeship in Yemen*. Richmond, Surrey: Curzon.

——— 2006. Endorsing indigenous knowledge: the role of masons and apprenticeship in sustaining vernacular architecture – the case of Djenné. In *Vernacular architecture in the twenty-first century: theory, education and practice* (eds) L. Asquith & M. Vellinga, 46-62. London: Taylor & Francis.

——— 2007. Crafting knowledge: the role of 'parsing and production' in the communication of skill-based knowledge amongst masons. In *Ways of knowing: new approaches in the anthropology of experience and learning* (ed.) M. Harris, 173-93. Oxford: Berghahn.

——— 2008. Muscles, morals and mind: craft apprenticeship and the formation of person. *British Journal of Educational Studies* **56**, 245-71.

MARKOVÁ, E. 1962. *Slovenské čipky* (Slovak laces). Bratislava: SVKL.

MIŠIK, V. 1988. *Škola paličkovania* (The school of lace-making). Bratislava: Alfa.

O'CONNOR, E. 2005. Embodied knowledge: the experience of meaning and the struggle towards proficiency in glassblowing. *Ethnography* **6**, 183-204.

PODOBA, J. 2005. On the periphery of the periphery: Slovak anthropology behind the ideological veil. In *Studying peoples in the people's democracies* (eds) C.M. Hann, M. Sárkány & P. Skalník, 245-55. Münster: LIT Verlag.

PRENTICE, R. 2008. Knowledge, skill and the inculcation of the anthropologist: reflections on learning to sew in the field. *Anthropology of Work Review* **29**: 3, 54-61.

REICHARD, G. 1934. *Spider woman: a story of Navajo weavers and chanters*. Glorietta, N.M.: Rio Grande Press.

RISATTI, H. 2007. *A theory of craft: function and aesthetic expression*. Chapel Hill: University of North Carolina Press.

SEDALOVÁ, Ľ. 1989. Čipky (Laces). *Národopisné Informacie* **89**: 1, 83-97.

SENNETT, R. 2008. *The craftsman*. New Haven: Yale University Press.

SIMPSON, E. 2006. Apprenticeship in western India. *Journal of the Royal Anthropological Institute* (N.S.) **12**, 151-71.

URTON, G. 1997. *The social life of numbers: a Quechua ontology of numbers and philosophy of arithmetic*. Houston: University of Texas Press.

ZAJONC, J. 1999. Niečo o autorskom práve (Some notes on copyright). *Slovenská Čipka* **2**, 22-4.

5

Embodied cognition and communication: studies with British fine woodworkers

TREVOR H.J. MARCHAND *School of Oriental and African Studies*

Introduction: toward a theory of embodied cognition

In 2005 I began research with woodwork trainees at the historic Building Crafts College in East London. The principal aim of the project is to advance my understanding of skill, learning, and identity among communities of craftspeople. To date, fieldwork has included two years of full-time training as a student in the fine woodwork programme and a continuing series of interviews with established furniture makers in the UK. The research has involved comparative analyses between the apprentice-style learning I documented among minaret-builders in Yemen (2001) and mud-brick masons in Mali (2009) and the institutional training provided at the college (2007a; 2008), together with theoretical explorations of motor cognition and embodied communication in teaching and learning practical trades (2007b; 2010). This chapter focuses on the latter, and I use the available space to elaborate a theory of the way actions are interpreted and generated *from* the bodies of co-practitioners.[1]

Pivotal to my studies with craftspeople is the idea that the mental representations we possess as humans are not restricted to those that can be defined in language and that comprise the constituents of propositional thinking (Marchand 2003). Rather, representations are acquired by a variety of cognitive domains, and form the respective bases of 'thinking' in those domains. Like Henry Plotkin (1993), I regard knowledge to be any state in an organism that bears a relationship to the world. Therefore an expanded definition of knowledge must include, as a minimum, thinking *with* sound imagery (e.g. music: see Jackendoff 1992: 11-14; Lerdahl & Jackendoff 1983), visual imagery (e.g. spatial and visual cognition: see Jackendoff & Landau 1992; Jacob & Jeannerod 2003; Marr 1982), and motor imagery (e.g. craft, dance, and sport: see Jeannerod 2006).

With regard to physical practice, I argue that representations generated in the motor domains of cognition form the constituent basis of a motor-based knowledge that makes possible the interpretation, understanding, and realization of practice. Thinking *with* and *through* action and movement involves, for instance, the assignment of motor-based interpretations to representations derived from the pairing of visually processed signals with observed actions, gestures, and postures. Motor cognition therefore needs to be open, at the very minimum, to information processed by visual cognition. It is also responsive to information supplied by a variety of other domains, and it evidently interfaces with language, since practice may be co-ordinated with verbal instruction and command.

In his seminal studies of motor cognition, neuropsychologist Marc Jeannerod observes that 'motor representations' (i.e. mental representations instantiated in the motor domains of cognition) are manifested in two possible ways: either as actualized physical actions and movement available to third-party observation; or alternatively as simulated motor imagery whereby one imaginatively 'feels' oneself (as differentiated from 'picturing' oneself) to be executing an action (Jeannerod 1994; 1999). The former corresponds to the conventional understanding of the way motor intelligence is realized. The latter more interestingly demonstrates that motor representations can be 'thought with' and 'reflected upon' without necessarily being enacted. This is achieved in a manner similar to the way we can entertain propositional thoughts and ideas without speaking them. Athletes, acrobats, and dancers can 'rehearse' exercises and routines by imaginatively 'feeling' their muscles and limbs wend their way systematically through the procedures. Guang Yue and Kelly J. Cole have demonstrated how this serves to improve performance and even condition the body (1992; see also Cross, Hamilton & Grafton 2006; and Oishi & Maeshima 2004). Indeed we all engage in this form of motor-based mental activity when imaginatively re-enacting familiar activities or preparing for new ones. Such mental rehearsal often involves both a visualization of the activity in the 'mind's eye' and motor-based simulation. The two represent distinct mental processes, but they are capable of playing complementary roles, as demonstrated by the experiments conducted by Angela Sirigu and Jean-René Duhamel (2001) on the mental manipulation of objects.

Like Jeannerod, I propose that skilled activities – and especially those enacted with the intention to teach or to demonstrate – are available to, and act upon, the motor cognition of an observing audience. It is in motor cognition that actions are parsed and interpreted, thereby eliciting simulated or actualized motor responses. In participant learning environments such as London's Building Crafts College, a trainee's on-line response to the instructor's example is typically imitative at both the action and programme levels. In other words, trainees try physically to copy the idiosyncratic details of the instructor's performance and imitate the hierarchical organization of actions, including bi-manual co-ordination and sub-routine structure of the overall procedures (Byrne 2003; Byrne & Russon 1998a). The trainee's interpretation and imitative enactment of the observed activity arise chiefly in motor cognition, and most likely in co-ordination with representations from cognitive domains processing other sorts of signals from the overall learning environment.

My thesis is inspired by the dynamic syntax approach to communication (Cann, Kempson & Marten 2005; Kempson, Meyer-Viol & Gabbay 2001). This linguistic theory requires some measure of explanation since the terrain will be unfamiliar to most readers. The model that I set out encompasses the anthropology of movement's concern with the 'semantics' and context-dependence of action interpretation (Farnell 1999), but extends beyond this project by centrally including the groundwork for describing a kinaesthetic- and proprioceptive-driven 'syntax' of bodily communication. Further progress in this research requires greater interdisciplinary collaboration and, critically, more dedicated ethnographic fieldwork systematically to record action 'dialogue' in context.

Multiple modes of communication

In everyday exchanges, spoken language is integrated with gestures and actions, all of which unfold in time and space and within the richly layered context of 'place'. The excerpt below was recorded during a morning lesson on technical drawing at the Building Crafts College and highlights the multiple modes of communication involved in teaching. The spoken dialogue in this excerpt has been transcribed directly from the natural language used in the particular situation and therefore includes pauses and fragmentation, and at times utterances that seemingly express only partial ideas. The intention to communicate ideas fully was in fact satisfied through the use of skilled action, objects, and visual material that complemented, or in some cases superseded, spoken language. I have tried to illustrate the content of the lesson, including the most salient actions and gestures, with a sort of 'thick description' of the event (see Fig. 1).

> **Workshop example one:**
> In the third week of term, the course instructor assembled the new cohort of fine woodwork students around a bench in the shop. The 'toolbox' session this morning would address the setting out of a full-scale rod drawing for a casement window that we would each individually build.[2] The instructor had already cut a length of white paper from the roll and taped it down evenly to a sheet of MDF board. He steadily surveyed the faces around him and then, like a conductor, drew attention to his lesson with an upheld pencil. 'So, sharp pencil!' he announced audibly, drowning out the lingering murmurs. 'At the moment, uh, 2H pencils are sufficient, but if you want to invest in, you know, sort of drawing pens ... or pencils, you can'.
>
> He then picked up a bevel-edged chisel from the bench top and began sharpening the pencil tip. 'So, notice the chisel is pointing *away* from me ... when I'm sharpening it'. On emphasizing the direction of his action, he shot a sideways glance at a student who negligently sliced his finger on a chisel the day before. The instructor's lips curled in a mocking grimace and the other trainees broke into a surge of chuckles. As the young man self-consciously inspected his wound with a bashful flush in his cheeks, a fellow trainee peered over his shoulder and bantered sardonically using his nickname 'Oh, I'm sorry Carlos my son ...'
>
> The instructor carried on with the lesson, now directing his gaze onto the open pages of a book to his left and signalling to the students to follow with renewed concentration. 'So I've ... I've got this book open. And this is, uh, "Building Craft Foundation", level one and two, at chapter three ... *communications*. It deals with scales. We'll be coming onto that when we do the second drawing,

Figure 1. A 'toolbox' session at the Building Crafts College. In this photo, the workshop instructor is giving a lesson on how to use a power router.

basically, the scale drawing'. He shifted focus to the sheet of blank drafting paper laid out on the bench top before him. 'But it's a communication, and what you're drawing here, this rod, is a communication ... between other trades'. And then moving back to the book, he pointed to a series of diagrams and tapped them with his finger. 'Here we've got drawing symbols and abbreviations ... And I'll just, I'll give you my sort of out ... overview, really ... of how drawings should be set out. And I'll be talking about that. I'll leave it on that page there, which is page 86'.

The instructor then held up a small wooden box with a long, narrow extension protruding through either end of its central axis. Scanning the assembly of students he asked, 'Okay, these are called what? ... Anyone know?' One of the young trainees standing in the background cautiously ventured a response in a subdued voice. 'Thumb ... thumb rules ...'

Suddenly the instructor's body stiffened and his face grew serious. The lesson was momentarily interrupted. He cast a cold stare across the workshop at a student who had just arrived, and demanded abruptly, 'Twenty to ten. Is that right? Your ... your arrival time. You've just arrived? Twenty to ten.' 'No', the student contested sheepishly, 'I saw you ... before now'. 'Have you?' retorted the instructor curtly. 'Well the first time I've seen you! Could you get your diary, and put twenty to ten down? Yeah. I didn't really feel your diary times reflected your true arrival times last week'.

The instructor resumed the lesson and altered his tone accordingly. 'So the first line I'm going to put down ... Sorry. What did we say this was?' he asked picking up the wooden box with the long extension and searching for a volunteer. Another student responded this time 'Thumb rule ruler ...' 'Yup, "*thumb rule*"', agreed the instructor, reiterating the correct name. 'Who's got a combination square handy?' he asked as he proceeded to draw the measured construction lines for the rod, applying different degrees of pressure to the lead to produce lines of varying quality and thickness. After the session, a basic set of drafting equipment was distributed to each student and we returned to our respective workbenches to produce drawings based on the example provided.

From this workshop example, a number of specific training issues are readily identifiable as well as a variety of methods for communicating the information. The instructor presented a selection of drawing instruments and an appropriate-size sheet of paper for our task. He briefly explained the role of a rod in producing architectural joinery; and with the aid of a textbook he introduced the concept of 'scale' and pointed to conventional symbols employed in technical drawing. Before proceeding to draw, the instructor demonstrated a convenient way to sharpen a pencil using a workbench tool. In doing so, he showed how to grip and gently angle the chisel, and he emphasized safe practice by directing the razor-sharp edge away from his body and limbs. The thumb rule was then introduced and the instructor demonstrated how to slide it smoothly along the edge of the MDF board, parallel to the bottom edge of the paper, to make straight lines. While drawing, he exhibited how varying line weights can be produced with a single pencil. In addition to the technical and safety content of his lesson, the teacher offered instruction on correct behaviour and comportment by sternly rebuking the late trainee for his tardiness and sloppy record-keeping. This exchange was also intended at establishing a shared understanding of hierarchy, authority, and responsibility in the workshop.

The teacher structured his demonstration to reflect the sequence of stages involved in setting out a rod drawing: from preparing paper and tools to establishing a set of conventions and producing the measured pencil lines. He employed a combination of spoken language, visual material, and physical actions to communicate his lesson. The verbal content included statements of information and a Socratic method of questioning that incited dialogue and promoted interactive learning. Words were used to articulate concepts and combined to express propositional thoughts and ideas. Tone and volume displayed emotion and conveyed emphasis, thereby providing listeners with additional context for interpreting utterances. The visual materials used by the instructor included diagrams contained in books; a display of the physical objects and implements required, and a trail of pencil lines made on his own sample drawing. Similar to the diagrams used by village lace-makers in Makovicky's study (this volume), the lines of his rod presented a set of instructions to the initiated reader for making a timber casement window and provided a benchmark reference for the student work. Most pertinent to learning technical drawing, however, was not the example of the drawing *on paper* but rather the example of the drawing *in progress*. Ultimately, woodwork trainees must acquire the necessary skills for producing technical drawings – not just recognizing and reading them – and, like learning any physical activity, this is achieved most effectively by observing and imitating the techniques of the hands and body.

At this point, a fundamental question arises about the relation between visual observation and physical action. Put simply, how do we do what we see? In watching another person in action, observed skills are not merely being processed by visual cognition and 'stored' as images that can be subsequently replayed in the mind's eye to guide imitation. We know from experience that our ability to re-imagine visually someone's expert performance carries no guarantee that we can re-enact the feat. (Visualize a trapeze artist in motion, and then try it!) I am suggesting, however, that watching another person's practice acts upon our motor-based understanding of the task. Visual imagery of bodily movement serves as input to our motor domains, where it is parsed into its component postures, gestures, and actions. These are mapped incrementally onto motor representations and an interpretation *from* the body is constructed.[3] Whereas sound is the principal medium of exchange of propositional thoughts and ideas in spoken language, vision is the primary medium of exchange between practitioner and observer. In the workshop, the instructor *shows* the trainees what to do: '*Watch* this!'

Motor-based understanding constitutes a knowing *how from* the body, as differentiated from merely knowing *that about* the body. It demands physical immersion in, or experience of, the same or a comparable activity. As with any sort of knowledge, the level of motor-based understanding is dependent on the individual's experience and direct physical engagement in the activity. The more experience one has of an activity, the finer the detail 'noticed' and grasped. Practical skill therefore develops *in* bodily practice: *in* repetition and rehearsal and *in* simulated motor imagery of the exercise. As discussed above, simulation is a motor-based 'imagining' of action which, like inner dialogue, can serve to re-form and hone performance. It is worth repeating that motor-based understanding of movement is not amenable to description or explanation in propositional thought or language, at least not easily or without being impoverished in the 'translation' between one cognitive domain and the other (Bloch 1998; Ryle 1949). This is why, as all performers, athletes, and craftspeople know, there is no substitute for practice when learning a trade or playing a sport.

In successful 'toolbox' sessions, students learn what the carpentry instructor intends to teach, though notably not in any universal manner. This means that varying degrees of parity have been achieved in the mental representations constructed by both the practising instructor and his observing trainees. In watching the instructor sharpen his pencil with a chisel, the individual trainees construct visual representations of the objects and the bi-manual actions involved. The principal aim of the instructor's lesson, however, is to achieve parity in motor cognition regarding skilled execution, whereby he and his trainees construct the same (or approximate) motor-based representation of time-ordered actions and procedures involved in physically sharpening the pencil or doing the rod drawing. In the next section I will show how the practitioner's and observer's representations of a skill-based activity are built incrementally in motor cognition, as in dialogue, each employing the exact same cognitive strategy.

Dynamic syntax and embodied communication

Workshop example two:
'Could you gather around!' commanded the instructor loudly. One by one the first-year trainees surrendered tools and timber to the tops of their workbenches and assembled around the teacher. He was stationed at the bench of a student who was well advanced in making the outer frame for his casement window project. The student was preparing to introduce a 5 mm-deep rebate[4] around the interior edges of the header, sill, and two jambs of the frame that would snugly accommodate the hinged window. Most trainees had never used the so-called 'rebate-and-fillister plane' that was needed for the job, so the instructor offered a toolbox demonstration. The rebate-and-fillister is a hand-operated plane fitted with a side fence and an adjustable depth stop that control the width and depth of the cut, respectively. Achieving a perfect ninety-degree angle in the rebate, however, proves challenging for novices.

One of the timber jambs was already fastened to the worktop with a 'G' cramp. The instructor grasped the plane by its cast-iron handle and lifted it into the air. 'Does anyone know what this is?' he asked. 'Rebate plane', someone answered confidently. 'Good', said the instructor flatly. 'And what do we use it for?' 'To put a rebate into the timber', retorted the same student. 'Mmmm ...', agreed the instructor, smirking. 'According to our drawings we're introducing a, uh ... 5 mm rebate into the frame. Make sure you're doing the right side ... that's the inside', he warned as he reached into the pocket of his white lab coat for a six-inch metal ruler. 'You can fix the depth by adjusting this stopper'. He loosened the small screw and measured 5 mm vertically to the tip of the blade. He then re-tightened that screw using the end of his ruler as a driver, and proceeded to loosen the fastenings for the fence. 'And move the fence over ... the exact width of our rebate', he instructed while sliding the fence along two shiny steel bars that projected perpendicularly from one side of the plane, and then he fixed it in place.

With a twist of his wrist, the instructor turned the tool bottom-side-up to make a final inspection of the stopper and fence in relation to the plane iron, verifying the width and depth with his ruler. He slipped the ruler back into his coat pocket and then gently pressed a thumb against the tip of the plane iron to check that it was sharp. 'Some of these in the cabinet might be dull ... so you might want to have a look'. He took a relaxed stance at one end of the clamped piece of timber, his body facing down the length of wood and one foot stepped in front of the other. He aligned the plane iron along the timber's edge, gripping the handle in his right hand and pressing the tool firmly inward toward the wood with his left. The small group of trainees observed quietly: some standing, others seated on wooden stools – arms folded, heads cocked to one side. Starting at one end, with his torso gently twisted and right elbow raised, the instructor drove the rebate plane forward along the length of timber, producing a wood shaving that curled upward and over the plane iron. With a contraction of his forearm and elbow he pulled the plane back along the same path and into the initial position. Then forward again. The motion this time was rough and ragged, and the plane iron bit deeply into the grain. He made a puckered look at the thick shavings. 'Take it off slowly ... these should be thin', he advised as he pried the wood curls from the mouth of the plane with his fingers. He adjusted the plane iron, reducing the blade's extension, and then re-adjusted the depth-stop with his ruler.

The instructor took up his stance and resumed planing. As he progressed, his actions became more gracefully co-ordinated in a series of economic and repetitive movements, and the plane now skated along the face-edge of the timber, forward and backward, with mechanical rhythm. A succession of wispy wood curls pushed upward from the mouth, and every so often the instructor stopped to remove the accumulation of shavings. The resinous odour of pine was pungent and pleasing. Gradually and evenly, he worked the plane over the entire length of the timber's edge, moving along from one end toward the other. He calibrated the downward pressure applied to the tool in response to the changing character of the wood, and he maintained a constant lateral pressure against the side of the plank by pushing the instrument inward with his left hand. His centre of gravity remained fixed, held in balance by the motions of the exercise. Nearly all bodily movement was concentrated in the steady, fluid extensions and contractions of his arms. 'You have to watch not to go off at an angle. Keep it nice and straight'. As the depth of the rebate sunk closer to the pencil line drawn at 5 mm, the instructor monitored the vertical position of the cutting edge more frequently. When the task was completed, he took the metal ruler from his pocket, this time to check that the width and depth of the stepped cut corresponded to the rod drawing. The rebate angle was perfectly square and the dimensions were consistent along the entire length. Pleased with the results, he unclamped the timber window jamb from the worktop and passed it around for the trainees to inspect with both their eyes and fingers; some even held the fresh-cut wood to their noses to savour its scent.

Posture, facial expression, gesture, and deictic pointing regularly serve as scaffolding to the concepts and ideas expressed by words. As mentioned previously, these layers of communicated information provide additional context for the listener's (time-*linear* and incremental) interpretation of an utterance as it is realized, word by word, by a speaker. In workshop lessons like the one described above, the spoken content of the communication is small in comparison with the physical demonstration. In cases of skill teaching and learning, utterances typically recede to a secondary form of communication, providing supplementary context for the observer's (time-*ordered* and incremental) motor-based interpretation of an activity.

Dynamic syntax (hereafter 'DS') offers a promising model for better describing the nature of communication, and more specifically the cognitive activities of processing and producing communicative content (see Cann *et al.* 2005; Kempson *et al.* 2001).[5] DS starts from the premise that 'understanding is prior to speaking' in early language acquisition, and accordingly makes the analysis of 'understanding' central to its project. Unlike linguistic theories that define grammar as a use-neutral competence that underpins performance,[6] DS proposes a grammar formalism that directly reflects the dynamics of parsing natural language. Thus 'knowing a language is knowing how to parse it' (Cann *et al.* 2005: 1). From this standpoint, the structural properties of language are described in direct relation to the hearer's cognitive tasks of processing dialogue and deriving an understanding of what has been said. In doing so, DS simultaneously addresses how words and what they are taken to mean combine *within* sentences (i.e. the syntactic and semantic aspects of compositionality), and how the on-line interpretation of words is made in relation to a context already established, minimally, by the preceding dialogue. Significantly, what the hearer constructs in processing dialogue is not a representation of structure defined over words in a sentence, but a representation of meaning assigned to an utterance. So the 'grammaticality' of an utterance is not determined by a distinct set of syntactic rules, but rather grammaticality is a measure of 'parsibility' (i.e. the success of the utterance in supplying information for the construction of a fully meaningful representation). Parsing natural language is ultimately recognized as a 'meaning-making' exercise.

Of direct relevance to the theory of embodied cognition and communication I am espousing, DS subscribes to a representational theory of mind (RTM), whereby what we can know of the world is essentially and necessarily mind-dependent. All information received from our total environment is cognitively mediated and meaningfully represented as mind-internal concepts. For example, when we see an object, what we possess in mind is not the 'thing' itself but rather a representation processed by our visual apparatus and subjected to our faculties of reasoning about what it is. Likewise, when we hear an utterance (or think *with* language), it is not the words themselves that are entertained in our conceptual understanding of what is said, but rather the concepts they map onto and the propositional representations they combine to create in what Fodor (1975) coined the 'language of thought' (LOT). Therefore the notion of 'context', too, refers not to external surroundings (as usually implied in anthropology), but rather context is individually possessed as a mind-internal repertoire of existing concepts and representations, acquired, constructed, and modified in an ongoing manner from environmental stimuli.

More interestingly, it is widely agreed in pragmatics that our mind-internal representations of what we see, hear, touch, smell, and so on, have more 'meaning' than what is made perceptually available by the stimulus. There is a 'systematic gap between the information provided by the stimulus itself and the information we recover from it' (Cann *et al.* 2005: 21). In other words, the meaning recovered from a unit of stimuli (i.e. a word, something heard, a thing seen, an odour, etc.) is 'under-specified' and requires processes of inference, drawing upon other information available from context to enrich the semantic content of that initial representation and derive fuller meaning (Sperber & Wilson 1986). As I finished typing the preceding sentence, I glimpsed a small, black object glide swiftly past my open window and into the foliage of a nearby Ceanothus shrub. Moments later, a serenade of distinctive birdsong broke the silence. Drawing upon the context of representations mapped from other stimuli, including the pattern of movement (saliently, 'through the air') and the subsequent twittering issued from the direction of the shrub, I infer quite automatically and quite assuredly that the small, black object I spotted was a 'blackbird'.

In the toolbox session described in my example above, a hypothetical observer who lacks any formation in carpentry would visually process some imagistic representation of the rebate plane that the instructor held in the air, but they might more vaguely 'see' (i.e. entertain a representation with semantic content) a HAND-TOOL.[7] By contrast, a woodwork trainee with some basic hand-tool experience might 'see' a WOOD-PLANE, and another with greater familiarity in the trade might 'see' a REBATE-AND-FILLISTER PLANE. The construction of a representation from visually processed signals is situational and context-dependent. The same holds true for words in language. When a woodwork trainee later pondered whether to use a hand-tool or a power-tool for putting a rebate into his window frame, the instructor told him to 'Use a plane!' The word 'plane', in itself, supplies insufficient information. Having just attended the toolbox session, however, the trainee, in parsing the instructor's string, mapped that lexical input onto the concept PLANE which was enriched to construct a more meaningful representation describing the exact type of plane needed for the task. The trainee went directly to the tool storage and retrieved a rebate-and-fillister plane.

The idea that representations mapped from the stimulus are 'semantically' under-specified, and require enrichment from additional information supplied by context, is generally agreed. But DS takes an important step further in extending the notion of 'under-specification' to the syntactic structure of a representation mapped from the stimulus. Without delving too deeply into the mechanics of syntactic under-specification, it may be manifested in natural language as, for example, 'word actions'.[8] This implies that words map to representations that, in addition to having semantic content, also project structural information about what sorts of other representations they can combine with; and/or project a sequence of actions to recover further information that will update and enrich their meaning in context. For example, representations corresponding to verbs such as 'give' (representation GIVE) are essentially three-place-predicate formulas that project 'requirements' to recover representations of a subject, object, and indirect object (i.e. GIVE $\rightarrow$ who(?), what(?) and to whom(?)). All requirements may be satisfied by information supplied by the parse strategy or from existing context. For example:

Jack: How do you protect your furniture?
Anna: I give three coats of tung oil.

Anna's response does not explicitly supply the indirect object (i.e. 'furniture', or the corresponding pronoun 'it'), but she nevertheless provides sufficient information for Jack to construct a fully specified proposition since both interlocutors possess some representation FURNITURE in their individual context recovered from Jack's preceding question. In other words, as Jack processes Anna's response on a word-by-word basis, the representation he is constructing for 'give' (GIVE) will become fully specified by information recovered from his parse strategy and by the representation FURNITURE recovered from the existing dialogue context.

To summarize, dynamic syntax proposes that spoken language is construed as a signal generated and received as sound waves. The hearer's task involves parsing the information made available by an utterance in natural language, and progressively assigning interpretation with the goal of constructing a mental representation with propositional content that closely matches that of the speaker's intent. This is the quintessence of 'successful communication'. Fundamental to the DS framework, parsing proceeds incrementally on a word-by-word basis as lexical input is received in the real time of dialogue. Parsing involves mapping some signal onto a mind-internal concept, but also simultaneously enriching that initially under-specified information and satisfying the structural requirements it introduces by using information provided by other representations retrieved from context and with updates made available by subsequent parse strategies.

Once again, context consists strictly of mind-internal representations, and minimally includes representations constructed up to any given point in the dialogue, including that under construction. Context also presumably includes representations mapped from perceptually processed stimuli from the total environment as well as representations (or 'knowledge') that one already possesses about one's fellow interlocutors or the subject of dialogue. As we have seen, lexical items are under-specified in terms of their semantic content and syntactic structure, and DS claims that under-specification of meaning and structure pertains to all environmental stimuli supplied to cognition. In turn, the property of under-specification introduces requirements that drive the update process to satisfy them. The incremental enrichment of meaning and structure relative to some context progresses the growth of some fully specified proposition formulated in the language of thought (LOT).

Because DS seeks to establish 'a grammar formalism that reflects the incremental way in which context-dependent interpretation can be built on-line' (Kempson, Cann & Purver 2006: 2), the often-presumed division of cognitive labour between syntax and semantic processing is blurred, and context is recognized as playing a key role in all aspects of language-processing. Inspirationally, this firmly challenges the long-dominant idea that our human capacity for language is an encapsulated modular domain, and promotes a rethinking of language as embedded within a more general cognitive system that enables us to retrieve and process information from our continual interaction with our environment. It also opens a space for serious consideration of the cognitive relations between spoken language and other forms of dialogue. In the remainder of this section I will suggest how the DS model of language contributes toward my hypothesis about the nature of skill learning and embodied communication.

Practice theory suggests that we learn by example. So like language-learning, 'understanding' is conceived as being prior to 'practising' techniques of the body. I have adopted this starting-point in modelling the cognitive processes that give rise to 'embodied understanding', and subsequently to the physical capacity for imitation and creative production. In establishing the framework for this exercise, it is important to note that understanding action and movement *from* the body is achieved neither by constructing fully specified imagistic representations of what has been seen, nor by formulating linguistic propositions that describe what has been done. Understanding, instead, is arrived at in motor cognition and expressed as motor representations. I reiterate that these are formulated, like all other representations, in the language of thought (LOT), and as such, they are constituted by a syntactic combination of motor representations.

In the toolbox session described above, the assembled trainees concertedly watch the instructor's demonstration of how to use the rebate-and-fillister plane. I propose that information processed by vision provides input to their motor cognition. The instructor's stance, his grasp of the tool, the directional pressure he exerts with his body, and the fluid extension and retraction of his arms are disarticulated into component postures and actions and assigned kinaesthetic and proprioceptive interpretation. Notably, the content of such interpretation is not a semantic depiction of what that practice *means* but rather a motor-based one describing the *sense* and *feeling* of doing it.[9] Like parsing natural language or any other signal perceptually received from the environment, parsing in the motor domain proceeds incrementally and in the real time of the observed performance. I differentiate the procedural aspect of motor parsing from natural-language parsing, however, by substituting the notion of time-linear with a 'time-ordered' one. I argue elsewhere (2007b; 2010) that the actions, gestures, and postures that constitute a skilled movement unfold in time and in an orderly fashion, but not in a strictly linear sense like the word-by-word sequence of an utterance. Several co-ordinated actions and positions may be simultaneously enacted by different parts of the body at any point during a complex movement, and thus the construction and compositional properties of corresponding representations must be conceived of in a multi-dimensional way, reflecting the nature of physical movement itself in space. This interesting difference between parsing natural language and parsing movement might also explain the challenge to articulate in natural language *that* which one knows *how* to do.

Under-specification and the dynamics of update form the core of natural-language structure and reflect the dynamics of language-processing. I contend that the same is true for the communication of physical practice, as exemplified in craft (see Portisch, Makovicky, Venkatessan, and Dilley, this volume) and sport (see Downey, this volume). As the constituent actions of a movement are parsed from the stream of input supplied by vision to motor cognition, they are assigned some initial, under-specified interpretation. Since understanding precedes response in communication, the assignment of a motor-based interpretation to the stimulus first instantiates simulated motor imagery, and not a corresponding actualized physical action. It is necessary first to describe what the content of this sort of interpretation might consist of before offering an explanation of how under-specification applies in this case. Elsewhere (Marchand 2010) I have written that the content of a motor-based interpretation is not semantic in nature: it pertains neither to the meaning of the action, nor to aesthetic judgements, nor to its possible symbolic connotations. Interpretation containing these aforementioned types of information is formulated within a propositional thinking *about* the action (or gesture). By contrast, a motor-based interpretation contains kinaesthetic and proprioceptive information directly related to the physical character and co-ordinated bodily mechanics involved in performing some action.[10] More specifically, kinaesthetic information represents the corporeal *sensation* associated with that action: the *feeling* of muscular extension and contraction; the *feeling* of muscular relaxation and tension; the *feeling* of flow, disruption, and vibration in action; and the *feeling* of applying force or exerting pressure. The proprioceptive content represents an embodied *sense* of balance and an interior *sense* of the relational positioning of digits, limbs, and other body parts to each other.

In parsing the constituent actions in a movement, the motor-based interpretations assigned to them will therefore be under-specified minimally in terms of kinaesthetic and proprioceptive content. Enrichment is achieved via the parse strategy, which operates incrementally and in a time-ordered manner over the physical movement and relative to some context. To repeat, context is individually possessed as a set of mind-internal representations. And in motor cognition, context is minimally defined by the motor representations constructed up to, and including, the current one under construction in the parse task. An observer's context is also likely to include representations mapped from other stimuli in the social and material environment where the practice is performed, and possibly from existing relevant experience in the given (or comparable) activity. In the last workshop example, for instance, a trainee's existing knowledge of the context may include mental representations corresponding to the softwood properties of the material being planed. Instantiation of this representation may inform the kinaesthetic content of his motor-based interpretation of the instructor's applied pressure with the hand plane.

But more than being under-specified in terms of kinaesthetic and proprioceptive content, I also venture that the motor representations corresponding to the constituent actions, gestures, and postures of a movement are syntactically under-specified. In other words, representations corresponding to parsed actions introduce requirements regarding what other sorts of motor representations they may combine with to enact a completed movement in which all conditions are satisfied. I refer again to the toolbox session. When the instructor takes up his stance at one end of the clamped timber, his demonstration commences by aligning the plane with the timber's edge using his arms carefully to position the tool at this spot. With the plane grasped firmly in both hands using a certain configuration of wrists, palms, and fingers, he then exerts directional forces upon the wood surface, applying pressure both downward with his left hand and laterally with his right before starting to plane. His torso at this point is gently twisted to the left, facing in toward the workbench, and his elbows are bent and raised in readiness to drive the plane along the timber length. His body is poised for action, like a swimmer on the starting block (Marchand 2008).

In observing the instructor bend and raise his elbows into ready position, the trainee's motor-based parse progressively disarticulates the movement into its component (and sometimes simultaneous) actions and maps these in an incremental and time-ordered manner to corresponding motor representations of simulated motor imagery.[11] These constituent representations introduce structural requirements regarding the co-ordinated arrangements of simultaneously entertained motor representations that they may enter into; plus requirements concerning the sorts of actions with which they need to combine in order to arrive at a fully specified representation of movement.

More straightforwardly, in parsing the instructor's bending and raising of his right elbow in the context of wielding the plane, the kinaesthetic and proprioceptive properties of that instantiated representation introduce requirements to combine in simultaneous fashion with actions of the left arm and the torso that, together in co-ordination, yield a *feeling* of motor control over the procedures and *sense* of balance in their execution. It also introduces requirements regarding the sorts of subsequent actions the right arm itself must enact in order to complete some fluid movement of that limb. In this case, an extension of the right arm is required to release the sprung muscles and the bend in the elbow. (Conversely, if the instructor suddenly, and violently, twisted his right elbow laterally rather than following through with the anticipated extension, it would not only produce a 'wrong' *feeling* in the observer, but may even provoke him or her to cringe with simulated discomfort and pain!) And information made available by the broader context of the planing exercise will be drawn upon to satisfy that combinational requirement.

In summary, structural requirements introduced by successive motor-based representations drive the process of update to satisfy under-specifications with kinaesthetic and proprioceptive content and structural information that complete a fully specified representation of a movement relative to some context. Once again, it is important to note that in the case of motor-based representations, as differentiated from linguistic propositional ones, I am suggesting that the property of under-specification may not induce a strictly time-linear sequence of incremental updates. Rather, plural (possibly several) updates are likely to be processed simultaneously, reflecting the complex and three-dimensional nature of movement. Stefan Vogt and David Carey have similarly noted that 'even simple pattern learning appears to involve the extraction of complex features rather than the formation of linear associations' (1998: 706).

Practice is regularly – though not exclusively – learned through observation and a synthesis of action-level and programme-level imitation (Byrne & Russon 1998*a*; 1998*b*), so my discussion has focused on the parse process applied to information made available to the motor domain via vision. But language, too, can be employed to convey and receive instructions about *how* to do something.[12] Since parsing natural language constructs propositional representations expressed in LOT, the informational content of these representations is equally available as input to motor cognition, and accordingly parsed there to construct motor representations. The woodwork instructor can command a trainee to: 'Hold the plane with both hands. Line it up along the edge of the timber. Press in against the wood, and down, to keep it in position. And plane with long, even, forward strokes ....'

To repeat, natural language is parsed in the incremental, time-linear order that words are received as input, and thus the construction of corresponding propositional representations is equally incremental and time-linear. This also means that the informational content associated with that representation is made available as input to motor cognition in the same incremental, time-linear way. But, as we have seen, skilled practices and movements regularly comprise numerous actions simultaneously performed by different parts of the body, and in an immeasurable variety of possible combinations. Language-production and -processing, by contrast, is constrained by time-linear sequencing, making it impossible to capture the complexity of three-dimensional movement with words. Verbal instructions are necessarily impoverished because linguistic propositions can only convey information about one salient action at a time. Other simultaneous and possibly crucial actions to the movement are either eliminated from the instruction altogether or (re)arranged to follow one after the other. Propositional representations flatten three-dimensional practice into the sequential order imposed by language, thereby rendering simultaneity time-linear.

Vision, on the other hand, has the capacity to construct multi-dimensional representations.[13] The dimensional quality in the arrangement of information provided as input to motor cognition is arguably more akin to the multi-dimensional array of informational processing that I have suggested occurs there. It would therefore be more cognitively efficient to access input from vision than from linguistic propositions in constructing motor representations, not necessarily because of the sort of information that vision supplies, but because of the structural configuration of that information as input. Language loses the 'simultaneity' of practice that vision can capture. Arguably more effective than vision for learning skill and acquiring practice is to have one's positions, postures, and movements physically manipulated and guided by another person. This occurs regularly in disciplining the comportment of children or teaching them sport, and less frequently in formal learning environments (see Downey, this volume). Tactile guidance makes direct links to motor cognition, enabling the motor-based interpretation of the receiver to capture the fully dimensional arrangement of the simultaneous and time-ordered components of an activity.

As a concluding thought to this section: *if* all mental representations are expressed in the language of thought (LOT), as Fodor claims; and all mental representations are syntactically structured, as upheld by DS; and different cognitive domains (e.g. propositional, visual, motor) impose distinct dimensional arrangements on their respective compositionality rules, as I have suggested, *then* what distinguishes propositional, visual, and embodied ways of knowing is not a matter of difference in the nature of the constituent concepts they acquire or employ, but rather a difference in the way that their respective concepts, as units of information, combine to form fully specified representations. It is therefore due to the combination rules pertaining to each domain that a different effect (or way of 'thinking') is produced (e.g. an idea, an image, or a movement). Indeed this may explain in cognitive terms the difference between *knowing how* and *knowing that*, and provide the ontological basis for an enduring popular sense of a mind-body dualism.

Conclusion: modelling mimicry and shared performance

During a toolbox session on the topic of screws and screwdrivers, the instructor stressed the importance of selecting the appropriate tool for the task. After discussing the purpose of cabinet screwdrivers with examples for the trainees to inspect, he introduced an assortment of Posidriv™ and Phillips-head screwdrivers with cross-shaped tips of varying size. In mid-sentence, while cautioning about the consequences of not matching tip size to screw gauge, one of the students abruptly interjected and finished off the warning for him.

> *Instructor:* When choosing a Phillips screwdriver, make sure the tip is the right size for your screw. If
>   it doesn't fit snugly in the cross-shaped slot, it's likely to ...
> *Trainee:* Strip the head!

This phenomenon of one interlocutor completing the string of another occurs regularly in spoken dialogue. Linguists coin this event 'shared utterance', which succinctly describes the participation of two (or more) interlocutors in completing the vocal statement of an idea or proposition. In this concluding section I will demonstrate how shared performance also occurs in the realm of practice. By mapping the processes of both parsing and production engaged by participating practitioners, I intend to show how a fluid swap of roles may take place between them.

Workshop example three:

A first-year trainee clamped a 2,500 mm length of redwood pine timber to the top of his workbench. It had been machined to a thickness of 45 mm and width of 100, and would be a stile for the panel door he was constructing. He carefully measured and marked the position of the mortises with a pencil, and incised parallel lines onto either side of the timber with a marking gauge. From the bench top, he picked up a 15 mm mortise chisel in his left hand and grasped a heavy wooden mallet with his right. He positioned himself behind the end of the timber and self-consciously separated his feet by a short stride, keeping a slight spring in his knees. Eyeing the markings, the trainee carefully lowered the sharp end of his chisel onto the wood face, lining up the squared edge of its bevelled tip between the incised lines. He paused in concentration, feeling the weight of the mallet in his palm, and then raised it just 15 cm or so over the handle of the chisel, which he held steadily upright. As he did so, he drew his body in close with head hung awkwardly, peering down over his work. The shop instructor moved toward the trainee's bench and observed silently, standing to one side. The mallet came down gently on the first hit, barely puncturing the smooth redwood surface. The trainee scrutinized the position of the cut to make sure the blade of the tool remained within the incised boundaries. Feeling assured, he raised the mallet back into position, hovering just above the top of the chisel handle. He shifted balance slightly and checked the position of his arms before bringing the mallet down in a staccato of short, quick taps, driving the sharp steel slowly into the softwood timber. As he paused to verify progress, the instructor stepped in closer saying, 'At this rate, you'll be at it 'til Christmas'. The trainee paused, shuffled his feet into position and re-composed his focus, then knocked the head of the chisel again, this time applying a little more force in his cramped movement. He looked searchingly with a side glance and the instructor motioned for him to pause. The trainee handed over the tools and surrendered his place behind the timber. The instructor positioned the chisel blade with a steady left hand, establishing a comfortable space between him and the tool. He looked to his student to draw attention to the instrument and his readied posture. 'Check to see it's ninety degrees', he said referring to the chisel, 'otherwise you'll go at, uh, an angle or bruise the edge of your mortise'. With a fluid movement of his right arm, the instructor raised the mallet above his shoulder line and brought it down with a resounding blow, driving the chisel deep into the pinewood. The trainee shook his head slowly up and down, monitoring the demonstration and focusing on the instructor's overall posture and wielding of the tools. The instructor drove the chisel in twice more before cleaning out the chips of wood with its sharp end and blowing out the remainder. The student shook his head again and reclaimed his tools. He found his footing, cautiously placed his chisel between the incised lines and checked to see it was straight. Biting down onto his lower lip, he took a deep breath and resumed his task, extending the arm that held the chisel in place and increasing the leverage in his hammering.

In this workshop example, both the trainee and instructor alternate between observing and practising. The trainee's initial display with the mortise chisel provided the stimulus for the instructor's motor-based parse. The representations of simulated motor imagery entertained by the observing instructor, and enriched with information supplied by the context of this particular tool-wielding exercise, instantiated a 'wrong' kinaesthetic *feeling* for the movement, and 'illogical' compositionality of parsed actions. In other words, there was a failure to construct a fully specified representation in motor cognition. The instructor therefore motioned for his student to stop and he offered a demonstration of 'correct' procedures. The two swapped positions, whereby the trainee took on the parser role and the instructor became the producer of the action. Information derived from the visually processed stimulus was accessed by the trainee's motor cognition in the real time of the demonstration. His parse disarticulated the instructor's stance, grasps, and movements and assigned motor-based interpretation to the input in an incremental and time-ordered manner, as described in the previous section. The resulting representation was then retrieved from context and re-used by the trainee to align (though not necessarily replicate) his renewed activity with the instructor's demonstration and thereby complete the task.

The next example conveys a yet more fluid swapping of roles between practitioners, whereby one carpentry trainee takes over from the other on several occasions to complete movements and tasks in progress (see Fig. 2).

Workshop example four:

I was preparing to glue up my bedside cabinet project. My Arts-and-Crafts-inspired design consisted of twenty-four individual components that fitted together with mortise-and-tenon and stub-tenon joints. All components had to be glued and cramped together at one time, so the assemblage had to be performed systematically and rather quickly. The cabinet components were numbered and orientated with pencil marks, and arranged on the worktop in sequential order; a pot of PVA carpenter's glue, application brush, clean rag, and wooden mallet stood nearby; and a selection of metal cramps were readied for bracing the drying structure. Before starting, I asked my colleague Toby to stand on the opposite side of my workbench and lend a hand with the task. As we proceeded, our individual

Figure 2. My 'Arts-and-Crafts' bedside cabinet assembled with mortise-and-tenon joints.

activities became progressively co-ordinated with one another. In the absence of explicit instructions, Toby sensed when to intervene with his hands for steadying the components I was joining, when to pass the mallet for tapping tenons into place, or when to pick up the cloth for wiping away excess glue from the joints. The markings on the arranged timber members also guided Toby's activities, like mine, and he selected and passed the pieces as needed.

Gluing up is often an intense exercise for novices, demanding concentration and efficiency, and leaving little room for verbal negotiation. On occasion, I explicitly called out the tool required or, with short utterances, directed Toby's attention to where his assistance was most needed. For the most part, however, few words were exchanged. When reaching for timber components or implements on the worktop with my right hand while precariously holding the pieces of the cabinet together with my left, Toby sometimes intercepted my manual actions, picked up the necessary object, and either passed it to me or fluidly executed the task I initiated. As we commenced the final stage of cramping the assembled table, I extended my reach toward the pile of metal cramps on the worktop. I intended to use a small G-cramp first to brace the as-yet-unfitted table top to the supporting rails on the underside. Toby again intercepted my motion, but grasped a long sash cramp instead, and he began adjusting it across two table legs at a position where the tenons of the cross rail joined the mortises in the legs. I paused, ready to object, but in briefly observing his procedure I realizd the advantage of his method. By closing the joints between the legs and cross-rails on all four sides of the table, the frame of the structure would be 'squared', thereby making it easier to ease the table top into its correct position. As he turned the 'tommy bars' to squeeze the sash-cramp jaws, I picked up a second sash cramp and executed parallel procedures on the table legs nearest me.

On the face of it, there is nothing extraordinary in the above example. We all recognize that activities are shared and co-ordinated between people, similar in manner to the way that spoken dialogue is routinely shared between speakers. This is perhaps most evident in manual work activities, team sports, and dance, but it is equally apparent in everyday practices such as gardening or cooking together; reaching or grasping for objects or utensils; or intercepting to open the door for another person. What is worthy of closer consideration, however, is the manner by which such uptake and completion of another interlocutor/co-practitioner's goal is cognitively achieved.

Before exploring the cognitive operations that give rise to 'shared performance', I turn once again to dynamic syntax to consider briefly how the phenomenon of 'shared utterance' is modelled. In describing the parsing task in the previous section, it was stated that the hearer incrementally constructs a context-dependent interpretation of a string as it is received on a word-by-word basis in dialogue. The time-linear parse strategy maps each lexical item to an initially under-specified representation which is successively enriched and updated by information supplied by the parse routine or recovered from context. At any point in the dialogue, context minimally comprises all completed representations and any currently under construction (i.e. those still requiring semantic and structural update).

Notably, DS also establishes that a speaker, in the course of generating an utterance, employs the exact same cognitive strategies as her parsing interlocutor in incrementally constructing a meaningful representation corresponding to what she says. This means that, typically, speakers do not have a fully formulated representation 'in their head' of what they wish to say. Rather, a speaker has some 'idea' of what she intends to communicate, and this takes shape as a fully formulated representation *in* the process of generating a string on a word-by-word basis. Presumably this holds true whether an idea is being expressed vocally to a third party, typed on a laptop, written in a letter, or silently composed in one's thoughts. The speaker's possession of an initial idea (or goal) of what she wishes to communicate is the key factor differentiating the nature of her task from that of the hearer. At each incremental step in producing the utterance, the speaker's lexical selection is made against the goal, the sole criteria being that her choice of word progress the growth of the representation toward realizing her communicative intent.

Therefore, because speaker and hearer employ the same cognitive procedures in constructing a meaningful representation as a string of words is generated, and because both individually possess the same context at any given point in the dialogue, the parser may find himself in the cognitive position to perform a so-called 'abduction' step, thereby leaping to the conclusion of what the speaker is going to say. In so doing, he is completing his own representation of meaning and so he need not make any higher-level hypotheses about the speaker's intent or mental states (Purver & Kempson 2004). Having performed the abduction step, the parser may choose to interject and finish the utterance (as in the example at the start of this section), thus hijacking the speaker's role and making the original speaker the parser. This swapping of roles is perpetuated in dialogue.

As I discuss in my introduction to this volume, there is no guarantee that the intervening interlocutor will have completed a representation that corresponds to what the initial speaker had in mind to convey. In such cases, one or more possibilities may arise: the communication may break down altogether; the initial speaker may recuperate her role as producer and supply the necessary information for re-establishing her communicative intent; or, feasibly, the dialogue may take a turn following the new direction introduced by the 'abductor'. In the latter case, the speaker-cum-hearer who assumes the parsing role will continue to construct her representation from where it was cut short, incrementally enriching and updating it with the new information supplied by the abductor. Evidently, the completed representations that they will both possess will differ from that which they would have constructed if the initial speaker would have been allowed to complete her utterance. In this manner, interlocutors are continually modifying and redirecting the representations that they and their listeners are constructing. To my mind, this powerfully illustrates the 'social production of knowledge' and reveals the everyday junctures where meaning-making, belief formation, 'common sense', and 'truths' take shape.

I also contend that, like shared utterance, 'shared performance' occurs frequently, and the underlying cognitive operations of the phenomenon can be explicated in an equally straightforward manner. In observing an activity, the parser's task was earlier described as involving the disarticulation of a movement into its constituent actions, gestures, and postures, and mapping these to motor representations. Doing so equates to what Jeannerod (2006) calls an embodied simulation of the activity, and this entails a *feeling* for the movement without physically actualizing it. Motor representations are defined minimally by their kinaesthetic and proprioceptive content, and compositionality is multi-dimensional, reflecting the complex three-dimensional nature of motor activity. The parser incrementally constructs a full motor representation of movement in a time-ordered manner using (often simultaneous) information supplied, on-line, by a practitioner. Motor representations are enriched and updated using information recovered both from the ongoing parse routine and from the context of existing representations. Context, I have stressed, is individually shared by observer and practitioner; and, at any point in the activity, each possesses the same (or closely approximate) set of completed motor representations plus any currently under construction.

As in the case of spoken dialogue, I suggest that the practitioner of a task employs the very same cognitive operations as the observer in incrementally constructing a fully defined motor representation corresponding to the physical activity he generates.

Again, the only difference is that, from the start, the practitioner has in 'mind' (i.e. motor cognition) what it is he intends to do, if only as a vague 'motor sketch' or 'goal'. Like language production, this initial goal serves as a subsumption check against which his incremental and time-ordered selection of actions, gestures and postures is made, instantiating actualized movement. The only condition guiding selection from his existing motor repertoire is that all choices progress the growth of the motor representation toward satisfying what it is he has in mind to *do* (or, in the case of an instructor, what it is he has in mind to demonstrate to his observing pupils).

So, finally, because observer and practitioner employ the same motor cognitive operations in their respective roles as parser and producer of an activity, and because both share the same motor context, at any given point in a movement the observer may find herself in the 'motor-ready' position to perform an abduction step. Like the hearer described above, the parsing-observer thereby completes her motor representation before the practitioner finishes his movement, and in so doing she may interrupt the activity and take over. This swapping of roles was illustrated in workshop examples three and four, and the exchange between co-practitioners in the latter example was shown to be fluid.

In watching me assemble my bedside cabinet, Toby incrementally constructed an on-line kinaesthetic and proprioceptive interpretation of my actions, gestures, and postures as I produced them. The example records how, on several occasions, Toby arrived at a completed embodied simulation (or motor representation) of my as yet unfinished movements, and he intervened to complete the given task. In the instance when he intercepted my reach and picked up a long sash cramp, his interpretation of which object or actions were required for completing my initiated activity was enriched and updated by information recovered from the context he already possessed. In addition to the set of motor representations that he individually constructed as a co-practitioner in our activity together, Toby's context contained existing representations acquired from his prior woodworking experience with the tools and objects to hand. Toby's selection of a cramp and cramping method differed from what I had in mind to 'use' and 'do'. Now in the observer's seat, my parse of his actions resulted in unanticipated growth in both the propositional representation (i.e. my 'reasoning' for selecting a certain tool) and motor representation (i.e. motor procedures for assembling the furniture) that I had hitherto been constructing *in* practice. Effectively, this resulted in a revised understanding of and subsequent change to my own carpentry practice and procedures. I maintain that it is precisely this phenomenon that drives skill learning and acquisition, and prompts revision *in* practice.

Shared utterance and shared performance demonstrate how the making of things, including dialogue and material artefacts, is a shared activity between situated interlocutors and practitioners, each with his or her own agency and individual contribution to the enterprise. At every turn in the process, there lies the possibility of misinterpretation, or new interpretation, and the carrying forward of ideas and practices in novel directions. Making things is therefore making knowledge. By carefully studying these micro-processes, we stand a better chance of describing the mechanics of social and cultural change.

NOTES

The research for this study was funded by a three-year Fellowship from the Economic and Social Research Council (RES-000-27-0159). I would like to thank my woodwork instructors and fellow trainees at the

Building Crafts College for sharing their carpentry and learning experiences with me. I would also like to thank Ruth Kempson for her valuable comments on earlier drafts of this chapter and an anonymous reviewer for their insightful editorial suggestions.

[1] Earlier versions of this theory and variations of the ideas expressed here have been published in Marchand (2007*b*; 2008; 2010), and I have taken the liberty to paraphrase a small number of the key theoretical passages from these texts since they succinctly express the ideas I am trying to develop and convey in the present chapter.

[2] A rod is a 1:1 scale drawing that shows all important joints and measurements for the making and assembly of a piece, and it is used to mark out the timber and as a reference throughout production.

[3] Vision likely includes a multitude of Fodorian first-order modules that process different types of information, including object description, spatial relations, and movement (Fodor 1983). In observing grasps, gestures, or skilled actions, representations generated by these modules would seemingly interface with motor cognition and inform relevant aspects of motor-based understanding and performance.

[4] In a woodworking context, the definition of a 'rebate' (also referred to as 'rabbet') is a step-shaped recess cut along the edge or in the face of a piece of wood (*The concise Oxford dictionary*). Fillister is more specifically the rebate on the edge of a sash bar of a window to hold the putty and glass pane.

[5] These works express the cognitive processes and conceptual representations established by the parsing routine in calculus and with binary tree structures familiar to syntactic analyses. I do not describe these here, but rather present a discussion of the key ideas that directly relate to an anthropological (re-)thinking of practice and embodied cognition.

[6] The most significant example of this kind is Chomsky's theory of Universal Grammar (1965), which set the agenda in linguistics for the next three decades.

[7] Following conventions used in literature on representational theory of mind, I am using UPPERCASE words to indicate that I am referring to some conceptual representation that corresponds to the equivalent word(s), and not the word(s) itself/themselves.

[8] See Cann *et al.* (2005) for other forms of syntactic under-specification, including 'left-dislocation structure' of an utterance.

[9] Motor mirror neurons very likely play a key role in this process. See for example Oztop, Kawato & Arbib (2006).

[10] Kinaesthetic: (Greek) *kineo* 'move' + *aisthesis* (Greek) 'sensation'; proprioceptive: (Latin) *proprius* 'own' + receptive.

[11] This is possibly the function of motor mirror neurons located in the Broca's area of the brain. Motor mirror neurons fire in the same configuration both when observing and when performing an action, and are believed to be directly implicated in our human ability to learn grasps and motor actions.

[12] In the case of blind persons, tactile and haptic input is also assumed to be represented in LOT, and the informational content of these representations is presumably made available to the motor domain to be processed as motor representations comprised of kinaesthetic and proprioceptive content.

[13] See Marr (1982) for an explanation of the '2½D sketch' in visual cognition.

REFERENCES

BLOCH, M. 1998. Language, anthropology and cognitive science. In *How we think they think*, 3-21. Boulder, Colo.: Westview.

BYRNE, R.W. 2003. Imitation as behaviour parsing. *Philosophical Transactions of the Royal Society, B, Biological Sciences* **358**, 529-36.

——— & A.E. RUSSON 1998*a*. Learning by imitation: a hierarchical approach. *Behavioral and Brain Sciences* **21**, 667-84.

——— & ——— 1998*b*. Common ground on which to approach the origins of higher cognition. *Behavioral and Brain Sciences* **21**, 709-17.

CANN, R., R. KEMPSON & L. MARTEN 2005. *The dynamics of language: an introduction*. Amsterdam: Elsevier.

CHOMSKY, N. 1965. *Aspects of the theory of syntax*. Cambridge, Mass.: MIT Press

CROSS, E., A.F. DE C. HAMILTON & S.T. GRAFTON 2006. Building a motor simulation de novo: observation of dance by dancers. *NeuroImage* **31**, 1257-67.

FARNELL, B. 1999. Moving bodies, acting selves. *Annual Review of Anthropology* **28**, 341-73.

FODOR, J. 1975. *The language of thought*. Cambridge, Mass.: Harvard University Press.

——— 1983. *The modularity of mind*. Cambridge, Mass.: MIT Press.

JACKENDOFF, R. 1992. *Languages of the mind: essays on mental representation*. Cambridge, Mass.: MIT Press.

———— & B. LANDAU 1992. Spatial language and spatial cognition. In *Languages of the mind: essays on mental representation*, R. Jackendoff, 99-124. Cambridge, Mass.: MIT Press.

JACOB, P. & M. JEANNEROD 2003. *Ways of seeing: the scope and limits of visual cognition.* Oxford: University Press.

JEANNEROD, M. 1994. The representing brain: neural correlates of motor intention and imagery. *Behavioral and Brain Sciences* **17**, 187-245.

———— 1999. Mental imaging of motor activity in humans. *Institut des Sciences Cognitives Working Papers* **99-8** (available on-line: *http://www.isc.cnrs.fr/wp/wp99-8.htm*, accessed 11 January 2010).

———— 2006. *Motor cognition: what action tells the self.* Oxford: University Press.

KEMPSON, R., R. CANN & M. PURVER 2006. Talking and listening: dialogue and the grammar-pragmatics interface (available on-line: *http://www.kcl.ac.uk/content/1/c6/03/20/96/Pomona-Kempson-et-al-Dialogue-Pragmatics.pdf*, accessed 15 January 2010).

————, W. MEYER-VIOL & D. GABBAY 2001. *Dynamic syntax: the flow of language understanding.* Oxford: Blackwell.

LERDAHL, F. & R. JACKENDOFF 1983. An overview of hierarchical structure in music. *Music Perception* **1**, 229-52.

MARCHAND, T.H.J. 2001. *Minaret building and apprenticeship in Yemen.* Richmond, Surrey: Curzon.

———— 2003. A possible explanation for the lack of explanation; or 'why the master builder can't explain what he knows': introducing informational atomism against a 'definitional' definition of concepts. In *Negotiating local knowledge* (eds) J. Pottier, A. Bicker & P. Sillitoe, 30-50. London: Pluto.

———— 2007a. Vocational migrants and a tradition of longing. *Traditional Dwellings & Settlements Review* **XIX**, 23-40.

———— 2007b. Crafting knowledge: the role of 'parsing and production' in the communication of skill-based knowledge among masons. In *Ways of knowing: new approaches in the anthropology of experience and learning* (ed.) M. Harris, 173-93. Oxford: Berghahn.

———— 2008. Muscles, moral and mind: craft apprenticeship and the formation of person. *British Journal of Educational Studies* **56**, 245-71.

———— 2009. *The masons of Djenné.* Bloomington: University of Indiana Press.

———— 2010. Embodied cognition, communication and the making of place and identity: reflections on fieldwork with masons. In *Human nature as capacity: an ethnographic approach* (ed.) N. Rapport. Oxford: Berghahn.

MARR, D. 1982. *Vision.* San Francisco: Freeman.

OISHI, K. & T. MAESHIMA 2004. Autonomic nervous system activities during motor imagery in elite athletes. *Journal of Clinical Neurophysiology* **21**, 170-9.

OZTOP, E., M. KAWATO & M. ARBIB 2006. Mirror neurons and imitation: a computationally guided view. *Neural Networks* **19** (Special issue on the brain mechanisms of imitation learning), 254-71.

PLOTKIN, H. 1993. *Darwin machines and the nature of knowledge.* Cambridge, Mass.: Harvard University Press.

PURVER, D. & R. KEMPSON 2004. Context-based incremental generation for dialogue. *Proceedings of the 3rd International Conference on Natural Language Generation* (INLG04), Careys Manor, Brockenhurst, Hampshire.

RYLE, G. 1949. *The concept of mind.* Chicago: University Press.

SIRIGU, A. & J.R. DUHAMEL 2001. Motor and visual imagery as two complementary but neurally dissociable mental processes. *Journal of Cognitive Neural Science* **13**, 910-19.

SPERBER, D. & D. WILSON 1986. *Relevance: communication and cognition.* Oxford: Blackwell.

VOGT, S. & D. CAREY 1998. Toward a microanalysis of imitative actions. *Behavioral and Brain Sciences* **21**, 705-6.

YUE, G. & K.J. COLE 1992. Strength increase from the motor programme: comparison of training with maximal voluntary and imagined muscle contractions. *Journal of Neurophysiology* **67**, 1114-23.

6

Footprints through the weather-world: walking, breathing, knowing

TIM INGOLD *University of Aberdeen*

We can't go over it.
We can't go under it.
Oh no!
We've got to go through it!

Rosen & Oxenbury 1989

'We're going on a bear hunt', sings the traditional nursery rhyme. 'What a beautiful day!' On their way to encounter the bear, our intrepid, would-be hunters walk through long grass that goes 'swishy swashy' as they pass, a deep river that goes 'splash splosh', oozy mud that goes 'squelch squerch', a dark forest where they go 'stumble trip', and a whirling snowstorm that howls 'hoooo woooo'. It turns out to be a chastening experience, and the youngsters return a little wiser and less foolhardy than when they set out. The story is a beautiful illustration of the intimate relation between becoming knowledgeable, walking along, and the experience of weather. By *becoming knowledgeable* I mean that knowledge is grown along the myriad paths we take as we make our ways through the world in the course of everyday activities, rather than assembled from information obtained from numerous fixed locations. Thus it is by *walking along* from place to place, and not by building up from local particulars, that we come to know what we do. Yet as we walk, we do not so much traverse the exterior surface of the world as negotiate a way through a zone of admixture and interchange between the more or less solid substances of the earth and the volatile medium of air. It is in this zone that all terrestrial life is lived. As inhabitants of this zone we are continually subject to those fluxes of the medium we call weather. The *experience of weather* lies at the root of our moods and motivations; indeed it is the very temperament of our being. It is therefore critical to the relation between bodily movement and the formation of knowledge.

My objective in this chapter is to investigate the relation between these components of ambulatory knowing, pedestrian movement, and temperate experience. I shall proceed in four steps. First, I shall explore the meaning of what we take to be the *ground*. From there, I move on to consider the formation of *paths and tracks*. Thirdly, acknowledging that as we walk the ground we also breathe the air, I shall attend to the *wind*. Finally, I shall turn to the implications of these explorations of ground, path, and wind for our understanding of *knowledge* and of how it is formed.

Before proceeding, let me take a moment to situate my investigation within the context of the present collection. The chapters comprising the collection were originally written for a series of seminars on *The transmission of knowledge*. Like many of my fellow contributors, however, I am convinced that 'transmission' is quite the wrong word to describe the ways in which people come to know what they do. I have set out the reasons for my conviction elsewhere (Ingold 2000a; 2001; 2009; see also Ingold & Hallam 2007: 5-6), and will not repeat them here. As Marchand explains in his preface to this collection, it was in part because of a general dissatisfaction with the notion of transmission that the volume has been renamed *Making knowledge*. Yet even the notion of making, I contend, needs to be qualified. If knowledge is indeed made, then making has to be understood in the sense implied when we say of people that they 'make their way' in the world. It is not a construction, governed by cognitive mechanisms of one sort or another, but an improvisatory movement – of 'going along' or wayfaring – that is open-ended and knows no final destination. It is precisely this sense of knowledge-making, which is equally knowledge-growing, that I attempt to establish in this chapter.

My argument has a critical corollary, however, which distinguishes it from most other contributions to this collection. It has become almost an anthropological cliché to describe the relation between knowledge and the body by resort to the idea of 'embodiment'. Yet a mindful body that knows and remembers must also live and breathe. A living, breathing body is at once a body-on-the-ground and a body-in-the-air. Earth and sky, then, are not components of an external environment with which the progressively 'knowledged-up' (socialized or encultured) body interacts. They are rather regions of the body's very existence, without which no knowing or remembering would be possible at all. 'Inside me', confessed Saint Augustine, 'in the vast cloisters of my memory ... are the sky, the earth and the sea, ready at my summons, together with everything that I have ever perceived in them by my senses' (cited in Carruthers 1998: 29). What follows may be read as a protest against ways of theorizing the embodiment of knowledge that proceed, to the contrary, as though earth and sky – indeed the world itself – were extrinsic to what mindful bodies *are*. It is a protest against psychologistic approaches to 'grounded cognition', of the kind advocated by Emma Cohen (this volume), that effectively put the ground inside the brain, leaving individuals stranded in an unspecified 'environment' which is invoked merely for the purposes of allowing the body to have something material to interact with. The increasing regard for the neurological correlates of knowing has, it seems, been matched by an increasing disregard for the marvellous complexities of the world we inhabit, indeed for life itself. To restore ways of knowing to the processes of life, we must put this trend into reverse.

On the ground

Human beings are terrestrial creatures; they live on the ground. That much appears at first glance to be obvious. But what *is* the ground? As a first approximation, we might suppose that it is a portion of the surface of the earth that is evident to the senses of an upright body. 'To my senses', wrote Immanuel Kant, the earth appears as 'a flat surface, with a circular horizon' (1933: 606). This surface, for Kant, lies at the very foundation of human experience: it is 'the stage on which the play of our skills proceeds [and] the ground on which our knowledge is acquired and applied' (Kant 1970: 257). Everything that exists and that might form the object of our perception is placed upon this surface, rather as properties and scenery might be set upon the stage of a theatre. Beneath the surface lies the domain of formless matter, the physical stuff of the world. And above it lies the domain of immaterial form, of pure ideas or concepts, which the mind is said to bring to the evidence of the senses in order to organize the piecemeal data of experience into a systematic knowledge of the world as a whole – knowledge which Kant imagined to be arrayed as if on the surface of a sphere, at once continuous and finite in extent. With his feet firmly planted on the level ground and his mind soaring in the sphere of reason, the Kantian subject was above all a seeker after knowledge.[1] It was Karl Marx who subsequently put the subject to work, through a process of labour that saw the earth turned into an instrument of his purpose. The earth, Marx declared, is 'the most general instrument of labour ... since it provides the worker with the platform for all his operations, and supplies a field of employment for his activity' (1930: 173). What for Kant was a stage became, for Marx, a production platform, not merely furnished but materially transformed through human activity. Yet the ground still appears as a *substratum* for such activity, an interface between the mental and the material where the sheer physicality of the world comes hard up against the creativity of human endeavour.

More than a century later, James Gibson returned to the significance of the ground in his pioneering work on the ecology of visual perception. He begins, again, with what sounds like a truism: 'The *ground* refers, of course, to the surface of the earth' (1979: 33, original emphasis). There is much in common between Gibson's understanding of this surface and what both Marx and Kant had to say about it. For Marx's idea of the instrumental or use-value of the earth, Gibson substitutes the notion of *affordance*. Thus the ground surface is a substratum that affords support for a terrestrial biped or quadruped. It is 'stand-on-able, ... walk-on-able and run-over-able' (Gibson 1979: 127). In the limiting case of what Gibson calls the 'open environment', void of content, the ground would be realized as a perfectly level plain, receding without interruption to the great circle of the horizon. That, as we have seen, was Kant's view as well. There is one key difference, however. For in Gibson's thinking the ground has none of the metaphysical significance that it had for Kant or even Marx. It does not mark the boundary between the mental and the material or between conceptual reason and sensory experience; nor does it separate the consciousness of the labourer from the soil on which he works. It does not, in short, envelop the material world but rather comprises an interface, *within a world of materials*, between the relatively solid *substances* of the earth and the relatively volatile *medium* of the air (Gibson 1979: 16).[2] When Marx declared, in the *Communist manifesto* of 1848, that 'all that is solid melts into air', he was referring metaphorically to the evaporation, in bourgeois society, of the 'fixed, fast-frozen relations' of pre-capitalist modes of production, and not to any process of nature (Marx & Engels 1978: 476). For Gibson, by contrast, solidity is what distinguishes the substances of the earth from the gaseous medium above, a distinction that is revealed to perception as the ground surface. If the solid earth were to melt into air, then the ground would simply disappear (Gibson 1979: 22).

With the earth below and the sky above, and supported on the ground, the Gibsonian perceiver is placed in the midst of the phenomenal world rather than banished to its exterior surface. He is, in that sense, an inhabitant. He has air to breathe, and a platform to stand on. Yet an open environment, comprising the ground surface alone, would not in itself be habitable. Arguing this point, Gibson compares the ground to the floor of a room. In an empty, unfurnished room one could stand, walk, or even run on the floor, but do little else. In any inhabited house, however, the rooms are cluttered with furniture, and it is this clutter that makes possible all the other, everyday activities that are carried on there (as well as hindering some activities like running about). Likewise, Gibson reasoned, a plain devoid of features, though it might afford standing and walking, would in all other respects be a scene of utter desolation. It could harbour no life, and could not therefore serve as an environment for any animate being. In Gibson's words 'the *furniture* of the earth, like the furnishings of a room, is what makes it livable' (1979: 78, original emphasis). Like the room, the earth is cluttered with all manner of things which afford the diverse activities of its innumerable inhabitants. There are objects, which may be attached or detached, enclosures such as caves and burrows, convexities such as hills, concavities such as hollows, and apertures such as cracks and openings. Indeed it seems that any ordinary environment would be so cluttered up that its inhabitants would be unlikely ever to come directly into contact with the ground at all.

This result is deeply paradoxical. On the one hand, Gibson insists that the ground is 'the literal *basis* of the terrestrial environment', 'the underlying surface of support', and even 'the reference surface for all other surfaces' (1979: 10, 33, original emphasis). In that sense it should be fundamentally *there*, before all else. And yet, on the other hand, it is a surface that can only be arrived at through a process of abstraction and reconstruction: by excising every variation or particular from the environment of which it is a part, remodelling it as a piece of furniture or scenery, and then reconstructing the scene by imagining each piece placed on a pre-prepared and absolutely featureless floor. As a child I built a model railway, of which I was very proud. The most important part of the layout, however, was not the line but the landscape of hills and valleys through which it ran, made out of wire-netting, papier mâché, and plaster, all of which rested on a plane sheet of softwood mounted on a wooden frame and legs. This sheet, known as the baseboard, was indeed an underlying surface of support and the very basis of my model. But it was completely hidden from view by the 'clutter' I had constructed on it. Had the miniature people and animals that I had placed in my landscape been capable of movement, they would not have been walking across the ground of the baseboard but clambering over the scenery! It would have made no difference whether they were up on a hill-top or down in a valley, for both were part of the clutter. In the real world, by contrast, there is nothing equivalent to the baseboard of my model. It is a figment of the imagination. Making his way over hill and through valley, the walker treads the ground itself, experiencing its rising and falling in the alternation of close and distant horizons, and in the greater or lesser degrees of muscular exertion entailed in first toiling against, and then surrendering to, the force of gravity. Real hills and valleys, in short, do not rest upon the foundation of the earth's surface, as the scenery of my model rested on the baseboard, but are themselves formations of that surface.

How, then, is this surface to be understood? Our example of the walker already suggests one part of the answer. The ground is perceived *kinaesthetically*, in movement. If we say of the ground of a hill that it 'rises up', this is not because the ground itself is on the move but because we feel its contours in our own bodily exercise (Bachelard 1964: 10-11; see also Ingold 2000b: 203-4). Even if we view the hill from a distance, we sense its rise in the ocular movement of our focal attention as it scans the upward-sloping line of the horizon. Moreover, far from comprising a featureless and perfectly level plane, the ground appears *infinitely variegated*. These variations are not just of contour but also of substance, colouration, and texture. For all that clutter that Gibson supposed to be placed upon the ground is actually intrinsic to its very constitution. Of course it can be observed at different scales, from close-up to far away, and each will reveal different patterns, textures, and grains. Whatever the scale of observation we adopt, however, it is liable to appear just as puckered, mottled, and polymorphic. In that sense the ground surface has a fractal quality, whence follows a third characteristic: it is *composite*. It is, if you will, the surface of all surfaces, matted from the interweaving of a miscellany of different materials, each with its own peculiar properties. An analogy might be drawn with a textile, whose surface is not the same as those of all the strands of which it is woven, but is nevertheless constituted by them. Finally and perhaps most critically, the ground surface is not pre-existent but undergoes *continuous generation*. Recall that for Gibson, surfaces persist only to the extent that solid substances resist transformation into the gaseous state, or do not 'melt into air'. The presence of the surface, he thinks, is proof of the separation and immiscibility of substances and medium (Gibson 1979: 22). In the living world, however, the ground surface persists not in spite of reactions between substances and medium, but because of them. Indeed it is through such reactions that the ground is formed in the first place.

Much of the earth's surface is covered in vegetation. Plants grow *in* the ground, not *on* it, as their roots penetrate deep into the soil while their stems and leaves mingle with the open air, rustling in its currents.[3] Delving into the earth, we find the tangle of vegetation becoming ever more densely packed, so that it is often impossible to determine with any precision where 'ground level' actually lies. What matters for the plant is that it should have access to light, so that in practice the ground is not so much a coherent surface as a limit of illumination. The plant's growth is fuelled by a photosynthetic reaction which binds carbon dioxide in the air with moisture already absorbed into the soil from the atmosphere and taken up by the roots, releasing the oxygen which we and other animals breathe. When the plant eventually dies and decomposes, its material deposit adds to the layer of soil, rich in nutrients, from which further growth issues. In this sense the earth is perpetually growing over, which is why archaeologists have to dig to discover evidence of past lives (Ingold 2007b: S33). Clearly, then, the ground is not inert. To the contrary, it is the most active of surfaces, the primary site of those reactions, of which photosynthesis is the most fundamental, on which all life depends. Wherever life is going on, earthly substances are binding with the medium of air in the ongoing formation of the ground. Or as Martin Heidegger put it, in rather more poetic language, the earth 'is the serving bearer, blossoming and fruiting, spreading out in rock and water, rising up into plant and animal' (1971: 149). In short, thanks to its exposure to light, moisture, and currents of air – to sun, rain, and wind – the earth is forever bursting forth, not destroying the ground in consequence but creating it.

It is not, then, the surface of the earth that maintains the separation of substances and medium, or confines them to their respective domains. It is rather its *surfacing*.

By this I mean the engineering of the ground surface by coating it with a layer of hard and resistant material such as concrete or asphalt, as in road building or laying the foundations for urban development. The objective of such engineering is to convert the ground into the kind of surface that theorists of modernity always thought it was – level, homogeneous, pre-existent and inert (Ingold 2008: 1808-9). It is to make the earth into a stage, platform, or baseboard, or, in a word, into an *infrastructure*, upon which the superstructure of the city can be erected. Hard sur-facing, I contend, is the definitive characteristic of the built environment. In such an environment, life is truly lived on or above the ground and not in it. Plants grow in pots, people in apartments, fed and watered from remote sources. The built environ-ment, as Gibson said of environments in general, is cluttered with manifold objects whose only connection with any piece of ground is that they happen to have been set up on it. Were all the clutter removed, we would indeed be confronted with a scene of desolation. The hard-surfaced world, devoid of furnishing, is featureless and barren. Nothing can grow there. This is an extreme, however, that is never realized in practice, even in the most heavily engineered of environments. For unless it is con-stantly maintained and reinforced, hard surfacing cannot withstand the elemental forces of the sky and earth that erode it from above and subvert it from below. Eventually, it cracks and crumbles, and as it does so – as the substances beneath are exposed again to the light, moisture, and currents of the air – the earth once more bursts into life, overwhelming human attempts to cover it up.

Along the path

This distinction between the surface of the earth and its surfacing provides us with a key criterion by which to draw another, between the path or track and the road. Of course a road can be many things, as can a path, and the distinction I propose here is merely heuristic. But it serves to highlight the contrast between two modalities of movement which I call, respectively, wayfaring and transport (Ingold 2007c: 75-84). The wayfarer is a being who, in following a path of life, negotiates or improvises a passage as he goes *along*. In his movement as in life, his concern is to seek a way through: not to reach a specific destination or terminus but to keep on going. Though he may pause to rest, even returning repeatedly and circuitously to the same place to do so, every period of rest punctuates an ongoing movement. For wherever he is, and so long as life goes on, there is somewhere further he can go. Along the way, events take place, observations are made, and life unfolds. Transport, by contrast, carries the passenger *across* a pre-prepared, planar surface. The movement is a lateral displacement rather than a lineal progression, and connects a point of embarkation with a terminus. The passenger's concern is literally to get from A to B, ideally in as short a time as possible. What happens along the way is of no consequence, and is banished from memory or conscious awareness. In the perfect case, the passenger is delivered at the terminus in a condition identical to that in which he set out, as though nothing at all had happened in between. Unlike the continual *tactical* manoeuvring of the wayfarer, picking his way along the ground, the passenger's career may be understood as a series of *strategic* moves from location to location – rather like the 'moves', in draughts or chess, of a piece across the board.[4]

In practice, however, pure transport is an ideal that can no more be actualized than can the dream of being in two places at once. Time passes and life goes on, even while the passenger is in transit. And it does so, as we have seen, thanks to the fact that the world is *not* fully surfaced. Every road is a strip of hard-surfacing, laid down in preparation for the boots that march[5] or the vehicles that roll over it, and is more or less unmarked by their passage. But while the road provides the infrastructural support for transporting persons and their effects from point to point, quotidian life proceeds for the most part along winding paths that infiltrate the ground on either side (Ingold & Lee Vergunst 2008: 12-14). Inhabitants are wayfarers and not passengers; for them the road is an obstacle rather than a conduit – just another potentially dangerous feature of the terrain to be negotiated. Where the path differs from the road is that it is a cumulative trace, not so much engineered in advance as generated in the course of pedestrian movement itself. And by the same token, the path is marked in the ground, not laid over it. One could perhaps compare wayfaring with drawing: as the draughtsman traces a line with his pencil, so the wayfarer – walking along – paces a line with his feet. The painter Paul Klee had explicit resort to this comparison in his definition of drawing as 'taking a line for a walk' (1961: 105). Subsequently, in his landmark work of 1967, *A line made by walking*, sculptor Richard Long turned the metaphor into an actuality, creating a linear path in a grassy meadow by walking repeatedly up and down. Reviewing a recent exhibition of Long's work, Robert Macfarlane observes that the artist's 'legs are his stylus, his feet the nib with which he inscribes his traces on the world'. Walking becomes an act of inscription, of writing in the original sense of drawing a sharp point over a surface, of furrowing a track (Macfarlane 2009).

There are nevertheless important differences between walking and drawing which complicate the idea of path-making as a simple process of inscribing the ground. For a start, the walker does not set out upon a blank sheet. In the case of drawing, suggests art historian James Elkins, the first mark 'is born in blindness' (1996: 234). The draughtsman may begin with a figure in mind, or the outline of a shape, that he intends to realize on paper. Yet on the sheet before him there is initially nothing to see. Only as the picture evolves does blindness give way – though never fully – to vision, while the mental image correspondingly fades. The pedestrian is blind in a different way. It is not that he cannot see anything in the field of vision. On the contrary, since the ground is a fractal surface there is no limit to the variety it offers to his inspection. What he cannot see, however, either in his mind's eye or on the ground, is the overall pattern or design traced by his movement. This is due to the factor of scale. *Relative to the expanse of his walking*, the pedestrian's eyes are simply too close to the ground. To see the designs, he would have to fly with the birds, as in some societies shamans are reputed to do (indeed the exceptional cases of walked figures, such as the Nazca lines of highland Peru, seem to be premised on the idea of a shamanic or god's-eye view).[6] Ordinarily, however, the wayfarer is not a walker of shapes or outlines, and his vision unfolds at ground level, as he goes along, rather than from a superior and stationary vantage-point. To put it the other way around: if drawing were like ordinary walking, then the draughtsman's eyes would have to be located not in his head but somewhere near the tip of his pencil. For this reason, I believe it is misleading to compare the ground surface, as does the architect Francesco Careri, to a palimpsest upon which successive figures are superimposed, one upon the other. According to Careri, the surface of walking 'is not a white page, but an intricate design of historical and geographical sedimentation on which to simply add one more layer' (2002: 150). Path-making, however, does not so much add another figurative layer to the ground surface as weave another strand of movement *into* it.

A further difference between walking and drawing hinges on the contrasting action potentials of the hands and feet. The hand, liberated in the course of anatomical evolution from the function of supporting the body, is free to manipulate an inscribing tool which can cut a groove or deposit a trace as a more or less enduring record of its gestures. Such inscriptions can appear as continuous lines. But the feet, bearing the full weight of the body, *impress* the ground rather than inscribing it. Although the movement of walking is continuous, each footfall makes a separate impression. For the path to appear along the ground as a continuous line it must be walked many times, or by many people, so as to iron out the incidence of individual treads. On many surfaces, the traces left by these treads are so subtle as to be barely visible. Sometimes they leave no trace at all. The ground of a footpath may be just as variegated as that of the terrain through which it winds, and can only be discerned because of the way passing feet have compressed the soil, created or altered patterns of plant growth, rearranged gravel, or polished the surfaces of rocks and stones. No material need be added or scratched away. When Long made his famous line by walking the length of a meadow, we can only make it out thanks to the way grass stems bent and flattened by his footsteps caught the light (Macfarlane 2009). He has not cut the line with his boots, nor has material been deposited – as, for example, when lines are painted on grass to mark out a sports-ground. Another example comes from northern Namibia, where indigenous Akhoe Hai//om hunter-gatherers, according to their ethnographer Thomas Widlok (2008: 60), have unwittingly created paths through the desert, primarily between water-pans, in the form of lines of mangetti trees. As they went on their way, people would chew the highly prized nuts of these trees, periodically spitting out the hard kernels from which new trees grew. And although the trees have a short life-span, once the path is made it is conducive to further use as the trees provide food in the form of nuts, shade from the hot sun, and water that collects in the hollows of old trunks.

Inscriptions, then, are one thing; impressions another. This difference, in turn, invites some reflection on the phenomenon of footprints. One can read movement and direction from a footprint just as one can from an inscription – not, however, as the trace of a gesture, but rather as a record of changing pressure distributions at the interface between the walking body and the ground. In attending to surface texture as well as outline, it is a reading that is as much tactile as visual. Distinct footprints are registered most clearly not on hard surfaces but on those which, being soft and malleable, are easily impressed, such as the surfaces of snow, sand, mud, and moss, or – as Sherlock Holmes observed in the case of 'The crooked man' – a grassy lawn. 'There had been a man in the room', said Holmes, 'and he had crossed the lawn coming from the road. I was able to obtain five very clear impressions of his footmarks ... He had apparently rushed across the lawn, for his toe marks were much deeper than his heels' (Doyle 1959: 146). Yet precisely because soft surfaces do not readily hold their form, footprints tend to be relatively ephemeral. Snow may be covered by further falls or may eventually melt away, sand may be sculpted anew by the wind or washed by the tide, mud may be dissolved by the rain, and moss or grass may grow over again. Footprints thus have a temporal existence, a duration, which is bound to the very dynamics of the ground to which they belong: to the cycles of organic growth and decay, of the weather, and of the seasons. The ground, as we have seen, is matted from diverse materials. Footprints are impressed in the mat.

   Although inscriptions and impressions register differently in the surfaces they mark, they have in common that they are the traces of a moving body as it goes along. In this regard they are equally opposed to another species of mark that I call the *stamp*, made by imposing a ready-made design from above on a hard surface. In the field of writing, for example, this is what distinguishes the work of the scribe from that of the printer, or the pen from the press. As the ancient metaphor of the text implies, the lettering hand of the scribe or calligrapher leaves a trail of ink in its wake just as does the shuttling hand of the weaver of tapestries in laying the weft (Ingold 2007c: 68-71). The printer, by contrast, imposes a composition pre-assembled from discrete typographic elements, and set in the galley, upon a uniform and resistant surface made ready to receive it. To the modern author of printed works, according to Michel de Certeau (1984: 134-5), the page appears as a blank space awaiting the imprint of a composition of his own design. De Certeau compares the author to the colonial conqueror who confronts a territory, exorcized of all ambiguity, and erased of its past, as a surface on which to rewrite history. By setting his stamp upon the ground, the conqueror stakes a claim. This is precisely what Friedrich Engels had in mind when he declared that in the course of its historical transformation 'man alone has succeeded in impressing his stamp on nature' (1934: 34). He was referring to the imprint of a human design – 'premeditated, planned action directed towards definite preconceived ends' (1934: 178) – upon a surfaced world. Here, the surface is configured as an interface between the mental and the material: intentions already engraven in the mind are stamped on the solid earth.
   But footprints are not stamps.[7] They differ from stamps in their texture, in their temporality, and in their embeddedness in the ground of habitation (Ingold & Lee Vergunst 2008: 7-8). The designs of footprints are not ready-made, nor are they imposed from above *upon* a hard surface. They are rather made as a human being or other animal walks or runs along, *in* a surface that is soft, pliable, or absorbent. Thus whereas the stamp connotes immobility and omnipresence, footprints register emplaced movement. Far from staking a claim, the indigenous inhabitant leaves foot-prints in the ground as clues to his whereabouts and intentions, and for others to follow. While a trained eye and touch can read much from a single footprint, even more can be read from a series of prints. Such a series, observed in sequence, comprises a track. If the same track is trodden often enough, the many individual prints merge into a continuous path. One cannot, then, read individual movements from a path, but only those commonly or collectively made.
   One striking characteristic of such movements, and the paths they create, is that they are nearly always winding and hardly ever straight. In this regard, Long's *Line made by walking* is exceptional, since it is perfectly rectilinear. Paths are not generally straight for the same reason that it is virtually impossible to draw a perfectly straight line freehand without the aid of a ruler. Indeed, with allowances for the differences between walking and drawing noted above, the contrast between drawing a line freehand and with a ruler is precisely akin to that between wayfaring and transport (Ingold 2007c: 161-2). If, in transport, the passenger has 'found the way', as a connection between points, even before setting out, so also, in drawing a line with a ruler, the edge of the ruler is lined up against the points to be connected before putting pencil to paper. In drawing freehand, by contrast, one has always to keep an eye on where the pencil is going, making adjustments while on the move. So too the wayfarer, as he goes along, has continually to attend to his path, adjusting or 'fine-tuning' his movement as the journey

unfolds. Only when he has reached a place can he truly be said to have found his way there. In de Certeau's terms, wayfaring is tactical rather than strategic: its paths are 'wandering' or 'errant' (1984: xviii). To wander is to follow a course that is sinuous instead of straight, or literally, to *wind along*. And it is to winding's namesake, the wind, that I now turn.

In the wind

Tom Brown is a tracker from New Jersey who learned his skills as a boy following a chance meeting with an old Apache scout by the name of Stalking Wolf. A track, Brown tells us, is a temporary thing:

> Unless the mud goes hard and turns gradually to stone, tracks do not last. They fade, and as they dry, the wind sweeps them relentlessly level to ease its way across the ground. Tracks exist at the interface where the sky drags along the surface of the earth. They exist for a relatively brief time in a narrow level *near the surface of the ground* where the wind and the weather move across, changing the temperature and building information into the track. Wind pushes the tracks flat; rain tries to wash them away (Brown 1978: 6, my emphasis).

Brown's intuition that tracks exist not on the ground surface but near it resonates with our earlier characterization of the ground as a surface that itself undergoes continual formation within an unstable zone of interpenetration in which the substances of the earth mingle and bind with the medium of air. These blending reactions, as we have seen, are fundamental to all life. But if that is so, then we should surely acknowledge that the track or path is as much an aerial phenomenon as a terrestrial one. Formed by creatures – human or non-human – that must perforce breathe the air as they walk the ground, it is not only impressed in the earth but suspended in the currents of wind and weather that, dragging the earth's surface, conspire to erase it. Looking for a way to express this essential ambiguity of the track, as at once terrestrial and aerial, Brown evidently found it by splitting the difference. 'Near' the ground surface, it is not quite of the earth and not quite of the air, but of both simultaneously. The synonymy between the *wind* of the meandering path and the *wind* of the swirling air may, then, be more than accidental.

Elsewhere, in an essay on the nature and history of the line (Ingold 2007c), I have suggested that lines come in two principal kinds: traces and threads. Traces are formed on surfaces; threads are strung through the air. My argument was that these two manifestations of line are readily inter-convertible. In the formation of surfaces, threads are converted into traces; in their dissolution, traces are converted into threads. Is the path, then, a trace or a thread? Recognizing that it passes through a world of substances and medium in constant interchange, where surfaces are perpetually forming and dissolving, we should perhaps answer that the path is neither one nor the other, but rather 'thread becoming trace' or 'trace becoming thread'. In his ethnographic account of the significance of wind among Khoisan hunter-gatherers of southern Africa, Chris Low provides a wonderful example of the former, describing how, for the Khoisan, 'wind connects the hunter with the prey like a thread leading from one body to another' (2007: S75). The thread is essentially one of scent – the smell of the animal wafted through the air. As every animal has its distinctive smell, the whole environment is riddled with such scent-threads, binding its human and non-human inhabitants into an intricate web and percolating the very depths of their awareness. People even spoke of the threads as vibrating inside them, making a ringing sound. In tracking an animal whose scent is wafted towards you, it is essential to move *against* the wind, lest the animal be alerted to your intentions. Thus you start at the end of the thread and gradually wind it up, leaving the trace of your movement behind you as you advance on your quarry (Low 2007: S75-7). Among the Aboriginal people of Yarralin, in the Australian Northwest Territory, the converse transformation occurs as tracks left by ancestral Dreamings on the earth's surface, in the era of world creation, are perceived as *strings* akin to the long streaks that appear across the sky at sunset, or in forked lightning, and along which dreaded *kaya* beings, mediators between earth and sky and between life and death, drop to earth or pull people up (Rose 2000: 52-6, 92-5).

If the path is at once a trace and a thread, both on the ground and in the air, so too the pedestrian body simultaneously walks and breathes.[8] Exhalation follows inhalation as step follows step in a closely coupled, rhythmic alternation. However, the tendency, to which I have already alluded, to envision the material world as a clutter of solid objects mounted on a baseboard – like the landscape of my model railway – has led in the writings of philosophers and theorists to a certain suppression of the aerial dimension of bodily movement and experience. While emphasizing the solid forms of the landscape, they have neglected the fluxes of the medium in which they are immersed. In a word, they have shut out the weather. Yet even the residents of the hyper-modern city have to contend with the weather, despite their best efforts to banish it to the exterior of their air-conditioned, temperature-regulated, artificially lit, and glass-enclosed buildings. For the walker out of doors, however, the weather is no spectacle to be admired through picture windows but an all-enveloping infusion which steeps his entire being. As I have argued elsewhere (Ingold 2005), the weather is not so much what we perceive as what we perceive *in*. We see in sunlight whose shades and colours reveal more about the composition and textures of the ground surface than about the shapes of objects, we hear these textures in the rain from the sounds of drops falling on diverse materials, and we touch and smell in the keen wind that – piercing the body – opens it up and sharpens its haptic and olfactory responses.[9] Indeed a strong wind can so overwhelm the senses as virtually to drown out the perception of contact with the ground. 'Around, up, above, what wind-walks!', exclaimed Gerard Manley Hopkins in his poem 'Hurrahing in Harvest' (Hopkins 1972: 27). The wind-walker does not, however, literally fly. The philosopher Gaston Bachelard compares him to a reed. Like the reed, the walker remains earthbound. Dynamically, however, as Bachelard observes, the one is the *reverse* of the other. Whereas the reed bends backwards in the wind, the walker leans forwards, tilting against the current. 'His walking stick pierces the hurricane, makes holes in the earth, thrusts through the wind' (Bachelard 1983: 162).

Given its centrality to life and experience, the absence of weather from anthropological accounts of human ways of being and knowing is little short of extraordinary. This cannot be due to its neglect in our fieldnotes, since I am sure that the notes of most ethnographers are full of references to weather phenomena, as indeed mine are. I began my entry for every day of fieldwork in Finnish Lapland with a brief description of what the weather was like. But when I came to sort and rearrange my notes, in the process that ethnographers rather grandly call 'analysis', these descriptions dropped out. I did not know what to do with them. My omission, then, was not one of observation. It lay more in the lack of any conceptual framework within which to accommodate anything as protean and temperamental as the weather. I doubt whether I have been alone in this.

It has been conventional in both anthropology and archaeology to think of the 'material world' as comprising the two broad components of *landscape* and *artefacts* (Gosden 1999: 152). Much attention has been paid to the ways in which people engage with the things of this world, to the apparent capacity of things to act back, and to the 'hybrid' agencies that are formed when persons and things combine in the production of effects. In all of this, however, no one has given a thought to the air.[10] The reason, I contend, is that so long as we suppose that all that is material is locked up in the congealed forms of the landscape and in the solid objects resting on its surface – or in what the archaeologist Bjørnar Olsen calls 'the hard physicality of the world' (2003: 88) – then the air is literally unthinkable. As a material medium that has escaped the bounds of materiality, it would be a contradiction in terms. We would be forced to conclude either that air does not exist, or that it is actually immaterial and therefore of no consequence. And if that is so, then there could be no weather in the world.

This conclusion is not only contrary to experience but patently absurd. To draw the limits of materiality around the surfaces of the landscape and artefacts would be to leave the inhabitants of the landscape and the users of artefacts in a vacuum. They would be unable to breathe. Nor could anything grow. Let us, then, readmit the air as an essential material constituent of the inhabited world. This is easily done, yet is not without consequences for the way we think about our relations with the environment. One consequence is that we can no longer imagine that all such relations take the form of interactions between persons and things, or that they necessarily arise from the conjoint action of persons and things assembled in hybrid networks. For the air is not a person or a thing, or indeed an entity of any kind, and cannot therefore comprise part of any networked assembly. It is rather, quite simply, a *medium* which, as Gibson pointed out, affords locomotion, respiration, and perception. Ironically, in his reconstruction of the lived environment as a furnished floor, the medium appears to vanish from Gibson's account, leaving an empty void. It is as though, in between the clutter, the environment were riddled with holes. 'It is into these holes', Gibson declared, 'that the birds fly' (Gibson 1979: 106). In the real world, of course, birds fly in the air, not in holes. Indeed their flight is made possible thanks to air currents and vortices partly set up through the movements of their wings. But this does not make the bird into a bird-air hybrid, any more than the fact that we humans ordinarily walk in the air turns us into human-air hybrids. It is merely to recognize that for persons or things to interact at all they must be immersed in the flows, forces, and pressure gradients of the surrounding media. Cut out from such currents, they would be *dead*.

In short, the medium is not so much an interactant as the very condition of interaction. It is only *because* of their suspension in the currents of the medium that things can interact. The point may best be demonstrated by flying a kite. A kite-in-the-air behaves very much like a living being. It seems to possess an agency of its own. Buoyed up by the wind and swooping in its currents, the kite strains at the thread linking it to the hand of the human flyer. On the ground the flyer, also bathed in the air, feels the tension in the thread, and 'plays' the kite by alternately loosening it and reining it in. An interaction is going on between the flyer and the kite, which is perhaps so close that one might better speak of the whole performance as the action of a flyer-kite hybrid. But this interaction could not take place were it not for the fact that both flyer and kite are jointly immersed in the current of air. Were the current stilled, the kite would crumple and drop, lifeless and inert like a dead bird. This leads me to one last observation. If the medium is a condition of interaction, then it follows that the quality of that interaction will be tempered by what is going on in the medium, that is, by the weather. Such, indeed, is our experience. With its twin connotations of mixing or blending and fine-tuning, the verb *to temper* captures perfectly the way the fluxes of the medium comprise the ever-present undercurrent for our actions as we go along in the world. By way of our immersion in the medium, we are constituted not as hybrid but as *temperate* (and temperamental) beings. The fact that a whole suite of words derived from this common root refer interchangeably both to the characteristics of the weather and to human moods and motivations is sufficient proof that the two are not just analogous but fundamentally identical.[11] Both refer to the conditioning of interaction by our suspension in the medium. And if the weather conditions our interaction with people and things, then, by the same token, it also conditions how we know them. This brings me to my final theme, namely the formation of knowledge.

Know as you go

I began with Kant, and it is to him that I now return. I have referred to his postulate that the surface of the earth is given to experience as a flat and uniform substratum upon which lie all things that might form the objects of perception. Placed at a particular point on this surface, the perceiver can acquire a more or less complete knowledge of things lying within the circle of the horizon. What he can never know, however, is how much more there is still to be known. Imagining himself in this predicament, Kant admitted that 'I know the limits of my actual knowledge of the earth at any given time, but not the limits of all possible geography' (1933: 606). In such a situation there could be no possibility of systematic knowledge, no way of fitting what is known so far within an overall conception of the whole. To explain how such knowledge nevertheless lies within the grasp of human reason, Kant drew a sophisticated analogy between the topology of the mind and that of the earth's surface. Let us suppose that our perceiver already knows, *a priori*, that – contrary to the evidence of his senses – the earth is not flat but spherical in form. His situation is then transformed. For, as the extent of the surface is finite and potentially calculable, he is able to estimate not only the limits of his present knowledge, but also the limits of the entire, potentially knowable world. And if the knowable world is spherical, Kant argued, so, likewise, is the world of knowledge.

> Our reason is not like a plane indefinitely far extended, the limits of which we know in a general way only; but must rather be compared to a sphere, the radius of which can be determined from the curvature of the arc of its surface – that is to say, from the nature of synthetic *a priori* propositions – and whereby we can likewise specify with certainty its volume and its limits (1933: 607-8).

Knowledge is thus arrayed upon the spherical surface of the mind, just as the objects of knowledge are arrayed upon the spherical surface of the earth.

Let us imagine a Kantian traveller (Ingold 2000b: 212-13). Traversing the earth's surface, he picks up data from here and there, cumulatively fitting local particulars into nested conceptual frames of ever-wider, and ultimately global, span. Thus as he travels *across* the surface his knowledge is architectonically built *up*, as a superstructure, upon the curved foundation of his reason. Reconstructing the world from the pieces he collects, the mind's hard but initially empty surface is furnished with content. The traveller is, in effect, a mental map-maker. And as is the rule in cartography, his observations are taken from a series of fixed points rather than *en route* from one place to another. His moves serve no other purpose than to carry himself and his equipment – that is to say, the mind and its body – from one stationary locus of observation to another. His ideal mode of travel, then, is transport. In his observations he measures up the world *as if* it were a full-scale model, calculating lengths and altitudes in relation to an imaginary base conventionally mounted at sea-level (conveniently ignoring the fact, as every mariner knows, that the surface of the ocean is *not* level and in any case rises and falls with the tides). Perhaps this will suffice to show how closely linked is the Kantian conception of knowledge, and of the limits to knowledge, to certain presuppositions about the ground, and about movement, that we have explored in previous sections. These presuppositions, as we have seen, are not realistic in practice and bear little relation to the lived experience of inhabitants.[12] For inhabitants are wayfarers: they move through the world rather than across its outer surface. And their knowledge, as I shall now show, is not built *up* but grows *along* the paths they take, both on the ground and in the air.

Recall that for Kant, the ground on which knowledge is acquired and applied is apprehended from a certain point, bounded by its horizon; this ground is uniform, homogeneous, and fully laid out in advance. In the experience of the wayfarer, by contrast, the ground is apprehended in the passage from place to place, 'in histories of movement and changing horizons along the way' (Ingold 2000b: 227). It is infinitely variegated, composite, and undergoes continuous generation. If this is what the ground of knowing is like, then what kind of knowledge results? Consider first the factor of movement. For the wayfarer, movement is not ancillary to knowing – not merely a means of getting from point to point in order to collect the raw data of sensation for subsequent modelling in the mind. Rather, moving *is* knowing. *The wayfarer knows as he goes along.* Proceeding on his way, his life unfolds: he grows older and wiser. Thus the growth of his knowledge is equivalent to the maturation of his own person, and like the latter it continues throughout life. What distinguishes the expert from the novice, then, is not that the mind of the former is more richly furnished with content – as though with every increment of learning yet more representations were packed inside the head – but a greater sensitivity to cues in the environment and a greater capacity to respond to these cues with judgement and precision. The difference, if you will, is not one of how much you know but of how well you know. Someone who knows well is able to *tell*, in the sense not only of being able to recount stories of the world, but also of having a finely tempered perceptual awareness of his surroundings. Sherlock Holmes, to revert to an earlier example, was supremely knowledgeable in this sense. Though he liked to present himself as a master of deduction, his true skill lay in *abduction* (Gell 1998: 14-16) – in the ability to draw an entire thread of antecedent events from the examination of, say, a single footprint. The skill of a tracker such as the Apache scout, Stalking Wolf, or his disciple Tom Brown, is just the same.

In short, whereas the Kantian traveller reasons over a map in his mind, the wayfarer draws a tale from impressions in the ground. Less a surveyor than a narrator, his aim is not to 'classify and arrange', or 'to place every experience in its class' (Kant 1970: 257-8), but rather to situate each impression in relation to the occurrences that paved the way for it, presently concur with it, and follow along after. In this sense his knowledge is not classificatory but storied, not totalizing and synoptic but open-ended and exploratory (Ingold 2009). Walking along, as architectural theorist Jane Rendell explains, provides a way of understanding sites in flux in a manner that questions the logic of measuring, surveying and drawing a location from a series of fixed and static viewpoints. When we walk we encounter sites in motion and in relation to one another, suggesting that things seem different depending on whether we are 'coming to' or 'going from' (Rendell 2006: 188).

This leads us to the second property of the ground surface to be considered: that it is infinitely variegated. If there were, in the wayfarer's mind, a surface analogous to the surface of the earth, then it would not be that of a perfectly rounded globe but would rather be as wrinkled and puckered, at every scale, as the ground surface itself. Indeed the convolutions of neural tissue in the brain would furnish a better analogy than the bulbous dome of the skull. I do not think, however, that any analogies are needed. For the ground of knowing – or, if we must use the term, of cognition – is not an internal neural substrate that resembles the ground outside but the very ground we walk, where earth and sky are tempered in the ongoing production of life. As Gregory Bateson insisted (1973: 429), the mind is not bounded by the body but extends along the multiple sensory pathways that bind every living being into the texture of the world. These pathways, as we have seen, are both traced on the ground as tangible tracks and threaded through the air as trails of scent.

Walking along, then, is not the behavioural output of a mind encased within a pedestrian body. It is rather, in itself, a way of thinking and knowing – 'an activity that takes place through the heart and mind as much as through the feet' (Rendell 2006: 190). Like the dancer, the walker is *thinking in movement*. 'What is distinctive about thinking in movement', writes dance philosopher Maxine Sheets-Johnstone, 'is not that the flow of thought is kinetic, but that the thought itself is. It is motional through and through' (1999: 486). The motional thought, however, runs along the ground. Thus the complex surface of the ground is inextricably caught up in the very process of thinking and knowing. It is part of what Andy Clark (1998) has called the mind's 'wideware': those essential supports for cognition that lie beyond the body and its brain. In this regard the ground is an instrument, not only in the blunt sense that we need it to stand on, but also in the sense that without it we would lose much of our capacity to know. If its variations were erased and covered over by a hard surface, we would still be able to stand and walk but could no longer know as we go along. Just as there is no seeing for the draughtsman confronting a blank sheet of paper, so there is no knowing for the wayfarer on a surfaced earth. His walking would be reduced to the mere mechanics of locomotion, of getting from point to point. In reality, however, not only does the extended mind of the wayfarer infiltrate the ground along myriad pathways, but also, and inevitably, it tangles with the minds of fellow inhabitants. Thus the ground comprises a domain in which the lives and minds of its human and non-human inhabitants are comprehensively bound up with one another. It is, as we have already seen, a composite, woven from diverse materials, and its surface is that of all surfaces. By the same token, the knowledge that runs in the ground is that of all knowledges. Or in a word, it is *social*. It is when it percolates the ground, tangling with the trails of other beings, and not on some transcendent surface of reason, that mindfulness enters the realm of the social.

I have already suggested that the growth of knowledge, for the wayfarer, is part and parcel of his own development and maturation as an embodied being. Through the repeated practice of travelling the same trails – a practice which gradually converts tracks into paths – every nuance of the ground surface is incorporated into what Bachelard would call his 'muscular consciousness' (1964: 11). But the body is not a sink.

As a number of contributions to this collection demonstrate, and as I have argued elsewhere (Ingold 2006: 77-8), conscious awareness does not retreat with practice, or subside into the murky depths of unconscious automatism, but rather increases in concentration and intensity with the fluency of action, along the ever-extending path-ways of the body's sensory entanglement in the lifeworld. It is not only the wayfarer, however, who grows. The ground he walks is growing too – 'rising up', as Heidegger wrote, 'into plant and animal' (1971: 149). The ground, in short, is continually coming into being along with its inhabitants. Like the tissues of plants and the bodies of animals, knowledge grows from the ground of the social. As inhabitants go their ways, following in the footsteps of predecessors, so the ground and the knowledge that grows from it are always in formation and never complete. Yet nothing would grow at all were it not for the currents of air that sweep the ground and the sunlight that bathes the bodies of its inhabitants. 'To be alive', writes Alphonso Lingis, 'is to enjoy the light, enjoy the support of the ground, the open paths and the buoyancy of the air' (1998: 17). Only a living body can know, and if knowledge is embodied, this is only because the body, in turn, is *enwinded* (Ingold 2007b: S32). Or in the words of environmental philosopher David Macauley, 'with our heads immersed in the thickness of the atmosphere or our lungs and limbs engaged with the surrounding winds, we breathe, think and dream in the regions of the air' (2005: 307).

Though it may not exactly melt into air, the body certainly walks, breathes, feels, and knows in it. Thus is knowledge formed along paths of movement in the weather-world. The ground from which knowledge grows is indeed the very same ground that – like the children on their bear hunt – we all walk in our everyday excursions, through calm and storm, swishing grass and root-riddled woods, sun-baked mud and rain-sodden ooze. I hope to have shown, in this chapter, that far from being subsidiary to the constitution of knowledge, this ground, and the ways we walk it, lies at its very core. We can't go over it; we can't go under it; we just have to go through it.

NOTES

The research on which this chapter is based was carried out during my tenure of a Professorial Fellowship funded by the UK Economic and Social Research Council over the three years 2005-8 (award number RES-051-27-0129). I am very grateful to the Council for its support. Earlier versions were presented to the workshop on *The transmission of knowledge* organized by Trevor Marchand at the School of Oriental and African Studies, University of London (September 2007), to the Departments of Anthropology at Goldsmiths College, London (October 2007) and the University of Toronto (March 2008), and to the Departments of Archaeology at the Universities of Cambridge (February 2008) and Lund (November 2008). I have benefited greatly from the comments of participants on all these occasions.

[1] Throughout this chapter, I employ the third-person singular pronoun in its masculine form. This is of no significance whatever for my argument, and readers are welcome to substitute the feminine form if they wish.

[2] On the distinction between the material world and the world of materials, see Ingold (2007a: 14).

[3] Once when I presented this chapter to an archaeological seminar, this observation drew a caustic response from a particularly distinguished member of the audience. How, he wondered, could such statements of the downright obvious, as that 'plants grow in the ground, not on it', possibly advance our understanding? To this, my answer was that the most obvious truths are often those most easily forgotten. It sometimes pays to remind ourselves of them, lest we allow ourselves to be beguiled by an ontology that consigns the living world to the inertia of its objective representation.

[4] The distinction between tactical and strategic movements is drawn from the work of Michel de Certeau (1984: xviii-xix).

[5] Marching is the form of pedestrian movement that approximates most closely to transport. Unlike the wayfarer, whose movement continually responds to an ongoing perceptual monitoring of the country through which he passes, the pedestrian on the march notices nothing. Before his steadfast, unswerving gaze,

the country passes unobserved, while his straightened legs and booted feet beat out a purely mechanical oscillation.

[6] Alfred Gell (1998: 86-90) analyses the Cretan labyrinth on the same premise. His argument is that the pattern of the labyrinth serves an apotropaic purpose, protecting those ensconced behind the surfaces on which it is inscribed from external aggression. Fascinated by the pattern, aggressors are waylaid by the cognitive conundrum it presents and never make it through to the other side. Though this may be true of some kinds of pattern, I believe that as an explanation of the labyrinth it is wide of the mark (Ingold 2007c: 53-7).

[7] In this respect it might be interesting to compare Engels's rhetoric of the human stamp, epitomizing the colonial mentality of the nineteenth century, with the twenty-first-century rhetoric of the carbon footprint. Whereas the stamp is hard and conspicuous, the footprint is vaporous and invisible.

[8] To get a measure of the magnitude of the phenomenon we are dealing with, it is worth bearing in mind that an average human being breathes approximately 15 litres of air per minute, and takes some 10,000 steps per day.

[9] On sunshine and shadows, see Baxandall (1995: 120-5); on hearing ground surfaces in the rain, see Hull (1997: 26-7, 120); on touching in the wind, see Ingold (2007b: S29).

[10] In this regard, art historians and cultural geographers are apparently as guilty of omission as anthropologists, archaeologists, and students of material culture. Painters have, of course, long appreciated that to paint a 'landscape' is to blend both earth and sky into a single field whose illumination depends at every moment on the fluxes of the medium. Yet in commenting on their pictures, cultural geographers and art historians, according to John Thornes (2008), have had almost nothing to say about the skies, concentrating exclusively on depictions of the ground and the scenery displayed on it.

[11] Apart from *temper, temperate*, and *temperament*, we have *tempest* and *temperature*. Of course we feel the temperature from the air that surrounds us.

[12] The philosopher Alphonso Lingis offers further corroboration of this point. 'The ground', he writes, 'is not – save for astronauts and for the imagination of astronomers – the planet, an object which viewed from the distance is spherical. We do not feel ourselves on a platform supported by nothing but feel a reservoir of support extending indefinitely in depth' (Lingis 1998: 14).

REFERENCES

BACHELARD, G. 1964. *The poetics of space* (trans. M. Jolas). Boston: Beacon.
——— 1983. *Water and dreams: an essay on the imagination of matter* (trans. E.R. Farrell). Dallas: Pegasus Foundation.
BATESON, G. 1973. *Steps to an ecology of mind*. London: Fontana.
BAXANDALL, M. 1995. *Shadows and enlightenment*. New Haven: Yale University Press.
BROWN, T. 1978. *The tracker: the story of Tom Brown, Jr as told by William Jon Watkins*. New York: Prentice Hall.
CARERI, F. 2002. *Walkscapes: walking as an aesthetic practice*. Barcelona: Editorial Gustavo Gili.
CARRUTHERS, M. 1998. *The craft of thought: meditation, rhetoric and the making of images, 400-1200*. Cambridge: University Press.
CLARK, A. 1998. Where brain, body and world collide. *Daedalus: Journal of the American Academy of Arts and Sciences* (special issue on *The brain*) **127**, 257-80.
DE CERTEAU, M. 1984. *The practice of everyday life* (trans. S. Rendall). Berkeley: University of California Press.
DOYLE, SIR A.C. 1959. *The memoirs of Sherlock Holmes*. London: Penguin.
ELKINS, J. 1996. *The object stares back: on the nature of seeing*. New York: Simon & Schuster.
ENGELS, F. 1934. *Dialectics of nature* (trans. C. Dutton). Moscow: Progress.
GELL, A. 1998. *Art and agency: an anthropological theory*. Oxford: Clarendon Press.
GIBSON, J.J. 1979. *The ecological approach to visual perception*. Boston: Houghton Mifflin.
GOSDEN, C. 1999. *Anthropology and archaeology: a changing relationship*. London: Routledge.
HEIDEGGER, M. 1971. *Poetry, language, thought* (trans. A. Hofstadter). New York: Harper & Row.
HOPKINS, G.M. 1972. *Look up at the skies!* (ed. R. Warner). London: Bodley Head.
HULL, J. 1997. *On sight and insight: a journey into the world of blindness*. Oxford: Oneworld Publications.
INGOLD, T. 2000a. Evolving skills. In *Alas poor Darwin: arguments against evolutionary psychology* (eds) H. Rose & S. Rose, 225-46. London: Jonathan Cape; New York: Random House.
——— 2000b. *The perception of the environment: essays on livelihood, dwelling and skill*. London: Routledge.
——— 2001. From the transmission of representations to the education of attention. In *The debated mind: evolutionary psychology versus ethnography* (ed.) H. Whitehouse, 113-53. Oxford: Berg.
——— 2005. The eye of the storm: visual perception and the weather. *Visual Studies* **20**, 97-104.

——— 2006. Walking the plank: meditations on a process of skill. In *Defining technological literacy: towards an epistemological framework* (ed.) J.R. Dakers, 65-80. New York: Palgrave Macmillan.

——— 2007a. Materials against materiality. *Archaeological Dialogues* **14**, 1-16.

——— 2007b. Earth, sky, wind and weather. *Journal of the Royal Anthropological Institute* (N.S.) (special issue on *Wind, life, health: anthropological and historical perspectives*, eds C. Low & E. Hsu), S19-S38.

——— 2007c. *Lines: a brief history*. London: Routledge.

——— 2008. Bindings against boundaries: entanglements of life in an open world. *Environment and Planning A* **40**, 1796-810.

——— 2009. Stories against classification: transport, wayfaring and the integration of knowledge. In *Kinship and beyond: the genealogical model reconsidered* (eds) S. Bamford & J. Leach, 192-213. Oxford: Berghahn.

——— & E. HALLAM 2007. Creativity and cultural improvisation: an introduction. In *Creativity and cultural improvisation* (eds) E. Hallam & T. Ingold, 1-24. Oxford: Berg.

——— & J. LEE VERGUNST 2008. Introduction. In *Ways of walking: ethnography and practice on foot* (eds) T. Ingold & J. Lee Vergunst, 1-19. Aldershot: Ashgate.

KANT, I. 1933. *Immanuel Kant's critique of pure reason* (trans. N.K. Smith). London: Macmillan.

——— 1970. A translation of the introduction to Kant's *Physische Geographie*. In *Kant's concept of geography and its relation to recent geographical thought* (ed.) J.A. May, 255-64. Toronto: University Press.

KLEE, P. 1961. *Notebooks*, vol. 1: *The thinking eye* (ed. J. Spiller, trans. R. Manheim). London: Lund Humphries.

LINGIS, A. 1998. *The imperative*. Bloomington: Indiana University Press.

LOW, C. 2007. Khoisan wind: hunting and healing. *Journal of the Royal Anthropological Institute* (N.S.) (special issue on *Wind, life, health: anthropological and historical perspectives*, eds C. Low & E. Hsu), S71-S90.

MACAULEY, D. 2005. The flowering of environmental roots and the four elements in Presocratic philosophy: from Empedocles to Deleuze and Guattari. *Worldviews: Environment, Culture, Religion* **9**, 281-314.

MACFARLANE, R. 2009. Walk the line. *The Guardian, Features and Reviews*, 23 May, p. 16 (available on-line: *http://www.guardian.co.uk/artanddesign/2009/may/23/richard-long-photography-tate-britain*, accessed 11 January 2010).

MARX, K. 1930. *Capital*, vol. 1 (trans. E. and C. Paul). London: Dent.

——— & F. ENGELS 1978. Manifesto of the Communist Party. In *The Marx-Engels reader* (Second edition) (ed.) R.C. Tucker, 469-500. New York: Norton.

OLSEN, B. 2003. Material culture after text: re-membering things. *Norwegian Archaeological Review* **36**, 87-104.

RENDELL, J. 2006. *Art and architecture: a place between*. London: I.B. Tauris.

ROSE, D.B. 2000. *Dingo makes us human: life and land in an Australian Aboriginal culture*. Cambridge: University Press.

ROSEN, M. & H. OXENBURY (illustrator) 1989. *We're going on a bear hunt*. London: Walker Books.

SHEETS-JOHNSTONE, M. 1999. *The primacy of movement*. Amsterdam: John Benjamins.

THORNES, J.E. 2008. Cultural climatology and the representation of sky, atmosphere, weather and climate in selected art works of Constable, Monet and Eliasson. *Geoforum* **39**, 570-80.

WIDLOK, T. 2008. The dilemmas of walking: a comparative view. In *Ways of walking: ethnography and practice on foot* (eds) T. Ingold & J. Lee Vergunst, 51-66. Aldershot: Ashgate.

7

Unconscious culture and conscious nature: exploring East Javanese conceptions of the person through Bourdieu's lens

KONSTANTINOS RETSIKAS *School of Oriental and African Studies*

In her path-breaking analysis of Indonesian societies, Shelly Errington differentiates the societies of Eastern Indonesia from those of the Centrist Archipelago on the basis of the articulation of the principles of dualism and oneness. While Eastern Indonesia, she rightly observes, 'postulates unity but institutes fracture' (1987: 435), a move that results in pervasive systems of cosmological and social dualism that make exchanges possible and necessary, the Centrist Archipelago attempts to transcend dualities by positing a single, unitary source at the mythical beginning of the world and seeking to re-establish it in ritual occasions. The always unstable and contingent transcendences involved therein are accomplished within a field of practice that, as Benedict Anderson reminds us for Java, equates political power with the ability to combine opposing forces. The most dramatic manifestation of this emphasis is found in the *ardhanari* statues. 'In ancient Javanese art', Anderson writes, the

> combination [of opposites] does not take the form of the hermaphrodite of the Hellenistic world, an ambiguous transitional being between the sexes, but rather the form of a being in whom masculine and feminine characteristics are sharply juxtaposed ... [with] the left side of the statues [being] physiologically female, the right side male (1990: 28-9).

In the anthropological literature, the prime example of an equivalent project is Pierre Bourdieu's theory of habitus. In his eagerness to transcend the dichotomies of objectivism and subjectivism, social physics and social poetics, Bourdieu adopts the language of excess, a language predicated on oxymorons. The usual antinomies of determinism and freedom, conditioning and creativity, consciousness and the unconscious, or the individual and society that have permeated Western epistemology are reworked towards their ultimate reconciliation.

Within the space of four pages, Bourdieu defines the habitus as (i) 'structured structures predisposed to function as structuring structures' (1990: 53); (ii) 'a product of history [which] produces ... more history' (1990: 54); (iii) the 'internalization of externality', as well as the externalization of interiority (1990: 55); (iv) 'a spontaneity without consciousness or will' (1990: 56); and (v) the 'intentionless invention of regulated improvisation' (1990: 57).

Bourdieu's formulations have been assessed by several writers and from different angles, ranging from purely the phenomenological (Crossley 2001; Throop & Murphy 2002) to the cognitive (Lizardo 2004) and sociological (Jenkins 1992; King 2000), all stressing different shortcomings as well as major achievements. In this chapter, I am not so much interested in evaluating Bourdieu's concept of habitus for the purposes of cross-cultural analysis as in discussing it within a comparative framework with the explicit aim of highlighting two mutually constitutive processes: on the one hand, that of 'the making of knowledge about the ways other people make knowledge' (Marchand, Preface, this volume), and, on the other, that making manifest of anthropological knowledge and of charting the frontiers brought forth. I therefore proceed to conduct a thought experiment by means of bringing together Bourdieu and what can be construed as East Javanese conceptions of the person and the body. The purpose of this comparative experiment is to throw light on the condition of embodiment through the staging of a reciprocity of otherwise alien perspectives, and by these means to draw out anthropological knowns and elicit known unknowns. I contend that the pursuit of knowing as an ongoing process entails struggles to arrive at formulations that have to do as much as with what is known as with what remains stubbornly and nearly impossible to know. These struggles are instructive for they open up the necessary space for confronting the unnamed, meeting the unthinkable, and almost articulating the unsayable.

Knowledge of the unknowns that lay beyond the frontier is markedly different from ignorance (Dilley, this volume) in that the former denotes not so much a lack and a shortage that can be filled subsequently, but primarily a form of acute awareness that the capacities one is equipped with and the tools at one's disposal are grossly inadequate. The paradox that the awareness of the unnamed posits is intrinsically connected to the paradox that post-positivistic comparison involves. Commenting on Marilyn Strathern's remark that anthropologists should aim for 'comparison with the non-comparability of phenomena kept firmly in mind' (1990: 211), Michael Lambek and Andrew Strathern's apt differentiation of incomparability from incommensurability drives the point home. Incommensurability means that 'there is no neutral universal framework, no objectivist language in which alternative theories, paradigms, or cultures could be set side by side, point by point. However, incommensurability does not imply incomparability; it implies openness and multiplicity rather than absolute and categorical discriminations' (Lambek & Strathern 1998: 21). In the present chapter, I endeavour to grasp this un-representable openness which escapes *a priori* determinations and to create an epistemological position that makes incommensurability speak of the limits of anthropological knowledge as an enabling condition – the facing of the other as other rather than as a version of the self.

Using Boudieu's habitus is integral in this exercise for his work has been a constant inspiration for many anthropologists, including myself. His concept of habitus is also important for the conduct of a mediated dialogue, for both Bourdieu and my informants make a concerted effort to transcend dualisms. During the one-and-a-half year period that I stayed in Alas Niser – a semi-urban locality situated in the periphery of the municipality of Probolinggo in East Java – I was astounded by the eagerness people showed in pointing out that they are neither Madurese nor Javanese, but *orang campuran*, mixed people. To be a mixed person is commonly taken to rest on the merging of the juxtaposed embodied qualities and affective capacities of *halus* and *kasar*, roughly translated as refined and coarse, smooth and rough, elegant and crude, respectively. The epithets of *halus* and *kasar* are commonly used to establish various sorts of difference and hierarchy in Java, including those of ethnicity, gender, and social status. In addition, in portraying themselves as mixed, my interlocutors also pointed to the displacement of absolute distinctions between their sense of self and that of their others. Their conception of identity as mixed people is founded both on a certain degree of difference from their significant others and on a certain level of intimacy and amount of similarity with them. In other words, the acknowledgement of their derivation from Javanese and Madurese is integrally connected to claims of distinction.

What I wish to elaborate here is that the local universe of ethnic difference is built around a quite systematic and explicit form of knowledge that differentiates people according to habits. Styles of dress, types of food, manners of eating, speech tonalities, bodily postures, and overall comportment are highlighted as intimately related to modes of personhood. The first point of incommensurability derives from Bourdieu's account of habitus and body *hexis* as operating below the level of consciousness and hardly ever finding explicit linguistic expression. Indeed, Bourdieu's conception of habitus as the 'internalization of externality' and its placement 'beyond the grasp of consciousness' (1977: 93) is integral in allowing him to provide an answer as to how class inequality and domination are universally accepted as legitimate and reproduced.

A second issue is equally important. Bourdieu's definition of habitus as 'embodied history, internalized as second nature' (1990: 56) makes the distinction between nature and culture do a lot of analytical work. In what follows, I will argue that the line separating nurture and nature is significantly more blurred for my East Javanese interlocutors, for whom attention and care in the formation of the person start not with one's birth but rather much earlier, that is, with the seeking of appropriate parents, continues throughout the period of gestation, and carries on after birth. In other words, whereas Bourdieu along with the majority of social scientists postulates the discontinuity of nature and culture as axiomatic, my interlocutors assume a more or less continuous line predicated on notions of growth and maturation (see also Ingold 1991; Strathern 1980). In their case, habitus is not second nature, that is, society-turned-into-nature, but society-as-the-only-possible-nature. The importance of this incommensurability cannot be underestimated. Efforts to locate the social production of knowledge at the interface between bodies, environment, and human biology should confront the possibility that the analytical boundedness of such domains, and thus the ensuing problematic, is not universally applicable.

In line with several contributors to this volume, I reflect on the politics that underscore anthropology's making of knowledge, and emphasize the complexities of the relation between two different kinds of politics, our own and my informants. Taking Bourdieu as an example, I show how the natural equality of human beings corresponds to a shared axiomatic assumption, equally elemental and unreflective, making Bourdieu a true heir of the tradition of the European Enlightenment. His theory about the links between unconscious, hidden forms of knowledge and misrecognition is developed in an effort to account for the emergence and reproduction of social hierarchies. According to his account, the production and transmission of knowledge relating to the social and the personal are not only embedded within certain authority relations that regulate such flows by either facilitating or blocking them (see Dilley's chapter, this volume), but constitute the very arena in which domination operates. This line of thought is particularly apparent in Venkatesan's chapter (this volume), in which she shows how the acquisition of the skill of weaving, the technology that supports it, and its actual practice in everyday life are deeply politicized processes intimately related to acutely felt ambivalences about the social worth of weaving, of weavers, and of women versus men.

Fundamental insights into the effects of non-propositional, unconscious knowledge have to be approached with caution when they are brought to bear on societies that do not necessarily share the same assumptions about the constitution of the social and the human. In Java, the continuity conventionally attributed to a person's identity as far as his/her pre-natal and after-birth existence is concerned does not necessarily contribute to the masking of systems of social inequality, nor does it make identities assume forms which are fixed and given. Rather, systems of inequality are partially located within the domain of the actors' conscious awareness, and identities are locally recognized as predicated on the exercise of human agency. In this respect, I claim that in Java, hierarchy cannot be understood as the outcome of misrecognition, partly because of the alien status of the nature-culture dichotomy, and partly because some forms of knowledge and recognition deployed are explicit, overt, and propositional. As I have discussed elsewhere (Retsikas 2007a), the politics that inform human difference in this case acquire their particular impetus and dynamics not from a position that questions the assertion of hierarchy as un-natural, but from a perspective that works in tandem with it. The contestations of superiority involved in conceptualizations of ethnic per-sonhood in East Java are not undertaken within a framework permeated by the operation of the principle of (natural and jural) equality, but unfold within structures of encompassment capable of setting up a nested series of hierarchies. In literally combining both Javanese and Madurese modalities of being and acting, mixed persons seek to domesticate the superiority of Javanese *halus*-ness, and by encompassing it, they attempt to convert Javanese-ness into a part of a larger whole. The whole that mixed personhood instantiates corresponds to a further tier in the hierarchy of difference that accords mixed people a subject position of exceptional pre-eminence that is very much in line with *ardhanari* images of power.

The following descriptions of Javanese *halus*-ness, Madurese *kasar*-ness, and mixed persons' unstable and situational combination of the two are based on fieldwork involving a sort of apprenticeship on my part. I have narrated elsewhere (see Retsikas 2008) my own experiences of acquiring new habits in an East Java village to match my particular status during fieldwork, and of the ways that my body, potentially threatening and partially immoral as it was, was taken up and subjected both voluntarily and involuntarily to a process of inculcation of a new set of sensibilities and capacities for ethical action. This apprenticeship in unfamiliar ways of movement, dress, and speech is conveyed in this chapter by considering the ways that indigenous forms of knowing emphasize embodied subjectivity and sensorial inter-involvement with others and the ambient world, and which posit the assumption that being a person and acting and perceiving in a specific way are the same thing.[1]

Domination

Bourdieu's habitus is a concept tailored to account for processes of symbolic domination. The kinds of domination Bourdieu has in mind are twofold: class domination in Western, class-segregated societies (Bourdieu 2006) and gender inequality, as among the Kabyles of Algeria (Bourdieu 2001). Habitus's contribution to the legitimation and reproduction of social inequalities rests on two further concepts, those of *doxa* and *hexis*.

Doxa is 'the relationship of immediate adherence that is established in practice between a *habitus* and the field to which it belongs, the pre-verbal taking-for-granted of the world that flows from practical sense' (Bourdieu 1990: 68). A sort of 'enacted belief, instilled by childhood learning that treats the body as a living memory pad' (1990: 68), doxa capitalizes on the operation of habitus in converting objective structural positions into motor schemes and body automatisms so as to create and instil a sense of reality as given. The successful 'internal' replication of objective structures results in these external structures to being mistaken as natural. Their very arbitrariness is, in other words, concealed to all but the social scientist, the spirit of critical transcendence *par excellence*. Doxa describes the misrecognition of domination for it works so as to make the arbitrary character that social relations take in any given historical and cultural context inaccessible to the consciousness of social actors. Moreover, doxa expresses a certain somatization of social relations of domination that the concept of body hexis further explicates.

Bodily hexis is

> political mythology realised, *em-bodied*, turned into a permanent disposition, a durable way of standing, speaking, walking, and thereby feeling and thinking. [... In Kabyle society the] specifically feminine virtue, *lah'ia*, modesty, restraint, reserve orients the whole female body downwards, towards the ground, the inside, the house, whereas male excellence, *nif*, is asserted in movement upwards, outwards, towards other men (Bourdieu 1990: 69-70, original emphasis).

Behind such systems of distinction lie value systems. However, Bourdieu rightly warns against any assumptions about the determining influence of value systems, a common mistake committed by structuralists. The reason against such an approach is that such systems of distinction 'derive their symbolic efficacy from [the value systems'] practical translation into actions that go without saying' (1990: 71). Body hexis is therefore

> values given body, *made* body, by the hidden persuasion of an implicit pedagogy which can instil a whole cosmology ... and inscribe the most fundamental principles of the arbitrary content of a culture in seemingly innocuous details of bearing or physical and verbal manners, so putting them beyond the reach of consciousness and explicit statement (1990: 69, original emphasis).

Bourdieu's unconscious has very little in common with either Freud's (1991) or Lévi-Strauss's (1972) versions of the concept. His unconscious is the product of forgetting, always class- and gender-specific, cognitive as well as bodily. He writes: 'The unconscious ... is never anything other than the forgetting of history which history itself produces by realizing the objective structures that it generates in the quasi-structures of *habitus*' (Bourdieu 1990: 56). Social persons are made into who they are through the work of habitus, but this causative trajectory is concealed from their awareness. The forgetting of the social derivation of identity produces the misrecognition of the social as natural. The very naturalness of bodily and cognitive schemas contributes to the reproduction of social systems of distinction by making them appear really real, naturally natural.

Bourdieu's anti-essentialist thesis is manifested most clearly in his critique of Immanuel Kant's pure taste of judgement of the works of art, an exercise undertaken in *Distinction*. However, it is precisely here that internal problems surface regarding the equating of habitus with the unconscious. Kant's pure taste corresponds to bourgeois aesthetics founded on the privileging of form over function and disinterested pleasure over sensual and immediate gratification. Such aesthetics and sensibilities are for Bourdieu the outcome of class habitus and thus learned and acquired. They are acquired either through informal early socialization in the context of the family and/or formal education. The difference between the two modes of knowledge creation is of crucial importance here.

Bourdieu claims that while early acquisition is achieved through everyday exercises involving 'practical mimesis', mastery through formal education is based on voluntary, belated learning, itself employing a quasi-systematic discourse and a certain level of rationalization (2006: 66). In formal education, therefore, the principles of the pure taste of judgement do arise to consciousness as they receive explicit treatment by teachers and students alike. However, Bourdieu seems unwilling to pursue further the implications of formal learning for his overall theory of habitus, largely confining himself to an analysis of the hierarchization of the two modes of knowledge transmission, noting that members of the dominant class downgrade formal schooling as a mere substitute for the lack of deep-rooted, experiential familiarity with art.

The problematic nature of the relation between conscious and unconscious knowledge is obvious in other passages of *Distinction*, particularly in those pages where Bourdieu relates class struggle with the struggle over legitimate aesthetics. 'The art of eating and drinking', he writes, 'remains one of the few areas in which the working classes explicitly challenge the legitimate art of living. In the face of the new ethic of sobriety for the sake of slimness, peasants and especially industrial workers maintain an ethic of convivial indulgence [which] ... sweeps away restraints and reticence' (2006: 179). Working classes in France embark upon an explicit, conscious, and propositional denunciation of pure taste which is manifested not only in their unconscious preferences for fatty, heavy, and strong food, but also in their linguistic descriptions of upper-class bodies as stiff, of upper-class manners of eating as pretentious and contrived, and the valorization of virility, which upper classes perceive as vulgar and rough. It is important to note here that in describing such contestations, Bourdieu briefly abandons the language of habitus, and talks about antagonistic moralities and world-views, that is, systems of meaning characterized by a certain degree of rationalization and quasi-systematic description.

The issue of the relationship between body hexis and propositional knowledge is, however, partly addressed in his recognition of the semiotic functions of the body. The body, he writes, is 'doubly a social product: it derives its distinctive properties from its social conditions of production [and] from its objectification as to when perceived and named by others' (2006: 207). Such objectifications ultimately rest on 'the sign-bearing, sign-wearing body' (2006: 192). Gestures, postures, the pitch of the voice, manners of eating, food choices, and cosmetic usage are duly recognized as operating 'as social markers deriving their meaning and value from their position in the system of distinctive signs which they constitute and which is itself homologous with the system of social positions' (2006: 192). Despite these valuable insights, part of the problem remains, and this has to do with the fact that the semiotics of the body is usually situated well within the domain of language. Social actors are quite able to give more or less adequate commentary about their perception of others and are at least partly aware of the way others might perceive them. In the second case, they are also able strategically to employ a variety of bodily means so as to influence such perceptions. Indeed, what is highlighted by a number of make-over television programmes, such as *What Not to Wear* or *10 Years Younger*, and an array of fashion magazines for men and women is the significance that the body as a sign has assumed in late, consumption-driven capitalism. This in turn is very much connected with the emergence of a series of specialists who spell out the principles both of reading other people's bodies and of the art of affecting other people's perceptions of one's own body.

From France to Java

The body, too, is a central preoccupation for my interlocutors in Java. As Errington writes, 'In Java and much of the rest of island Southeast Asia, bodily behaviours – one's posture and demeanour, the tone of one's voice – are constantly attended to and read as signs of inner moral states' (1990: 17). Errington's observation is heir to a long tradition of anthropological work in the region that goes back to Anderson (1990), who was among the first to realize the importance of body semiosis. Both writers make amply clear that in this part of the world too, class hierarchy is conceived of as embodied. This is best exemplified in local conceptualizations of status distinctions that construe it as the result of differential accumulations of potency, and the latter's close association with the body. Both bodies and potency are made known through the effects they produce. The effects of potency, namely wealth, followers, knowledge, and political office, are taken to correspond to evidences or traces of its concentration. In what is a key reversal of Western assumptions, such evidences are not seen as the causes of status distinctions. Rather, they are generally construed to be visible manifestations of the presence (or absence) of potency.

This particular logic of conceptualizing hierarchies is also replicated in the domains of gender and ethnic difference. While those of gender have received proper attention by ethnographers (see Brenner 1998; Keeler 1990), the semiotic logic of ethnicity and its entanglements with embodiment have not received sufficient attention by ethnographers.

As mentioned, in both Java and Madura, the key conceptual distinction around which issues of social hierarchy revolve is that of *halus* and *kasar*. Most of the regional literature treats these concepts as part of the local value system, that is, as key metaphysical and ethical ideas. This is partly because of the influence that Clifford Geertz's interpretative style has exercised on the ethnography of Java. Against this analytical tendency, which effectively locates such concepts in the realm of the mind and belief, I have argued elsewhere that the *halus-kasar* distinction is better understood from the standpoint of phenomenology (Retsikas 2007a). Seen from this perspective, the two concepts correspond to an explicit form of knowledge about modes of being-in-the-world that links different ways of carrying out everyday activities with certain assumptions about the constitution of the persons involved. Therefore, at the heart of the *halus-kasar* distinction lies a particular take on embodiment according to which practices are defined as constitutive of persons, and persons as dependent on the very same practices that constitute them. Despite its strong affinities with Bourdieu's notion of habitus, this local understanding of embodiment does not dichotomize activities along biological and cultural lines.

Embodied difference

As noted above, the inhabitants of Probolinggo identify themselves as *orang campuran*, 'mixed people'. This identification owes its emergence to a series of demographic movements (Retsikas 2007b). Migrants from Madura and Central and western East Java have converged in the municipality of Probolinggo during the past two centuries. Though the area was populated in pre-modern times, the political upheavals of the eighteenth century caused large numbers of peasants to flee and large tracts of land to be taken over by tropical forest. The re-population of the area began in the early nineteenth century with the arrival of large numbers of Madurese migrants who reclaimed the land and put it into cultivation. Madurese migrants also settled in the town centre and port area, working as petty traders, pedicab drivers, and wage-labourers. In Alas Niser itself, young and relatively educated Javanese migrants from other places in Java arrived *en masse* from the late nineteenth century onwards in response to colonial and postcolonial needs for professionals in the administration.

The mixed personhood found in Probolinggo is the product of many factors; namely close co-habitation in ethnically mixed neighbourhoods, common participation in Islamic rituals, dense exchanges of food, and, most significantly, inter-ethnic marriages. The idiom of mixing recognizes the history of the divergent paths that lead to the present locality and highlights the active construction of homogeneity in the present. Spatial intermingling, ritual, and affinal exchanges have together engendered a new kind of persons that the term *orang campuran* encapsulates. In the words of an informant, the meaning of *orang campuran* is that a person is 'both of Javanese descent and Madurese descent, that one is both a person of Java and a person of Madura'.

Knowledge of whether a person is Javanese, Madurese, or mixed involves what Thomas Csordas has described as 'somatic modes of attention'. 'A somatic mode of attention means not only attention to and with one's own body, but includes attention to the bodies of others' (1993: 139). Attention is a conscious turning towards an 'object'. This turning towards furnishes knowledge, itself stemming from sensory engagement and experience. Somatic modes of attention lie at the heart of how difference is apprehended, bodily as well as cognitively. In this context, processes of knowing are founded on a reversibility – Merleau-Ponty's (1968) notion of the flesh – that constitutes a key characteristic of human embodied existence: namely the reversibility of the body as an object of knowledge and the body as the subject from which knowledge arises and which is brought into being at the same moment that knowledge is shaped. The paradoxical status of the body as both perceiving and perceived, both sensate and sensible, is the effect of its embeddedness within a social space produced and sustained by a multiplicity of perspectives. As perceiving, the body forms the subject for oneself; as perceived, it constitutes an object for others. The dynamics this inherent paradox unleashes are also replicated with respect to one's relation to one's own body. Hearing oneself speak, touching one's left hand with one's right hand, and looking at one's self in the mirror rather than simply collapsing the distinction between the object and the subject foreground difference as foundational in the experience of the self.

In East Java, as far as the experience of the other is concerned, it is significant to note that Madurese personhood is consistently and, for the most part, incontestably depicted by mixed people as coarse, crude, hard, and lacking in refinement. These are the basic connotations of *kasar*. In contrast, Javanese personhood is construed as gentle and smooth, capable of subtlety and excellent manners: the epitome of *halus*. However, not all adjectives qualifying Madurese personhood are negative. The Madurese are also depicted as brave, daring, adventurous, and hard-working. They are also said to be loud and stubborn, touchy and vengeful. But their loyalty, generosity, and fairness are a testament to their distinction. On the other hand, the Javanese are commonly construed as soft and delicate, timid and cool-tempered. In addition, they are judged to be lacking in desire for adventure, to be lazy and dishonest, or at least prone to dissimulation. Despite appearances to the contrary, such adjectival qualities are of social origin in the sense that they are revealed and constituted in social interaction. In other words, categorical qualities are inferred from everyday activity and conceptualized as embedded within a set of concrete indexical signs that are aesthetically and perceptually evaluated. Aesthetic and perceptual engagement with difference involves the senses.

The qualities of *kasar* and *halus* are closely associated with the visual impact of colours. Visual affects are taken as clues for deciphering the intentions of the perceived subject and a manifestation of his/her essence. Madurese dress habits are seen as involving a particular taste for gleaming and dazzlingly bright colours, in particular red, yellow, and green. The 'traditional' female attire is described as mixing and mingling several of these colours for the purpose of appearing beautiful and attractive. Similarly, Madurese masculinity is perceived as involving another visual contrast employing a combination of black, white, and red colours. In conjunction with state representations of 'traditional dress', Madurese men are portrayed in 'mixed' Probolinggo as going about their everyday lives wearing the *klabih pesa*, a black two-part cloth consisting of a short jacket and pair of trousers, and a *kaos dalem*, which is a red- and white-striped T-shirt.

By contrast, Javanese dress tastes and habits are qualified as calm and soft. Softness is taken to inhere in 'dark' colours such as white, black, ink blue, and brown. Dark colours form the basis of the batik textile designs for which the Central Javanese principalities of Jogjakarta and Surakarta are famous. Since at least the nineteenth century, both principalities have become synonymous with authentic 'Java'. According to John Pemberton (1994), the idea of 'Java' was invented by the indigenous courts so as to counteract the crisis of legitimacy they were facing due to their colonial domestication. Batik, along with other arts such as the shadow puppet theatre, is at the forefront of culture politics. During colonial times, batik designs were standardized and regulated by court edicts. More recently, they have undergone a second resurgence due to concerted efforts by the New Order state (1966-98) to build legitimacy through appeals to 'tradition'.

In today's Probolinggo, visual aesthetics are commonly taken as outward signs of inward states. Reddish colours and gleaming combinations are construed as manifesting the turbulent tensions imagined to inhabit the Madurese person and especially his or her inability to control socially undesired emotions (*nafsu*). Red indexes this dangerous lack of control. In contrast, the neutrality of Javanese colour tastes is taken to bespeak of introversion, timidity, and a refraining from public boasting. Soft appearances evince an interiority of smooth emotions brought about largely by the achievement of control.

In addition to sight, taste is stressed. Both scientific and local ecological knowledge describe the island of Madura as arid, dry, and infertile. This is largely the effect of a hot climate, extended periods of drought, the absence of large river systems, and the limestone composition of the soil. These particular ecological conditions render most of the island's land unsuitable for irrigated rice agriculture and have historically favoured the development of dry, rain-dependent fields (Husson 1995; Kuntowijoyo 1985). In the Madurese ecosystem, maize and cassava are cultivated alongside rice, with the former two being more important in both economic and dietary terms. In Probolinggo, the Madurese are generally construed as maize-eaters. Maize and cassava are seen as lacking in terms of nutritional value and described as the basic staple of poor peasants since they cannot afford to consume rice regularly and throughout the year. The devaluation of maize and cassava is partly conveyed by their characterization as *keras* (hard, tough, stony), a quality sensed by the teeth and the tongue. To the extent that Madurese persons are thought of as dependent on the consumption of *keras* food, the *keras* quality of food is seen as partaking in the qualities of those persons whose growth depends on its consumption. Furthermore, through the mediation of food, persons are construed as sharing the ecological characteristics of the land they work and inhabit.

In contrast, the staple diet of Javanese is said to consist of rice and is designated as *halus*. The soil of the island of Java is rich in volcanic elements and very fertile partly due to high level of rainfall. The rains ensure greater availability of water, which has in turn allowed for the development of irrigated agriculture (Whitten, Soeriaatmadja & Afiff 1996). The links between agriculture, levels of humidity, food texture, and personhood attested to above are also prevalent here. Javanese diet is construed as *halus* for it consists of rice, which is soft and juicy. In turn, Javanese persons are thought to exhibit a similar softness for they have matured through the consumption of soft substances.

The hierarchy that underlies the *halus-kasar* distinction has kinaesthetic effects too. Travel between the islands of Java and Madura is experienced as movement across an uneven terrain. The kinaesthetic experience of space is manifested in the verbs used to mark movement. Several first-generation Madurese migrants in Probolinggo who return to their villages in Madura for a short period of time to visit family and friends mark their movement across the Madura Straits with the verb *toron*, which literally means to climb down, to descend. Their return trip to Java is denoted by the verb *ongghe*, meaning to move upwards, to ascend. Here, hierarchy is perceived through travel and the movement of the whole body across space (see also Ingold, this volume).

In between the perceived uplands of Java and the lowlands of the island of Madura lies the land of mixed persons. According to my interlocutors, this land covers most of the eastern coast of East Java, from the north of Pasuruan down to the south of Situbondo and Asembagus, and from the mountains of Jember and Lumajang to the southern regions of Malang. Such a land is construed as both *halus* and *kasar*, less *kasar* than the land of Madura and less *halus* than the land of Java. By being more fertile, less hot, less dry, and more humid than the island of Madura, *camporan* land is thought of as giving life to persons of smoother appearance than those of Madura. In the same vein, *camporan* land is seen as being less fertile, hotter, drier, and less humid than Central Java. It is therefore conceived of as engendering persons with a more volatile temperament and more colourful appearance than those of 'authentic' Java.

A significant part of the conceptualization *and* experience of ethnic difference is played by the senses of speaking and hearing. Writing about the ways that speaking is related to both gender and status differences in Java, Ward Keeler notes that it is both the content of speech and its overall tone that are of particular importance to the Javanese. Noting that women are thought of as inferior to men partly because of their greater informality in deploying Javanese speech levels and their more casual tone, he observes that conveying 'information carries some threat of discord. If contrary to its receivers' wishes, [speech] may startle them, causing disarray to their thoughts and feelings, and so endangering both their health and self-possession' (Keeler 1990: 137). As a result, 'when addressing someone of significantly higher status than oneself, but even with one's near equals, one should attend carefully to the tenor of any encounter as well as to the information that is being exchanged' (1990: 142).

Owing to the risks and dangers inherent in communication, particular attention is paid to hearing and speaking. Both the Madurese and the Javanese languages consist of several speech levels. The difference between the two languages, as well as the differences between the distinct speech levels within each language, is construed in terms of the *halus-kasar* distinction. Here, the aural and oral qualities of speech are given as much attention as its content; the referential quality of the words containing information is as important as the sounds people produce and receive. Words are not simply 'carriers of referential meaning, but [meaning is to be found also] in the sounds of the words' (Stoller 1984: 568). In other words, language is a communicative activity taking place in a world created, animated, and experienced through sound.

In mixed Probolinggo, Madurese language is sensed as *kasar*, cacophonous and lacking the delicate, swirling melodies of Javanese. The relative inferiority of Madurese personhood therefore rests on the lesser degree of oral and auditory perfection a Madurese person is capable of displaying in linguistic interaction. *Kasar*-ness is largely a quality of the lower speech levels – *ngoko* in Javanese and *ta' abasah* in Madurese. The lower speech levels are employed in specific contexts, primarily among people of equal social standing who are engaged in long and intimate exchanges; and also from a social superior to a social inferior, but not vice versa. Such contexts permit the expression of relaxed conviviality that involves joking, teasing, gossiping, as well as dissatisfaction and frustration. The semiosis of these relations by *ngoko* is marked by *ngoko*'s blander and coarser sounds and a certain kind of speech performativity that relates to speaking faster and less evenly. The contrast with the long-drawn-out tonalities of the highest speech level, *krama*, is obvious. *Krama* is employed in formal occasions, when speaking to people one hardly knows or to whom one owes deference. *Krama* is characterized by an extremely stylized, slow, and flat mode of delivery. Indeed, Clifford Geertz observes that speaking in *krama* has 'a kind of stately pomp which can make the simplest conversation seem like a great ceremony' (1960: 254).

The anthropological literature on ethnicity has traditionally dealt with differences of language, diet, and dress from a symbolic and sociological point of view, construing such differences as resources that people draw upon according to circumstances so as to establish relative advantage (Barth 1969). Ethnic diacritics have been conceptualized as inhering on the surface of ethnic bodies, performing a primarily expressive function. However, the 'logic' of the material I have presented runs counter to such arguments, making the case that the whole body is the locus of difference. Javanese and Madurese are construed as different because they are experienced as having different bodies: bodies made up of distinct dispositions and capacities. Such dispositions and capacities are themselves traced to the undertaking of specific sets of practices and the formation of particular habits. Furthermore, the bodies to which practices give rise are recognized as being both a product and a condition for the reproduction of distinct modes of being-in-the-world.

My informants postulate that the relation between bodies and practices is characterized by the same circularity one detects in Bourdieu's theory of habitus. Both interlocutors in our imagined dialogue see practices as constitutive of bodies. Moreover, both interlocutors recognize human bodies as necessary for the reproduction and transmission of the very practices that constitute them. The two elements – bodies and practices – exist in a dialectical relation of mutual, reciprocal reinforcement with each term of the equation functioning as the index of the other. Bodies and practices can thus be described as fundamentally aligned or inexorably attuned to one another.

However, while Bourdieu allows very little space for change in one's habitus, noting that habitus corresponds to 'systems of durable ... dispositions' (1977: 72), my informants place disruptions in such alignments at the very centre of their understanding of the condition of embodiment. Indeed, their descriptions of Javanese and Madurese difference are made from the point of view of them being 'mixed'. This mixing is the result of demographic movements, an act of separation from the land and its products, and a break from engagements with people who are construed as being similar to oneself. As demonstrated elsewhere (Retsikas 2007b), movement necessitates the active fostering of relations with other types of land, and other kinds of people. Such relations result in changes of habits that the category of 'mixed people' encapsulates.

In apparent contrast to the pervasive presence of an explicit system of knowledge about the Javanese and the Madurese, the habits and practices that make 'mixed people' distinct are linguistically unelaborated and muted. My informants were unable or reluctant to provide narrative accounts of how this mixing has come about, how it is maintained, what it consists of, and how it differs from the 'pure' non-mixed categories. Indeed, my insistent questioning about the qualities and dispositions of 'mixed personhood' was met with short answers of the kind that 'we are all mixed persons' or that 'mixed persons are 50-50, neither *halus* nor wholly *kasar*, but both'. Such answers lacked the density, precision, and eloquence of animated descriptions of Javanese and Madurese personhood. The poverty of the verbal material was demonstrated repeatedly in the relative absence of exegetical accounts of the makings of mixed persons and the overabundance of matter-of-fact statements that described mixed persons as the direct result of inter-ethnic marriages. In a sense, the locals' sense of themselves as distinct was placed beyond the limits of propositional knowledge, with the dietary, dress, and language habits remaining linguistically unelaborated and un-marked.

As an anthropologist, I endeavour to conceptualize what my informants did or could not, spelling out the implicit, taken-for-granted nature of assumptions that lie at the centre of the category of mixed people. Elsewhere I have traced such assumptions to a series of historical conjectures and rites of commemoration (Retsikas 2007b). I have also pointed to particular enactments of kinship and affinity (Retsikas 2003) and a fluid conception of the person as manifested in gender oscillations made apparent in sorcery practices (Retsikas in press). I take the totality of such everyday practices to correspond to Bourdieu's habitus. What I find problematic in Bourdieu, however, is his placement of the entirety of habitus beyond the grasp of consciousness (see also Bloch 1991). The categories of *halus* and *kasar* are located within the domain of language as well as experience, providing the basis of a system of ethnic distinction of a semiotic and phenomenological import, serving as the foundation for the cognition and experience of hierarchy. On a different plane, I also find Bourdieu's strong emphasis on socialization as being especially problematic when applied to non-Western contexts. This question is the focus of the next section.

'Nature'

According to Bourdieu, habitus is acquired during socialization, with the family being the primary vehicle for the inculcation of the cognitive and bodily dispositions that accord to its class position. The durability of habitus is the result of early socialization experiences predicated on the assumed plasticity and malleability of what is mainly a *tabula rasa*. Some of these assumptions are shared by Hildred Geertz (1961), who in her well-received study of Javanese kinship notes that the Javanese family functions as the bridge between the individual and the wider society. In particular, she argues that the process of becoming Javanese is predicated on learning to have and display particular kinds of emotions such as shame or willed detachment. She found that this learning begins around the fifth or sixth year when the child, through a variety of techniques, slowly acquires the forms of mature behaviour the Javanese value most. While I do not dispute the impact early experiences have on children, what I wish to show here is that as far as my informants are concerned the effects of society are not assumed to begin with early childhood. Rather, the shaping of the person and its body is traced to activities that precede conception, continue during pregnancy, and, of course, extend beyond delivery.

Until recently, most marriages in Alas Niser were arranged by parents, with the majority of girls and boys getting married by the time they reached mid- to late teens. Though this is changing, the search for a spouse still involves parental consent and attention. Attention is paid especially to the social class background of the prospective spouse and in-laws. In general, the selection of *bhesan* (a term of address utilized reciprocally between the two sets of parents of a married couple) is guided by considerations accurately captured by the phrase *bebet-bobot-bibit* (heredity-wealth-moral character, Javanese). Ideally, the two *bhesan* will be at least approximate, if not identical. This approximation is believed to contribute towards the longevity and the fertility of the union.

The *bhesan* selection process is also held to contribute directly to the formation of the moral character of the children who result from the union. An appropriate quality of *bhesan* is to be 'good people'. 'Good people' means those who are not haughty, arrogant, or envious. It designates individuals who are on good terms with their relatives and neighbours, generous, and merciful. 'Good people' are pious Muslims, performing the five daily prayers, observing the fast, and giving alms. It is important to note here that the Javanese-Madurese distinction, despite its overt hierarchical tone, does not feature as a direct or significant concern in the *bhesan* selection process. Ethnic difference is made an explicit concern only when unions with either Chinese-Indonesians or Arab-Indonesians are contemplated – a rare occurrence.

The *bhesan* selection process is geared towards the transmission of sociality as a quality of the yet-to-be-born person. This transmission is held to be effected through the passing of substances, namely (uterine) blood and semen. Moreover, while in the womb, the foetus is conceptualized as an inherently social being for it is thought of as part of a sibling set. This set consists of one, two, or four additional entities, depending on whom one asks. According to the latter version, these entities are the amniotic fluid, the placenta, the blood, and the umbilical cord (*tretan se pa-empa*, Madurese). The foetus's four siblings are thought to play a life-supporting role during gestation. After birth, they are transformed into intangible cognitive aides, activating sense perception by inhabiting the nose, ears, eyes, and mouth. The fifth sense, *rasa* (touch/taste/feeling), corresponds to the fifth element of the set, that is, the whole body-person of the foetus.

As in other parts of Java and Madura, parents have to observe specific prohibitions that facilitate easy delivery and ensure that the child will be healthy (H. Geertz 1961; Niehof 1985). It is necessary that the expectant mother avoid eating sugar cane. Unless she does so, the baby at birth will start coming out, stop, and then start again in an indefinite cycle. The mother-to-be must also avoid lingering in doorways or accepting objects through an open door or window lest the child is born with a wide mouth. Both parents-to-be should avoid torturing animals, for the torture they inflict will be replicated in the child, who will suffer from bodily defects.

A very important ritual takes place in the seventh month of pregnancy. The ritual, called *tingkeban* (following upon [a wedding], Javanese) or *pelet beteng* (massaging the belly, Madurese), has been construed by Clifford Geertz as 'representing the introduction of the Javanese woman into motherhood' (1960: 39). While the mother-to-be is definitely one of the targets of ritual action, the foetus is another. Four actions are of particular importance in shaping the foetus. Firstly, the expectant mother is showered by senior female relatives with water mixed with petals from three different types of flowers. The water is poured with the use of a ladle made of half an unripe coconut and a branch of *kemuning* tree. Among pious Muslims families, the ladle is inscribed with Arabic script. The purpose of the ritual bath is to effect purity, while the Arabic letters are said to entice the foetus to become fluent in that language.

Following on, two unripe coconuts make their appearance. Among pious Muslims, the coconuts are decorated with recognizable human figures: the first with a male figure, the second with a female. Among less pious Muslims, the figures refer to the puppet theatre hero Arjuno and his wife Sumbroto. Arjuno, the most potent and handsome of all men, is described as the favourite figure of Hindu Gods from Java's pre-Islamic past. His wife is the exemplary woman, the most beautiful and loyal. Next, the two coconuts are made to drop from inside the expectant mother's clothes, an act that contributes to easy delivery. At the same time, the foetus is encouraged to model itself after the exemplars of masculinity and femininity.

The third ritual sequence relates to shaping the gender of the foetus. The father-to-be collects both coconuts and, using a large kitchen knife, strikes each one with a single blow. If neither splits, the birth is predicted to be difficult; if both split, it will be easy. If only one coconut splits, the un-split one indicates the gender of the child. Gender is taken to be shaped at least partly by the agency and skill of the father and partly by chance. In another locale in East Java, Rens Heringa (2007) describes this gendering as being achieved by the actions of women in preparing a fruit drink during the ritual proceedings. If the drink is bland, it will generate a boy; if it is sweet, it will produce a girl.

The final ritual act involves prayers and the collective recitation of particular passages of the Qur'an. *Sura Maryam*, *sura Yusuf*, *sura Muhammad*, and *sura Yasin* are recited, with the explicit intention of constituting the foetus as a moral Muslim subject. If the foetus is female, reading *sura Maryam* is thought to affect the foetus directly in the sense of making her character proximate to that of Maryam, the mother of Prophet Isa (Jesus). If the foetus is male, *sura Yusuf* and *sura Muhammad* are read aloud to entice the foetus to model himself after the exemplars of these two most revered figures. Finally, *sura Yasin*, considered the most important *sura* of all, is recited to induce the essence of the faith.

While Western culture and science construe gestation processes in purely biological terms, East Javanese conceptualize gestation as being a domain and a medium of sociality. The arbitrariness with which nature-culture distinctions are introduced becomes apparent when considering ideas and practices related to breast-feeding. Following childbirth, the new mother consumes large quantities of herbal medicines. The most important is *jamo pejjeen* (Madurese), made by boiling together a variety of ingredients. This homemade potion is believed to turn the mother's blood into breast-milk, and thereby into baby food. *Ebbu* Salmah, a midwife and mother of five, explained: 'Breast-milk is blood. The breast-milk that [resides] inside the mother is blood but [because of the medicine] it comes out white'. The belief that breast-milk is actually transmuted blood helps to explain the prohibition of marrying one's *tretan sosso* (milk sibling, Madurese), designating those who have sucked from the same teat.

The prohibition against marriage between milk siblings is spelled out in the Qur'an, where they are treated as equivalent to full siblings in matters of incest. As Janet Carsten observes among the Malay of peninsular Malaysia,

> It makes little sense in indigenous terms to label some ... activities as social and others as biological. ... If blood ... is acquired during gestation in the uterus and, after birth ... as people assert, is it then biological or social? The impossibility of answering this question merely underlines the unsatisfactory nature of this distinction (1995: 236-7).

Conclusions

Let me now sum up our imagined dialogue. For Bourdieu, habitus is a mechanism that captures the interplay of social relations and the body. As a mechanism of mediation between existing distributions of political and economic power and the formation of the subject, habitus gives rise to the 'socially informed body', with all its tastes and distastes, its compulsions and repulsions, with ... all its senses' (1997: 124, original emphasis). The socially informed body masks the very arbitrariness of systems of domination by making it appear that such systems are rooted in the body, and thereby easily mistaken as natural. Principles embodied in this way are fundamentally incontestable for they are placed beyond conscious awareness and misrecognized as pre- or a-social. Consent is acquired implicitly through appeal to assumed natural differences. Such principles resist deliberate transformation or explicit articulation, except, of course, by the privileged outside observer equipped with the tools of critical social science.

For my fieldwork interlocutors, social hierarchy is similarly rooted in the body. The principles involved in the establishment of such hierarchies, however, are at least partially situated within the domain of consciousness; they are both explicit and communicable to others, including the outside observer. These principles receive quasi-systematic linguistic treatment and are based on forms of moral knowledge and moral subjectivity that aim to further the production and reproduction of sociality. Persons are stratified according to the degree to which they embody morality. Mixed persons portray *halus* persons as coming very close to embodying moral perfection and instruct their children to behave in *halus* ways. Because hierarchy is partially subject to linguistic consciousness, it is also subject to subversion. *Halus*-ness is suspected of harbouring laziness, dissimulation, and passivity. *Kasar*-ness includes positive qualities such as generosity, hard work, and loyalty. On the one hand, these subversive evaluations destabilize the hierarchy that underpins the Madurese-Javanese distinction. On the other, they strengthen the overall value of hierarchy. I have argued elsewhere that for the people of Probolinggo, one of the consequences of the coining of the category of 'mixed persons' is clearly political, that is, of re-shaping the regional system of hierarchical ethnic difference (Retsikas 2007a). This re-shaping is based on the intention of removing Javanese *halus*-ness from the apex of the hierarchical pyramid and of promoting the political pre-eminence of 'mixed personhood'. From their perspective, this pre-eminence is founded on the ability of 'mixed persons' to encompass *halus*-ness as only one part of their constitution, and their concomitant capacity of embodying opposite qualities of being, namely both *halus* and *kasar*. My informants' silence surrounding the dispositional distinctiveness of being mixed also makes sense in this regard. Their eagerness to objectify others and to avoid being objectified themselves bespeaks of the power of the subject who desires to be always a 'who', never a 'what'.

Bodies (and persons) are not conceived in 'indigenous' terms as the product of pre- or a-social process; there are no assumptions made about a biological formation of bodies taking place before the social constitution of persons begins. Because of this, it is misleading to employ an analytical framework that radically dissociates the organism from the person and attributes their correspondence to the work of domination and the naturalization of arbitrariness. The concept of the 'socially informed body' only makes sense within an epistemological universe that opposes it to the natural, biological body. The thematization of the relationship between these two kinds of bodies sits at the heart of Bourdieu's assertion that the production of their correspondence is a deeply political act. In the social context I am researching, history is synonymous with genealogy, and the latter provides some of the links that connect bodies. Because acts of engendering persons are recognized as being social, persons are taken to correspond to the cumulative effect of such acts that encode the past and anticipate a reproductive future. Therefore, the dictum that persons 'embody history, internalized as *second nature*' (Bourdieu 1990: 56, my emphasis), is at least an awkward translation of what goes on in the minds and the bodies of my informants.

The reciprocity of perspectives involved in comparative exercises such as the one undertaken in this chapter necessitates the possibility of reversing the direction of explanation. 'Exploring East Javanese conceptions of the person through Bourdieu's lens' therefore calls for its corollary, that is, 'Exploring Bourdieu through an East Javanese lens'. The tensions produced by reciprocal gazes are analytically valuable. Their value lies in bringing to the surface fundamental incommensurabilities and in creating an opening for an undetermined epistemological space necessary for the articulation of the unthinkable and the unspeakable. The point of departure for the 'socially informed body' is that natural equality is a natural given and its purpose is to show how natural equality is transformed into social inequality. My interlocutors' notion of the body is radically different. For them, natural equality is a fiction and hierarchy is pervasive. Hierarchy is present from before conception, all the way to the grave and beyond. The formulations that underpin their understandings of embodied difference are intended to make this hierarchy sensible: that is, visible, audible, tactile, and felt, and thus somatically knowable in inter-subjective encounters. Moreover, as I have shown, this embodied hierarchy is neither stable nor fixed, but subject to innovative re-fashioning and strategic silence.

NOTE

[1] Some portions of the material presented here appeared in a previous article (Retsikas 2007a). However, with this material I am making a new argument.

REFERENCES

Anderson, B. 1990. The idea of power in Javanese culture. In *Language and power: exploring political cultures in Indonesia*, 17-77. Ithaca, N.Y.: Cornell University Press.

Barth, F. 1969. Introduction. In *Ethnic groups and boundaries* (ed.) F. Barth, 9-38. Oslo: Universitets Forlaget.

Bloch, M. 1991. Language, anthropology and cognitive science. *Man* (N.S.) **26**, 183-98.

Bourdieu, P. 1977. *Outline of a theory of practice* (trans. R. Nice). Cambridge: University Press.

——— 1990. *The logic of practice* (trans. R. Nice). Cambridge: Polity.

——— 2001. *Masculine domination* (trans. R. Nice). Cambridge: Polity.

——— 2006. *Distinction: a social critique of the judgment of taste* (trans. R. Nice). London: Routledge.

Brenner, S. 1998. *The domestication of desire: women, wealth, and modernity in Java*. Princeton: University Press.

Carsten, J. 1995. The substance of kinship and the heat of the hearth: feeding, personhood, and relatedness among Malayans in Pulau Langkawi. *American Ethnologist* **22**, 223-42.

Crossley, N. 2001. The phenomenological habitus and its construction. *Theory & Society* **30**, 81-120.

Csordas, T. 1993. Somatic modes of attention. *Cultural Anthropology* **8**, 135-56.

Errington, S. 1987. Incestous twins and house societies in insular Southeast Asia. *Cultural Anthropology* **2**, 403-44.

————— 1990. Recasting sex, gender, and power: a theoretical and regional overview. In *Power and difference: gender in island Southeast Asia* (ed.) J.M. Atkinson & S. Errington, 1-58. Stanford: University Press.

FREUD, S. 1991. *The interpretation of dreams* (trans. J. Strachey). London: Penguin.

GEERTZ, C. 1960. *The religion of Java*. Chicago: University Press.

GEERTZ, H. 1961. *The Javanese family: a study of kinship and socialization*. New York: Free Press of Glencoe.

HERINGA, R. 2007. Reconstructing the whole: seven months pregnancy ritual in Kerek, East Java. In *Kinship and food in South East Asia* (eds) M. Janowski & F. Kerlogue, 24-53. Copenhagen: Nias Press.

HUSSON, L. 1995. *La migration Madurese vers l'est de Java*. Paris: L'Harmattan.

INGOLD, T. 1991. Becoming persons: consciousness and sociality in human evolution. *Cultural Dynamics* 4, 335-78.

JENKINS, R. 1992. *Pierre Bourdieu*. London: Routledge.

KEELER, W. 1990. Speaking of gender in Java. In *Power and difference: gender in island Southeast Asia* (eds) J.M. Atkinson & S. Errington, 127-52. Stanford: University Press.

KING, A. 2000. Thinking with Bourdieu against Bourdieu: a practical critique of habitus. *Sociological Theory* 18, 417-33.

KUNTOWIJOYO 1985. Social change in an agrarian society: Madura 1850-1940. Ph.D. thesis, Columbia University. Ann Arbor, Mich.: University Microfilms International.

LAMBEK, M. & A. STRATHERN 1998. Introduction. In *Bodies and persons* (eds) M. Lambek & A. Strathern, 1-25. Cambridge: University Press.

LÉVI-STRAUSS, C. 1972. *The savage mind*. London: Weidenfeld & Nicolson.

LIZARDO, O. 2004. The cognitive origins of Bourdieu's habitus. *Journal for the Theory of Social Behaviour* 34, 375-401.

MERLEAU-PONTY, M. 1968. *The visible and the invisible* (ed. C. Lefort; trans. A. Lingis). Evanston, Ill.: Northwestern University Press.

NIEHOF, A. 1985. Women and fertility in Madura. Ph.D. thesis, University of Leiden.

PEMBERTON, J. 1994. *On the subject of 'Java'*. Ithaca, N.Y.: Cornell University Press.

RETSIKAS, K. 2003. 'People of mixed blood': ethnicity, personhood and sociality in east Java, Indonesia. Ph.D. thesis, University of Edinburgh.

————— 2007a. The power of the senses: ethnicity, history, and embodiment in East Java, Indonesia. *Indonesia and the Malay World* 35, 183-210.

————— 2007b. Being and place: movement, ancestors, and personhood in East Java, Indonesia. *Journal of the Royal Anthropological Institute* (N.S) 13, 969-86.

————— 2008. Knowledge from the body: fieldwork, power, and the acquisition of a new self. In *Knowing how to know: fieldwork and the ethnographic present* (ed.) N. Halstead, E. Hirsch & J. Okely, 110-29. Oxford: Berghahn.

————— in press. The sorcery of gender: sex, death, and difference in East Java, Indonesia. *South East Asia Research* 18.

STOLLER, P. 1984. Sound in Songhay cultural experience. *American Ethnologist* 11, 559-70.

STRATHERN, M. 1980. No nature, no culture: the Hagen case. In *Nature, culture and gender* (eds) M. MacCormack & M. Strathern, 174-222. Cambridge: University Press.

————— 1990. Negative strategies in Melanesia. In *Localizing strategies* (ed.) R. Fardon, 204-16. Edinburgh: Scottish Academic Press.

THROOP, C.J. & K.M. MURPHY 2002. Bourdieu and phenomenology: a critical assessment. *Anthropological Theory* 2, 185-207.

WHITTEN, T., R.E. SOERIAATMADJA & S.A. AFIFF (eds) 1996. *The ecology of Java and Bali*. Oxford: University Press.

8

Learning to weave; weaving to learn ... what?

SOUMHYA VENKATESAN *University of Manchester*

This chapter investigates two related questions, both of which stem from the larger project driving this special volume: the investigation of processes that define learning, thinking, and practice. My own material focuses on the embodied skill of weaving; in particular, the weaving of mats on hand looms in South India. Firstly, I am interested in the relationship between knowledge of and about weaving as a particular kind of activity, and action pertaining to this knowledge. Secondly, I explore how people learn how to weave, what they know about weaving prior to learning how to weave, and how this knowledge affects their ideas about what it is to weave or to be a weaver.

My main argument is that the acquisition of a skill is embedded in larger social knowledge about the value of the skill based on ideas about the body, gender, identity, politics, and economics. Acquiring, utilizing, or depending upon a skill positions individuals or groups in particular ways, not necessarily of their choosing. Just as gender, marital status, or one's position in a hierarchical order can influence what one can do socially, the things one can or does do (weave, cook, give birth) can locate a person or group by gendering, classing, or categorizing them. Therefore an interesting set of related questions is: what does learning a skill equip one to do, and does one want to do this in light of what and how one learns? In other words, what else is learned alongside the learning of a skill?

The above is closely intertwined with the question of identity and with the positive or negative identification with particular kinds of work, in this case the work of weaving. For Sandra Wallman (1979: 1-2), work is as much about social transactions as it is about material production. Work controls the identity as well as the economy of the worker. It is more and less than an economic activity. For the worker, work is a personal experience, her relation to the reality in which she lives. However, this personal experience is constrained by the logic of the system within which the person works. Thus, any analysis of work has to ask which forms of work in a given setting are thought to be socially or morally worthy and physically, spiritually, or intellectually fulfilling.

The account that follows focuses on two very different kinds of people: the Labbai Muslims of Pattamadai town in South India, who claim the weaving of high-quality mats as their 'traditional work' (*paramparai thozhil*), and 'Lila', a development practitioner employed by an NGO set up to develop traditional Indian craft. Lila is committed to the promotion of the mat-weaving industry and, relatedly, to enabling members of the group to continue making mats rather than give it up for other occupations. This involves helping weavers to overcome real and perceived problems with mat-weaving.

Lila, like the Labbais of Pattamadai, also learned how to weave. In exploring how and why she learned to weave and contrasting that with the ways in which the Labbais of Pattamadai arrive at the same skill, I suggest that embedded apprentice-style learning leads to a different kind of knowledge about weaving as compared to independent problem-solving styles of learning. Both modes of learning might lead to what Sennett (2008) terms 'material consciousness', that is, a sensitivity to, knowledge of, and ability to transform materials through tools and skill. But what each kind of practitioner *knows* about the work and worth of the skill may well be very different – each beginning *and* ending up with what might be termed a different consciousness of worth. Learning and knowing, then, cannot easily be separated, and, likewise, neither can the anthropology of learning and the anthropology of work.

Preservation, promotion, and development

Pattamadai is a small town in Tamilnadu state, South India. It has a population of around 13,000 people; the town's Labbai Muslim group numbers about 650. Since the end of the nineteenth century the Labbai Muslims of Pattamadai have been weaving very fine mats on hand looms using locally growing *korai* (a kind of sedge) as weft on a cotton warp. *Korai* mats are commonly woven throughout Tamilnadu and are used for a variety of purposes, including seating, bedding, and packing material. Pattamadai mats, however, are distinctive because of the time and skill required in their manufacture and for their resultant silk-like texture. Since 1953, when a Pattamadai mat was commissioned as a coronation gift for Queen Elizabeth II and was seen by the head of the All-India Handicrafts Board (see Nambiar 1964; Venkatesan 2009a; 2009b), the governments of both India and Tamilnadu state have taken an interest in the mats and in the mat-weavers, the former being identified as a traditional Indian craft and the latter as traditional Indian craft producers. A number of non-governmental organizations have also worked with Pattamadai weavers and traders.

The main aim of governmental and non-governmental development interventions is to ensure that Pattamadai mats continue to be made: this is considered important both for the sakes of the weavers, who would otherwise lose their livelihoods, and for the sake of the nation, which would otherwise lose a valuable element of its material and cultural heritage. Governmental support has included, among other things, the commission of mats for use in state gifting, invitations to weavers to attend specialist craft bazaars, and the bestowal of national awards for master-craft producers to three mat-weavers, two of whom were subsequently funded to train young people in the craft.

Non-governmental support has tended to focus more on markets and on product development. A Pattamadai mat of the highest quality can take up to a month to weave; this is reflected in its price. Furthermore, the silk-like texture of the mats makes them unfit for the normal uses to which mats are put in Tamilnadu (objects on which people sit or lie down). Weavers do not use the mats they weave, nor has there ever been a customary market for these objects (as reported by Pate 1917; Rao 1929). They are luxury goods for which demand needs to be created. NGOs such as the Madras Craft Foundation and the Crafts Council of India have liaised with government or worked on their own initiative to develop markets for the mats. Working as they mainly do with local Labbai mat-traders to whom weavers sell their mats (see Venkatesan 2006), few of the NGOs based in Pattamadai have much contact with weavers. The exception is one NGO that I will call here Craft Enterprises.

Craft Enterprises was a small NGO with an ambitious brief: to revitalize rural crafts and communities centred on craft production. The NGO, which existed from 1996 to 2001, when its funding ceased, worked with four artisanal groups in South India, including the Pattamadai mat-weavers. Central to Craft Enterprises' work was the presence of a 'facilitator', who would live with the craft group for the first year and build deep relationships with producers and acquire knowledge of their work. In this sense, Craft Enterprises was unusual among the other craft development agencies that worked with Pattamadai mats and weavers, but which had no real presence in the town. The Pattamadai facilitator, Lila, was, in some ways, like me, an anthropologist, living among the people with whom she worked. Unlike me, however, she had a very specific brief to promote and develop the mat-weaving industry. She and I became friends, bouncing ideas off one another and, for a while, sharing the house she was renting in Pattamadai after I arrived to begin fieldwork.[1]

Like other development agencies that have worked in Pattamadai, Craft Enterprises felt that establishing regular markets for the mats would be the most useful step. The NGO's strategy was to buy up 'super-fine mats' or mats of the highest quality (which local traders found difficult to sell and consequently weavers rarely wove) and then sell them in specialist craft exhibitions.[2] By 1996 Craft Enterprises was regularly buying super-fine mats from traders and, in November 1996, was able to sell them at a craft sale for what were perceived in Pattamadai as very high prices (£30-£50 per mat). The profits were used as working capital to buy more mats. In early 1997 some weavers of super-fine mats felt confident enough about the NGO's performance to request that the NGO buy mats directly from them rather than from traders. Lila then began to work directly and closely with eight weavers,[3] commissioning super-fine mats from them, collaborating on designs, holding regular sales in Indian cities, and ploughing the profits back into buying more mats. As a trader, the NGO was extremely effective. Weavers were paid good prices for their mats.[4] Every mat made by a weaver who worked with Craft Enterprises was bought by the NGO as soon as it came off the loom. Payments were made promptly. The weavers who worked with Craft Enterprises spoke exultantly of having escaped the 'exploitative practices of the local mat traders' (see Venkatesan 2006). Confidence in the future of super-fine mats, which had been on the wane, started to grow. Indeed, some of the weavers who began to work regularly with Craft Enterprises stopped weaving medium-quality (or fine) mats and switched to weaving super-fine mats exclusively. Enthusiasm, too, was high, and Lila would spend hours in weavers' homes working out new colour-ways and patterns. The NGO had clearly and successfully entered into a rhythm with the weavers of buying mats off the loom, thereby encouraging new mats to go on looms. The number of weavers regularly weaving super-fine mats was higher than it had ever been, and around eighty super-fine mats a year were being produced for Craft Enterprises.

Innovation and improvement

Once it looked like Craft Enterprises had managed to stabilize the production and sale of super-fine mats, Lila decided that she wanted to tackle problems with the mat-weaving loom, since, as she noted in her 1998 project report, 'after a few years of weaving, everyone complains of back, eye and knee problems'. She consulted the weavers about her plans to 'improve' the loom, but 'they insisted on a more "productive" loom for higher output rather than rectifying the physical discomfort due to bad posture forced by the loom'.

Despite the weavers' lack of interest in a loom that would promote better posture, Lila pressed ahead with the project with the support of Craft Enterprises. Her project report noted that a 'brief has been formulated to design a more ergonomic loom which would allow the weaver to stand and weave within a 2ft range thereby reducing the strain on the back, shoulders and eyes'.

Lila's first attempt to design an improved loom took the form of a collaboration between herself, an ergonomics expert, and a couple of weavers. The ergonomics expert spent two days in Pattamadai along with a yoga practitioner. They took videos of people weaving, spoke to a cloth-weaver in Pattamadai, and studied the cloth loom. In December 1998 the resulting loom was installed in Pattamadai and tested for two months. The weavers, however, were not enthusiastic: the prototype was expensive, large, and too different from what they were accustomed to. Lila decided to try again, reporting in 1999 as follows:

> We studied the new loom [which had not met with success] and the traditional loom and evolved a holistic guideline for designing the next model – upright sitting posture for comfortable weaving; details of structure to be simplified for manufacturing locally; should fit into existing spaces and conditions; should use existing practices in processes related to weaving such as warping and packing.

In addition to studying the loom that weavers used and the new loom that she had collaboratively designed with the ergonomics expert, Lila decided that she needed to master the entire weaving process – from setting up a loom to laying a warp to weaving and finishing a mat. Otherwise, she would not be able to grasp the problems with the existing loom; she would also not be able to design a viable alternative effectively.

Lila had by then spent a year living in Pattamadai and several years making short trips and, being technically proficient and very interested, had grasped the rudiments of weaving. She now decided to dedicate her time to constructing a loom of the kind used by the mat-weavers. In Bangalore, where she lived at the time, she constructed a scaled-down model of the loom, which she referred to as her 'toy loom'. She successfully wove a tiny 4 inch × 9 inch mat on this. While this miniature mat was much appreciated when Lila took it back to Pattamadai, the small loom was also of technical significance. It could be used to try out different warping configurations without going through the protracted task of laying out a warp on the full-size loom. The laying of the warp with even tension throughout is one of the most crucial aspects of not just fine and super-fine mat-weaving but of weaving in general.

Lila then designed a loom based on what she learned from her experience of constructing the 'toy loom', weaving on it and experimenting with warp configurations. Abdul, a weaver closely associated with Craft Enterprises, offered the yard in front of his house, and the newly designed loom was set up there in early 2000. Loom trials were carried out in the last fortnight of January 2000. Weavers who came forward to try the loom were to be compensated for their time with cash payments. While the loom trials were open to anyone who was interested, Lila strongly encouraged weavers closely associated with Craft Enterprises to come at fixed times and work on the loom. The mood seemed positive at the meeting where all this was decided. But even though weavers, especially those close to Lila, did stick to the trials timetable, they did not at all seem convinced about the need to design a new loom.

In Pattamadai in January 2001 I saw the new loom folded up in a corner of the veranda of Abdul's house, where it had been tested a year earlier. I asked him what he thought about it and received a non-committal answer: 'It is okay, but not suitable' (*paravaaillai, aanaal othuvarallai*). Today the loom continues to sit unused in a corner at another location.

Suitability and comfort

Lila, in trying to make a more comfortable loom, sought to enable people to work longer hours, thereby producing more. But comfort is a relative concept. Following Bourdieu, Wilk suggests that when standards are taken for granted, people operate on unspoken shared understanding and physical perception. This includes the concept of 'comfort' (Wilk 2001: 115). Wilk identifies this as naturalization. Submersive naturalization is deeply embedded in bodily practice and habit, profoundly shaping the 'sense of the possibility of any new tool' (2001: 115). Submersive naturalization is not passive, though it may appear so. People actively choose what they are accustomed to, feel comfortable with, and find suits their needs. Lila's loom was a technical masterpiece in some respects, but in others it simply did not suit the requirements of Pattamadai fine mat-weaving.

Weavers value symmetry within a mat with regard to its body, borders, and patterns. This is a strong aesthetic preference. On the extant loom, the mat is laid out fully for the weaver's inspection through every stage of its making. The weaver sits on a low stool placed underneath the warp (Fig. 1). As one section is woven, the stool is moved under it and the weaver sits on the newly woven section in order to continue weaving the next bit. When approximately 9 inches are woven, the weaver gets off the stool, crouches by the mat, and, placing one knuckled fist under and the other over the mat, starts to push

Figure 1. Regina works on a nearly completed mat.

the weft strands together. She thereby compacts the mat, making the fabric as tight as she can. The 9 inches are compacted down to around 5 inches. Once this is done, weaving is resumed, interrupted with periodic breaks to compact the fabric. Once the whole mat is woven, the weaver compacts it again, this time paying special attention to the borders and to any patterns. It is possible through careful compacting to correct any discrepancies between the widths of the different coloured border stripes, to ensure that the pattern emerges clearly, and even to rectify mistakes. Compacting is an extremely difficult task and is usually left to more experienced weavers as it is possible to damage the fabric or fail to achieve a sufficiently tight structure. The final compacting of a mat before cutting it off the loom is a crucial task, and less skilled weavers will often request more skilled ones to help. It is possible for an experienced person to ensure symmetry by making minute adjustments in packing.

One chief difference between the loom already in use in Pattamadai and Lila's loom is the height of the latter. Designed as a loom for a weaver to sit at on a bench (instead of on a low stool placed directly under the warp and just before the section to be woven), the new loom imposes certain changes in the layout of the mat as it is being woven (Fig. 2). Instead of the entire warp being laid out in front of the weaver so that the whole mat and its skeleton prior to weaving are visible, the warp in the modified loom is rolled up underneath the loom at the end furthest from the weaver. After the weaver weaves and packs a section of the mat, s/he rolls up the finished section underneath the warp. As the mat progresses, the rolled-up warp gradually unfolds before the weaver, is woven, compacted, and rolled up again.

On the loom commonly in use in Pattamadai, it is important to note that the weaver travels the length of the mat as s/he weaves it. At no stage in the weaving process is any part of the mat hidden from the weaver's or anyone else's eyes. This facilitates the general concern to ensure symmetry in border widths and patterning. The desire for symmetry is difficult to satisfy on Lila's loom. The weaver has to pay greater attention to the exact *number* of weft strands in different colours used throughout the mat, something that practitioners tend to measure with their eyes. In a household with many members, no single person monopolizes the loom. Should the person on the loom get up to attend to some task, someone else might move onto the loom and carry on weaving. The fact that the entire mat (the woven and yet-to-be woven sections) is visible to everyone considerably aids this way of working.

Even in households where weaving provides the main source of income, people spend a few hours on the loom and intersperse weaving with other activities. People sometimes take days off weaving if there is a marriage in the house or some other opportunity presents itself, or if they can afford it. In these instances, the loom is rolled up and put away, even with a half-done mat on it. Because of the whole new component of height on Lila's modified loom, it is not possible to roll it up and put it away in order to acquire more space.

Furthermore, the extant loom requires little financial investment. Most of its components are found to hand or quickly and cheaply fashioned by local carpenters. Wooden poles form the tripod and define the spatial limits of the loom at either end. A smooth stick inserted through the warp separates it into two interchangeable vertical layers through which weft strands can pass. The *kuchali*, or 'needle', used to insert weft strands through the warp is also made using a smooth stick with a hole on one end. There is only one component that is difficult to source and relatively expensive: this is the *achu*, or reed, which is used to space warp threads evenly and also to tighten the

Figure 2. Hassan Fathima sits at the new loom prototype.

weft.[5] The new loom has a few more complicated parts: pedals to move the warp up or down; a roller device to roll up and unroll woven sections and unwoven warp, respectively; a frame to lift the warp off the ground; and a high stool or bench. All of these have to be bought or somehow acquired, stored, and maintained. This requires more time, money, and storage space than most weavers are willing to spare. When there is a loom that works, why expend energy and resources on a new loom that, on the face of it, does not confer any significant advantage?

It is not that the weavers are closed to innovations. Indeed, a number have emerged from within the weaving group and have been taken up over the last century or so. All the weavers' own innovations, however, have tended to focus on shortening various processes, thereby speeding up the production of mats without significantly changing their quality. This includes laying the warp with shop-bought thread instead of yarn hand-spun in the home.

When it became clear that experienced weavers were not going to 'take to' Lila's loom, she wondered if she should focus her efforts on novice weavers who were not yet habituated to the extant loom. Indeed the site of the trials was crowded with older children and teenagers. And certainly, at least some of the technical problems could be ironed out over time. But I suggest that even those who were excited by the new loom and perhaps willing to use it may not be given the opportunity, resources, or encouragement by other households members to incorporate it into their weaving practice. This is because of a larger underlying issue that, notwithstanding her success in reviving the super-fine mat-weaving industry and her commitment to weaving and bettering work conditions, Lila could not change.

The problem is not with the *loom*; it is with *weaving*

Like Lila, I, too, learned how to weave. But unlike Lila, my learning was not orientated towards problem-solving, nor was it independent. I learned in the spaces in which the Labbais of Pattamadai learned. And like them, I learned that weaving is not highly valued by members of the group, even though it may be praised in public speech acts directed at development practitioners or elites with interests in Pattamadai mats. Notwithstanding Lila's and others' ideas about the national and personal importance of weaving and its relationship to a positive self-identity, few Labbais that I know learned how to weave with the intention of becoming weavers. They did so, or were encouraged to do so, in order to possess a skill that can earn them money.

Money (or, more accurately, the lack of it) causes much anxiety within Pattamadai Labbai households, few of which own agricultural land or have any financial safety nets. In addition to meeting day-to-day expenses, households also have to find money for life-cycle events. These include marriages, where large numbers of people, including every Labbai in the town, need to be feasted; menarche and circumcision celebrations; and funerals. In addition to these are expected and unexpected medical expenses and other expenditures. Borrowing from money-lenders (at high rates of interest) is common practice, as is participation in rolling credit and saving schemes. The above means that almost every Labbai household within Pattamadai requires the economic contribution of adult and teenaged women as well as of men and older boys. What kind of work is chosen for one, or chooses one, depends on the resources available; these include what other people do in the home, the social relationships that can be put to work, financial obligations and the ability to meet them, and, of course, opportunities and constraints.

Certain kinds of work, including securing highly valued jobs in the formal sectors of the economy, require inputs in the way of education beyond secondary-level schooling, which is expensive, especially as it defers the economic contribution of the individual to the household. If a household decides to educate one member at all, it is usually a male who benefits because of the concomitant sacrifices made by others. Other opportunities, including setting up as a trader (of mats, clothing, dry-goods, etc.), require capital, contacts, and specific personal qualities (see Venkatesan 2006). Trading is seen as risky yet worthwhile work. A man can test his powers of persuasion as well as his ability to buy cheap and sell dear. If he does well, he will see rewards. If not, he might have to move on to other kinds of work, including mat-weaving. Simmel's distinction between the producer and the trader is strikingly recognizable in Pattamadai: 'In trade, which alone makes possible unlimited combinations, intelligence always finds expansions and new territories, an achievement which is very difficult to achieve for the original producer with his lesser mobility' (Simmel, 1950: 403).

Most men see trading as a far more preferable alternative to the drudgery of weaving. The weaver cannot be mobile. The very nature of his occupation requires his physical presence at the loom, which is firmly fixed in space within the home. Men for whom weaving is the main source of livelihood see themselves as powerless and are likewise perceived by others. Local Labbai mat-traders to whom weavers sell their mats reinforce this. Traders frequently say that weaving is women's work, thereby feminizing all weavers.

Some men migrate for up to three years to the Middle East on labour contracts. Again, they or their households have to put up large sums of money in advance in order to secure jobs and work permits through agents. Men often speak of the jobs they do in the Middle East in dire terms, yet there is an element of excitement in the opportunity to travel and about the possible money to be earned. On their return from the Middle East, these men either make plans to return to the region on new contracts or they remain in Pattamadai, taking up weaving or trading.

Most men, then, move in and out of different occupations, some taking up mat-weaving during the interim periods. The work of weaving is associated with a lack of enterprise, ability, and opportunity, especially for men who need to weave regularly and not merely occasionally. Because it is based within the home, weaving is seen as work that keeps a man from making his mark in the public sphere. Weaving carries with it a whiff of lack of enterprise, ability, and opportunity.

Women do not venture far from their homes, so making a mark in the public sphere is a lesser issue than it is for men. Once Pattamadai Labbai girls reach menarche they are confined to their homes and immediate environs. From this time until their marriages, girls help around the house with cooking and are actively encouraged to learn household-based skills that can earn money. This is not only so that they can contribute economically; equally important is the concern to give a girl some resources that can hold her in good stead throughout her life. As the mother of a teenage girl said, 'We teach girls how to weave and to roll *beedis* [leaf-cigarettes] as a way of giving them a choice. A boy can always go out and work, but a girl cannot and she may need to have some way of making money after her marriage'.

Marriage alleviates some of the restrictions placed on young women, but they remain spatially bound to their homes and immediate environs. Few take up employment outside the home even if they need to earn money. In homes where women produce mats that are sold to local or other traders, weaving is recognized as crucial to household subsistence. Notwithstanding this, women often deplore the fact that they *need* to earn money. In the homes of 'people of means' (*vasadhi ullavanga*), women do not work. This ideal makes many women ambivalent about weaving as well as about other home-based income-generating activities, namely *beedi*-rolling, which is undertaken for large locally based companies. Certainly, many younger women say they prefer *beedi*-rolling to weaving because they can take their baskets of tobacco, leaves, and string to their verandas, sit with other girls, and chat as they work.

Payment for *beedi*-rolling is formally organized with a clear payment structure and schedule. By contrast, payment for mats, especially from local traders, is more informal. As noted above, weavers are necessarily dependent on traders to buy and sell on the mats that they make. Local traders do not always pay weavers straightaway for their mats, sometimes withholding payments or partial payments, especially when demand is low. Weavers speak about having to chase up traders day after day for payments due. At other times traders encourage weavers to take advances, thereby binding weavers to them when demand is high. At such times traders or their representatives cycle around the town to visit weavers with mats on their looms and lay claim to the mats, citing previous favours or advances that need repaying. Again, weavers who wish to sell elsewhere or are weaving for their own private purposes feel aggrieved and contrast the behaviour of the traders with that of *beedi* company representatives.

In conversation, men and women emphasize the hard physical labour involved in weaving. They claim that it causes back pain and stomach problems, it weakens eye-sight, and it can affect the reproductive health of young women. And yet, 'what choice do we have?' they ask. 'We need the money.' When there is money available, usually as a result of remittances from the Middle East, people stop weaving, only to take it up when money becomes tight again. It is not that weavers feel no pride or joy in their work. Indeed, sometimes they do. They also always take a great deal of care. If a weaver sees someone else's mat, he or she will comment on the quality of its fabric, its colours and design. But the negative aspects of weaving are emphasized a great deal more.

Making an analogy between weaving and cooking might be useful. Mainly under-taken by women, cooking is a necessary chore, although care is taken in preparing a meal. But there are times, on feast days or special events, when people delight in cooking fine and special dishes. On such occasions both men and women plan and cook the meal and there is much discussion about what to make, how it will be prepared, and by whom. Likewise, there are times when the routine work of making 'yet another mat' becomes charged with interest, enthusiasm, and ambition. For example, one year Khadeeja and her husband, Rahmatullah, who rarely weaves, collaborated on a mat that they wanted to enter into a government-run crafts competition. They spent a great deal of time and energy choosing the design to weave onto the mat (a peacock picked out in colourful silk threads). The mat took them over a month to finish and occasioned both anxiety and excitement, eventually winning an award in the compe-tition. The excitement that weaving generated here, however, is not habitually the case. Like Khadeeja's husband, many men who are capable of weaving do not necessarily want to – at least not all the time.

Marx makes a valuable distinction between work and labour and the very different ways in which each is perceived (see Corsin Jimenez 2003: 15). Work, for Marx, carries use-values. Work is something people enjoy for its own sake; it is its own worth. Labour, on the other hand, is integrated into an economic circuit. It is carried out for money and implies sacrifice and pain of a different order to that implied by work. It is fairly clear that Lila considers weaving as worthwhile work; it is something into which she is willing to invest significant effort. This is not the same for the majority of the Labbais of Pattamadai, for whom weaving is labour most of the time. Only very occasionally does it become worthwhile, usually as an opportunity for gaining public recognition through winning an award. For both male and female Labbai Muslims of Pattamadai, then, while learning how to weave is considered important for subsistence, being a weaver is not necessarily a desirable social status. Weaving here is a means of livelihood bringing in regular sums of money, but simultaneously adversely situating the weaver as powerless, weak, home-bound, and feminized.

Learning to weave, learning to be a weaver

I suggested earlier that the spaces and conditions under which one learns a skill like weaving affect what one *knows* about the skill and its associated ramifications. When I first arrived in Pattamadai and asked people directly about the weaving process and what it involved, I was offered a linear listing of the various processes. Simpson, whose questions about shipbuilding in western India received similar responses, suggests that such a discourse 'is an instantly recognizable form of explanation, which allows us to visualize/imagine the process – even if we are not equipped with the skills ... ourselves' (2006: 161). Furthermore, these kinds of narratives also serve to 'eradicate conflict, freeze the picture, engage with the expectations of the inquirer ..., and lend themselves too readily to re-description because they already exist in linear form' (2006: 161). It is description not exegesis, and it is certainly not the way one can understand what the Labbais of Pattamadai feel about mat-weaving. In a sense this is a form of description that meets the expectations of development practitioners and interested outsiders, without giving very much away.

When I persisted in asking about weaving, I was told that I should watch, see, try, and thus know what the physical work of weaving is all about. It was often suggested that this is not difficult work (in the sense of complicated or hard to get the hang of) even if it is laborious, tedious, and repetitive. One did not need formal training: one could pick it up by being attentive in spaces where weaving and related processes were going on and then have a go with occasional directed instruction. Indeed, as I found out when I learned how to weave in people's homes and later in a government-run apprenticeship scheme, one could pick up many weaving skills by simply 'being around and trying'.

There are many theories of learning that focus on learning as a social process. The following description of how people learn to weave resonates with Vygotsky's concept of the zone of proximal development, which traces the way in which a child observes, then works alongside an experienced adult, gradually becoming capable of doing everything (Goody 1989: 235). It resonates equally with Ingold's description of the learning of craft skills (2001). He describes how novices are encouraged to pay attention to skilled practitioners, to get a feel for things by trying and to engage in what Dilley (1999; following Bourdieu 1990) terms practical mimesis of more skilled practitioners. The constant and minute adjustments made by the weaver in response to the require- ments of the body, the loom, and the raw material, and the working out of problems in the process of weaving, are all testimony to the skilled practice of weaving, mastery over which, as Ingold claims for all craft skills, may be attained only through doing and not by applying prior knowledge to tools and raw materials.

Most people learn the various processes involved in mat-weaving by watching and imitating others. There is no prescribed progression of tasks. Novices try their hand first at whichever task appeals. Several of the tasks go on simultaneously. So, while one mat is on the loom, preparation may be ongoing for the next one(s). As noted above, there is rarely individual ownership over a mat, and different people may be involved in the various processes, from the preparation of the raw materials to the final removal of a mat from a loom.

When a weaving household buys a bundle of *korai* reeds, every reed has already been split vertically by the seller and dried. The reeds need to be soaked in water so that the pith at the centre rots, and the reed can be split into very fine strands. The *korai* is soaked for up to a week in the waters of the Kanadiyan canal, which flows through the town. Almost daily, someone from the household is at the canal to bathe or wash clothes. While there, they check their bundles and bring them home when the reeds are deemed ready. Once in the house, the bundles are opened and the wet reeds are separated and spread out. Whoever has brought the bundle back does this job. The next task, though, is a specialized one that normally only a more experienced weaver under- takes. Inexperienced persons might also try their hand at it, often sitting with more experienced ones and working alongside them.

A reed is picked up and the rotten pith is scraped away with a sharp knife. The rotten outer husk-like covering is also scraped away. What remains of the reed is held up and split into several fine strands. Depending on the level of skill of the person doing this, and the desired texture of the intended mat, between five and eight strands may be split from a single reed. A less skilled individual might only get two or three strands of even thickness throughout the length. But raw materials are cheap and, unless there is a shortage, the small number of strands is not seen as a significant problem – not initially anyway. All measuring is done by eye and hand, or by what one weaver described as *kann nidhanam*, the patient estimate of the eye. Once the split reeds are dyed or dried to their natural creamy-golden colour, they are ready for the loom.

The mat-weaving loom occupies a space of approximately 4 feet by 8 feet and is half a foot or so high. It remains rolled up until required, at which point it is tied to four embedded stakes in a corner of the main room of the house, or, if available, on a partially open weaving platform. The cotton warp needs to be laid before weaving can begin. This is a time-consuming task requiring two skilled people with proficiency in tying one particular kind of knot that demands quick and deft fingers. I had great difficulty learning to tie this knot. The elderly woman who showed me began slowly and patiently, and then, expressing increasing frustration, she muttered 'You can read and write and use a computer, but you cannot even tie a knot!' It was evident that she had gone through the same process with younger people in her household. Along with the other girls I discovered that learning how to tie the knot in isolation is a very different thing from actually employing it to ensure that the entire warp is made up throughout of a single continuous thread of even tension. Here, Ingold's distinction between the light experienced hand and the heavy hand of the novice rings true (2001: 24-5). It is not enough to know from watching and imitating, or being taught, or even trying something for oneself a few times. The ability to improvise in relation to the uneven thickness of a thread, the position of the knot, and so on, comes from experience and situated practice. Skill is an outcome not a prerequisite.

Once the loom is set up and the warp is prepared, anyone in the house who wants to weave the weft strands one by one through the warp, and who has arms long enough, does so. This process of inserting *korai* weft strands through the prepared warp is not difficult, and while a more experienced weaver who is around might give occasional instructions and come to the novice's aid when necessary, by and large the work is carried out in an atmosphere of benign neglect (following Lave & Wenger 1991: 94).

In the home, then, what we find is a combination of directed learning and picking up skill through watching, imitation, and 'having a go'. We also find selective specialization in different tasks connected to weaving.

While most learning takes place within the home or its environs, occasional opportunities to learn outside the house do present themselves. In 1999, 'Kamran' was appointed by the government as a trainer to teach mat-weaving to students who would each be paid a stipend to attend the six-week-long course. Since I was trying to learn to weave and was interested in how other people learned, I attended Kamran's sessions as often as possible. All of the trainees were female; indeed, had there been any young men at the training programme few households would have allowed their girls to attend.[6]

Kamran and a couple of experienced female weavers who were also enrolled as students prepared the looms. Most of the students had watched mothers and others in their homes, and had tried their hand at the various processes involved. Throughout the day the novices sat at the prepared looms and weaved using the *korai* that they had all assisted in preparing, each according to her individual ability. Kamran and the two experienced weaver 'students' helped with compacting and cut the mats off the loom when done.

Kamran harboured ambitions to be a mat-trader. The way in which he ran the apprenticeship training scheme provided him with mats that he could sell in his shop and in the craft bazaars he attended. He had no need to fear competition from the unmarried female apprentices since, as already mentioned, they were largely restricted to their homes. As far as the female trainees were concerned, their stipend received from the government made the course worthwhile. It also provided them an opportunity to leave their homes for a few hours a day and spend time in congenial company. There was a lot of giggling and chatter.

It became clear through listening and participating in various conversations that in the training space, as in their homes, the girls were learning ways of thinking about weaving. These included thinking about weaving as a means to earn money; as a resource if it became necessary for them to provide for their households after their marriages; as difficult work with meagre returns; as one thing they might do alongside other, more valuable things such as marrying, having children, and so on. Although they were happy to spend time outside their homes with others and receive a stipend, few were enthusiastic about the actual mats they were making or the tasks in which they were engaged. Part of the reason for this was that they knew that learning to weave (even as part of a government scheme) would not lead them to anywhere new. The girls felt certain that weaving would only continue to bind them to the spatial boundaries of their households, whether natal or marital. This was not a problem with weaving per se, but rather the issue was that they were Labbai Muslim girls learning to weave. Girls from other groups might be able to make something of the skill, but not them. In an illuminating conversation between me, a few Labbai girls, and two non-Muslim girls on the course,[7] the Labbai girls explored the possibilities that might arise for the non-Labbai girls as a result of the course. It was suggested that the non-Muslim girls, who were not restricted in the same ways as their Labbai counterparts, might go on to teach weaving in other towns as part of future governmental initiatives, or they might receive government jobs and travel. Learning to weave could open new worlds for them in ways that the Labbai girls did not feel were available to them.

Lave and Wenger point out in their model of situated peripheral learning that as a skill is learned, so too are the social values and attitudes within which the skill is practised (discussed in Herzfeld 2004: 51). As she weaves, the weaver is (at least some of the time) thinking about other things: keeping a peripheral eye on the children in the house; aware of the smells and requirements of cooking; feeling unease about the damage done by close attention to weaving to an already inflamed eye; aware of the nagging pain in the small of the back; worrying about how to raise money for the next debt re-payment or the marriage of a household member; or wondering whether the payment for the mat will be made promptly or whether the trader will pay only a small part, promising to pay the balance on receipt of yet another mat. And as she is learning how to weave, the novice is also learning gender-based expectations, attitudes to weaving, the satisfaction, the pain, the unequal relations of power between weavers and traders, and the belief that one puts in more than one gets out. The novice who weaves or engages in related processes rarely wants to be a weaver any more than do her mother, father, siblings, or contemporaries. She learns that becoming a weaver is a dead end rather than a stepping-stone to more interesting things.

The production and transmission of knowledge

In his introduction to this special volume, Marchand reflects on a fragment of conversation from his fieldwork: a trainee in a carpentry workshop completes his instructor's sentence about the suitability of oak for a particular project. The interjection directs the conversation into a discussion about the price of oak; the listener/reader is left in doubt as to whether this was what the instructor intended or whether there was something else she might have wanted to say about oak, but did not. Marchand's exploration of the shared production of knowledge suggests that sometimes, despite the best intentions, interlocutors may speak past each other in such a way that they fail to communicate. Lila's sensitive attempt to design an improved loom and its resultant failure has led me, too, to think about shared knowledge production and missed communication. How is it that Lila, who worked with the Pattamadai weavers for several years, learned to weave successfully, and helped revitalize the super-fine mat-weaving industry, nevertheless ended up spending time, energy, and resources on a project that was clearly of little interest and unsuited to its intended beneficiaries? I think that this is partly a result of the very different kinds of knowledge held by Lila and by the Labbais of Pattamadai about weaving and its desirability as an occupation

Lila came to Pattamadai with the very clear idea that the super-fine mat-weaving industry was equally valuable for the weavers as it is for the nation. Craft Enterprises' position was that weavers were giving up weaving because they had no other choice, and the NGO's role was to make that choice available through strategic support and through improving the conditions of work. The Labbais of Pattamadai, however, do not really see weaving as a choice. On the contrary, it is lack of choice that leads many of them to turn to weaving. This is rarely stated explicitly, and certainly never to development practitioners from whom weavers hope to benefit. Rather, in conversations with development practitioners, explicit complaints about weaving are made regarding the exploitative nature of the traders and the need for marketing support. To this extent, the kind of information transmitted is selected and selective. It pertains to areas that development practitioners are expected to address.

Toren (2009) argues strongly that 'we bring to any given encounter with any other our own unique history, that is, the history that we have lived, that makes us who we are, the history out of which we speak, and listen to, and understand others. We cannot help but assimilate others' terms to our own'. As a designer by training, a person with an abiding interest and commitment to craft, and someone with a good sense of the materials and processes, Lila values the Pattamadai mat-weaving industry, the skills of the weavers, and the objects they produce. As far as I could tell from my conversations with her over the years, she was aware that her enthusiasm for weaving surpassed that of the weavers. She certainly hoped that her efforts would make weaving a desirable option for the Labbais of Pattamadai. Indeed, her work in setting up a reliable and efficient system wherein the NGO would buy mats from weavers, making prompt payments and then selling on the mats in urban areas, is testimony to her recognition that weaving is first and foremost a matter of livelihood. Her attempt to improve the loom likewise came from her taking seriously weavers' grumblings (rarely couched as explicit complaints) about bodily troubles and discomfort caused by weaving.

Lila's loom is proof of her problem-solving capacities, but as far as the weavers were concerned, it was the wrong problem: it is not the *loom* that makes weaving laborious and painful; the problem is having to weave in the first place. In a sense, one might say that Lila took on board what was explicitly stated by weavers as the problems with weaving and she sought to resolve them. But the explicit complaints masked underlying implicitly held knowledge about weaving as undervalued labour. This was not something that could be explicitly tackled – nebulous and embedded as it is in the entirety of Pattamadai Labbai life. Lila's knowledge of weaving as worthwhile work in and of itself was something about which even the weavers she worked most closely with remained unconvinced.

A trader who was scornful of the entire project of improving the loom, while also curious about it, supplied his own reasons for its failure. 'This is women's work', he said, though being fully aware that some male weavers were participating in the trial, 'and women are not good at picking up new things'. I read his statement as one that positions weaving firmly in the sphere of women – weak, defenceless people who have few choices but make the most of what they have without seeking to improve their lot. What he was saying was that people who could successfully work with new ideas, incorporate new technologies, take advantage of new opportunities, would not be weavers. This, too, is common knowledge within Pattamadai and the reason why even those who can weave do not want to be weavers.

Conclusion

I suggested early on that Lila and I were similar in some ways. We were both interested in Pattamadai mat-weaving and both lived in Pattamadai among the weavers with whom we worked. The difference between us, however, is that, as a development practitioner, Lila knew what she was doing in Pattamadai in terms of developing the mat-weaving industry. Once she had settled down to her work, Lila's encounters with weavers were by and large directed and focused on production times, costs, training, sales, and designs. They were active and practical conversations about plans, problems, and possible solutions.

As the anthropologist, I did not know *exactly* what I was doing in Pattamadai (see Herzfeld 2007). I was around, interested, learning to weave or to cook, asking questions that sometimes led somewhere specific but most of the time opened up unanticipated conversations. Without being fully aware, I perhaps always knew about the low worth placed on weaving in Pattamadai. The lukewarm response to, and ultimate failure of, Lila's thoughtful attempt to modify the loom brought several conversations and insights together more clearly not only for me, but also for Lila, as we discussed in detail the project, its underpinnings, aims, and assumptions. Nevertheless, differences in what we conceived as our roles in Pattamadai persisted. When I finished my doctoral thesis and gave it to Lila to read, we had a telling conversation. She said she agreed with large parts of my analysis and understanding of the mat-weaving industry, but she had a question: what was I going to do now? Surprised, I said, 'Nothing. I guess people will read my work and it might inform their work'. Unsurprisingly this response did not satisfy her. Indeed, how could it, pointing as it does to the gulf between knowing for the sake of knowing and knowing in order to act?

Anthropologists have long been critical about 'development' (e.g. Escobar 1995; Ferguson 1994; Grillo & Stirrat 1997; Hobart 1993; however see Venkatesan & Yarrow 2010). As Herzfeld (2007) puts it, we are on the side of the marginalized – the same people whom development professionals seek to 'help'. The suspicion directed at development (and, by extension, development professionals) is often in diametric contrast to the value anthropologists place on 'local knowledge' and the attachment of the people with whom we work to their 'traditional practices', including artisanal or craft work. Indeed, anthropological studies of skill acquisition within artisanal groups have frequently focused on the kinds of skills that are valued both socially and by the individuals seeking to acquire them (an exception is Herzfeld 2004). This has given a particular flavour to anthropological understandings of artisanal work, and the value accorded to it – its world-creating abilities (Brouwer 1996), its rich symbolic content (e.g. Guss 1990) – analogically and to notions of embodied skill as doing rather than knowing (Ingold 2001). By contrast, this chapter has focused on a sensitive and thoughtful intervention made by a development practitioner among a group of artisanal producers who are themselves ambivalent about what they describe as their traditional occupation of mat-weaving. In doing so, I sought to explore the embodied and historicized production of knowledge by different kinds of person: the weavers of Pattamadai, a development professional, and, to a certain extent, an anthropologist.

I have argued in this chapter that when people learn craft skills in a socially embedded setting, they also learn how to think about the work this enskilment will enable them to do. The anthropology of learning in such cases has to incorporate the anthropology of work. When someone from a different social setting learns the same skill, they may acquire mastery over it but may not *know* what the skill entails for those who need to practise it.

A final word about knowledge. People in Pattamadai know that development initiatives come and go, even if individual development practitioners are completely committed to working with them. This is something they are prepared for. A development initiative may be beneficial while it lasts. When it is gone, it is business as usual (see Venkatesan 2006). Craft Enterprises no longer exists. Its funding ceased in 2001 and with it went the regular and stable market that it had created and nurtured. Although Lila has stopped working on modifying the loom, she continues to work with some weavers, designing and marketing mats. We remain in contact and she remains concerned about helping the mat-weaving industry. Most of the mat-weavers who worked with Crafts Enterprises have perforce had to return to the local traders who continue to buy mats when they need them and delay payments. The Labbais of Pattamadai continue to move in and out of weaving their high-quality mats as opportunities and constraints dictate. And they continue to know that weaving is not a choice, but a lack of choice.

NOTES

I am grateful to the people of Pattamadai for their friendship and for allowing me access to their homes and looms. I am also grateful to 'Lila' for years of conversations. Trevor Marchand's comments have been invaluable in thinking through this chapter. Other contributors to this book also provided valuable comments. Thanks to Christina Toren for permitting me to cite her unpublished paper. I am also thankful for feedback received at the *Transmission of knowledge* seminar series at SOAS and the Social Anthropology seminar at Manchester where versions of this chapter were presented. Any problems that remain are, of course, my responsibility.

[1] I began my doctoral fieldwork in Pattamadai in 1997, and each year throughout my Ph.D. and since completion I have spent several months there.

[2] Two qualities of mats are woven in Pattamadai. Medium-quality or 'fine mats' are of 50 count while high-quality or 'super-fine' mats are of 100-40 count, meaning every 9 inches of warp is made up of between 100 and 140 threads. Super-fine mats take thrice as long to make as fine mats and are consequently proportionately more expensive to buy from weavers.

[3] The number grew to eight by 1998 though dropped to six by 2000 as one weaver stopped working with the NGO and another gave up weaving altogether.

[4] The prices were established through consultation and discussion and were almost double what local traders would pay for the same mats. It must be remembered that Craft Enterprises, selling in more up-market spaces than local traders could access, could also market the mats for far higher prices than the Labbai traders of Pattamadai.

[5] The super-fine mat-weaving *achu*, like the cloth-weaving *achu*, has a wooden frame and very fine metal 'eyes'. Craft Enterprises located a maker of *achu* for sari-weavers and commissioned him to make

mat-weaving *achu*. This was successful, and several weavers bought new *achu* to replace their old and damaged ones (see Venkatesan 2009*a*: chap. 9 for more details).

[6] As a middle-aged married man, Kamran was not seen as a cause for concern. Further, the way in which the idiom of kinship is mobilized in Pattamadai means that most teenagers at the training programme refer to him as either a paternal or maternal 'uncle' (*mama, chacha, periappa*, etc.).

[7] Both of these girls were enrolled in accordance with the government ruling that members of scheduled and/or backward castes (SC/BC) be represented within the training scheme. Neither went on to weave.

REFERENCES

BOURDIEU, P. 1990. *The logic of practice* (trans. R. Nice). Stanford: Univesity Press.

BROUWER. J. 1996. *Makers of the world: caste, craft and mind*. Delhi: Oxford University Press.

CORSIN JIMENEZ, A. 2003. Working out personhood: notes on 'labour' and its anthropology. *Anthropology Today* **19**: 5, 14-17.

DILLEY, R. 1999. Ways of knowing, forms of power. *Cultural Dynamics* **11**, 33-55.

ESCOBAR, A. 1995. *Encountering development: the making and unmaking of the Third World*. Princeton: University Press.

FERGUSON, J. 1994. *The anti-politics machine: 'development', depoliticization, and bureaucratic power in Lesotho*. Minneapolis: University of Minnesota Press.

GOODY, E.N. 1989. Learning, apprenticeship and the division of labour. In *Apprenticeship: from theory to method and back again* (ed.) M.W. Coy, 233-56. Albany, N.Y.: SUNY Press.

GRILLO, R.D. & R.L. STIRRAT (eds) 1997. *Discourses of development: anthropological perspectives*. Oxford: Berg.

GUSS, D.M. 1990. *To weave and sing: art symbol and narrative in the South American rainforest*. Berkeley: University of California Press.

HERZFELD, M. 2004. *The body impolitic: artisans and artifice in the global hierarchy of value*. Chicago: University Press.

——— 2007. Deskilling, 'dumbing down' and the auditing of knowledge in the practical mastery of artisans and academics: an ethnographer's response to a global problem. In *Ways of knowing: new approaches in the anthropology of experience and learning* (ed.) M. Harris, 91-112. Oxford: Berghahn.

HOBART, M. 1993. *An anthropological critique of development: the growth of ignorance*. London: Routledge.

INGOLD, T. 2001. Beyond art and technology: the anthropology of skill. In *Anthropological perspectives on technology* (ed.) M.B. Schiffer, 17-32. Albuquerque: University of New Mexico Press.

LAVE, J. & E. WENGER 1991. *Situated learning: legitimate peripheral participation*. Cambridge: University Press.

NAMBIAR, P K. 1964. *Fine mats of Pattamadai*, vol. IX: *Madras*, part VII-A-IV: *Handicrafts and artisans of Madras State, Census of India 1961*. Madras: Census of India.

PATE, H.R. 1917. *Gazetteer of the Tinnelvelly district*, vol. 1: *Madras District Gazetteers*. Madras: Government Press.

RAO, N. 1929. *Report on survey of cottage industries*. Madras: Government Press.

SENNETT, R. 2008. *The craftsman*. London: Penguin.

SIMMEL, G. 1950. The stranger. In *The sociology of Georg Simmel* (ed.) K. Wolff, 402-8. New York: Free Press.

SIMPSON, E. 2006. Apprenticeship in western India. *Journal of the Royal Anthropological Institute* (N.S.) **12**, 151-71.

TOREN, C. 2009. Imagining the world that warrants our imagination – the revelation of ontogeny. Unpublished paper presented at the *Materializing the subject* conference, Manchester, February.

VENKATESAN, S. 2006. Shifting balances in a 'craft community': the mat-weavers of Pattamadai, South India. *Contributions to Indian Sociology* (N.S.) **40**, 63-89.

——— 2009*a*. *Craft matters: artisans, 'development' and the Indian nation*. Delhi: Orient Blackswan.

——— 2009*b*. Rethinking agency: persons and things in the heterotopia of 'traditional Indian craft'. *Journal of the Royal Anthropological Institute* (N.S.) **15**, 78-95.

——— & T. YARROW (eds) 2010. *Differentiating development: beyond an anthropology of critique*. Manuscript submitted for publication.

WALLMAN, S. 1979. Introduction. In *Social anthropology of work* (ed.) S. Wallman, 1-24. London: Academic Press.

WILK, R.R. 2001. Towards an anthropology of needs. In *Anthropological perspectives on technology* (ed.) M.B. Schiffer, 107-22. Albuquerque: University of New Mexico Press.

9

Reflections on knowledge practices and the problem of ignorance

Roy Dilley *University of St Andrews*

Much anthropological literature on knowledge regards the issue of knowing as a relatively unproblematic accumulation of what it is that people claim to know about the world, about their social relations, about their cosmology, and so forth. The anthropology of knowledge has grown apace over the last twenty-five years or so (Crick 1982), and knowledge posited as a salient category of anthropological investigation has become almost commonplace in our methods. We anthropologists freely talk too of 'bodily knowledge', as opposed to conceptual or cerebral knowledge. In addition, problems of anthropological inquiry have focused on the examination of how knowledge might be transmitted, communicated, passed on, or disseminated, to name but a few metaphors. But in a number of ways I consider the posing of these problems to be premature, for a prior issue has to be raised about knowledge, in whatever form, and about its reproduction through social relations. That topic is rarely considered, and it is the flip-side to knowledge, namely 'not knowing' or 'ignorance'. To talk of knowledge without recognition of the potential of ignorance is like speaking of velocity without a conception of distance.

My argument in brief is that knowledge and ignorance must be regarded as mutually constituting, not simply in terms of an opposition by means of which one is seen as the negation of the other, but also in terms of how a dialectic between knowledge and ignorance is played out in specific sets of social and political relations; indeed, how, too, moral value is placed upon knowledge and ignorance in various ways. If knowledge is transmitted, communicated, disseminated, or exchanged through social relations, it is given form and process by the potentiality of ignorance, of not-knowing, either as an absence in and of itself, or as a willed and intentional stance towards the world. If knowledge and ignorance are mutually constituting, then there must be consequences for the way in which they inform relations of learning. I aim to examine some of those consequences and implications below. Murray Last points out 'the importance of knowing about not-knowing', of the understandable 'reluctance in ethnography to record what people do not know ...; [for] it is hard enough to record what they do know' (1992: 393).[1] My goal in this chapter is to trace some features of the importance of knowing about not-knowing.

The first question to be addressed is the place of ignorance within the conceptual schemes laid out by anthropologists of knowledge, and more broadly within Western thought. These reflections are of a general and theoretical nature, but I hope to highlight the importance of not-knowing as a critical issue to be considered in investigations of knowledge; in particular, how we have framed our conceptions of ignorance and what kinds of moral loads they carry in different disciplinary domains. The second set of questions will refer to more ethnographically situated reflections on the relationship between knowledge and ignorance in specific contexts of social and political relations, such as those obtaining among Senegalese craftsmen or within French colonial practice.[2]

General orientations

My initial thoughts on these matters were triggered by a nineteenth-century St Andrews' philosopher, James Frederick Ferrier. He raised the problem of ignorance in relation to his discussion of epistemology in *Institutes of metaphysic* (1854). Father of the term of 'epistemology', Ferrier also gave birth to the idea of 'agnoiology', the theory of ignorance. Epistemology, the science of knowing and what is known, was contrasted with 'agnoiology', the doctrine of those things of which we are necessarily ignorant; that department of philosophy which inquires into the character and conditions of ignorance, according to the *Oxford English dictionary* (*OED*), or, in Ferrier's words 'the theory of true ignorance'. Ignorance was one element of his rationalist philosophical system, which comprised of epistemology, agnoiology, and ontology – theories of knowledge, ignorance, and being, respectively.[3]

The term 'epistemology' gained a wide currency in philosophical discourse as well as in more general English usage; yet the label of agnoiology never achieved a similar status, and as a concept was never developed theoretically to the same extent. Why this should be is a question philosophers are perhaps best equipped to answer. It would seem, none the less, as though ignorance is considered to be a blank space, and little can be said about blank spaces. What I take from Ferrier is the insight that the character and condition of ignorance are intimately linked to claims to knowledge: 'ignorance guarantees potential knowledge'. This reinforces the point that the one mutually informs the other, and although this may be an obvious point, it is one that we can elaborate on as anthropologists, especially if we introduce social relations into the equation, as well as the moral and political universes in which they are summoned as salient categories of thought.

Perhaps we should start this series of reflections by considering our own vocabulary referring to 'not knowing', and the semantic fields it defines. Our word 'ignorance' derives from the Latin '*ignorâre*', a compound meaning 'not to know' and comprising the negative prefix '*in*' or 'not' and the verb '*noscere*' (root – *nos*, to become acquainted with, to recognize, perceive, or acknowledge): that is, 'to know', in the sense of 'to perceive or apprehend' by the senses. The lack or want of knowledge might best be coined 'nescience', an absence about which philosophers have had little further to say after Ferrier. The term 'nescience' is derived from another Latin verb, '*scire*' (root – *scio*, to know or understand), meaning 'to know' by the mind rather than by the senses, and is prefixed by '*ne*' or 'not', giving the sense of 'not to know'. Our English verb 'to know' covers ground formerly occupied by several verbs, a distinction still retained in other languages, such as French, in which the separate meanings are captured by the verbs '*savoir*' and '*connaître*'.[4] Similarly, our English word 'ignorance', while derived from the Latin verb referring to not-knowing by the senses, has come to indicate not-knowing in both meanings.

Knowledge and nescience have not remained, however, timeless universals in a discourse of philosophical speculation, nor are they devoid of moral value; indeed, they are located in ethical discourses about knowing and not-knowing of different sorts. Specifically, they are subject to moral evaluation in theological reflection on the nature of knowledge and ignorance. A primal state of not-knowing in Christian theology is represented prior to the fall of humankind, and is overturned by the act of Eve offering Adam the fruit of the tree of knowledge. This primal state implies not only a state of ignorance, but also one of grace and innocence; it was only later transfigured into a state of knowledge and shame: 'For God doth know that in the day ye eat thereof, then your eyes shall be opened, and ye shall be a god, knowing good and evil' (Genesis 3, v. 5, King James version); 'And the eyes of them both were opened, and they knew that they were naked' (Genesis 3, v. 7).

In this context a state of ignorance bears a virtuous moral load; the primal state of not-knowing is a state of innocence that suggests a positive gloss on the morality of ignorance, a pristine condition in the history of humankind according to the Christian tradition. It was only after this act that Adam 'knew' Eve, in the sense of having carnal knowledge of her: 'And Adam knew his wife; and she conceived, and bare Cain' (Genesis 4, v. 1). Virginity, an absence of carnal knowledge, is here construed as a state of not-knowing, of ignorance and innocence, again a pristine condition that bears a positive moral value in Christian discourse. These are primarily referents to not-knowing by the senses, and they tend to carry positive valuations and moral connotations of innocence.

The state of ignorance as nescience, however, bears a different moral load, and it carries ethical imperatives for expunging ignorance by revealing knowledge of the divine message to mortal humankind. The imperative to engender learning has profound historical and institutional importance for the transmission of the Christian message. The state of being ignorant, a lack of knowledge, was discussed at great length from the time of the Middle Ages by theologians. Their concerns, which still echo today within Catholic theology, were focused on two aspects of this subject. On the one hand there was 'vincible' or 'wilful' ignorance that a person might reasonably be expected to overcome, and which could never be used as an excuse for sin. On the other, there was 'invincible' ignorance, which humans could not help or abate, and altogether excuses the person from guilt related to sins that he or she might commit unknowingly. In theological debate, therefore, the mere want of knowledge presumes no necessary liability or responsibility on the part of the human subject; but a state of ignorance which is imputable is a lack of knowledge about a thing or subject in a human being capable of knowing, and who has a requirement or some sort of social obligation to know. When ignorance is deliberately aimed at, when it is sought by a person for a particular purpose, then the consequences are severe from a theological standpoint. In short, nescience is not necessarily a mortal sin, but wilful ignorance is.[5]

These two senses of ignorance are reflected in the *OED* definitions of the term: ignorance is 'the fact or condition of being ignorant; a want of knowledge (general or specific)'; the second is ignorance as wilful and intentioned. The latter sense is captured by the verb 'to ignore', which used to mean 'not to know', but this meaning became obsolete in English by the 1700s. (This sense still exists in French, as in '*je l'ignore*' – 'I don't know'.) The verb in English carries also the meaning of 'to refuse to take notice of; not to recognise, to disregard intentionally, to leave out of account, to shut one's eyes to' (*OED*). One cluster of meanings, therefore, describes a sense of the limits to knowledge, the lack of knowing in some general or specific way. The second meaning involves intentionality, the direction of attention, a sense of agency and of an agent's consciousness.

These introductory remarks have highlighted a number of areas of investigation that I now want to take forward in a more explicitly anthropological way. In summary, there are a number of points to develop. First, our verb 'to know' captures in one semantic field at least two senses that remain distinct in other languages: 'to know by the senses' and 'to know by the mind'. Not-knowing in reference to each of these senses implies very different kinds of consequence. Not to know by the mind might be mistakenly understood as stupidity, but is captured by the term 'nescience', and in specific contexts carries a negative moral load. Not to know by the senses, a lack of awareness, is more ambiguous, and in certain contexts carries positive connotations. This Cartesian dualism appears to be significant to our own occidental ways of conceiving knowledge and ignorance; and knowing by the senses might be particularly pertinent to our conceptions of bodily knowledge, a subject to which I will turn below. Finally, the sense of not-knowing as the 'refusal to take notice of' will also be developed later.

An anthropology of ignorance

The kinds of question that appear to me to be perfectly well within an anthropological domain of competence, rather than a philosophical or theological one, relate to the place of ignorance in specific social and cultural situations. For example: What are the social consequences of ignorance? What do social practices of knowledge and ways of knowing tell us about conceptions of ignorance in any particular social milieu? Do all claims to knowledge cast a shadow that is to be demarcated as a domain of ignorance? Are accounts of knowledge and their shadow accounts of ignorance always mutually defining, to paraphrase Fardon (1990)? In this work, an ethnographic treatment of Chamba knowledge and ignorance in West Africa, Fardon limits himself to 'not knowing' and 'not paying attention to' as two crucial aspects of accounts of ignorance.[6] This preliminary limitation is necessary since there is simply not space here to trace through other, more subtle ways by which not-knowing may be construed, such as social memory and forgetfulness; presence and absence; deskilling and audit;[7] ideology, repression, and masking; strategy and power. I will ignore, too, literary reflections on ignorance, such as Milan Kundera's emigrants (2002), whose nostalgia and sense of not-knowing are mixed in painful relations of hope and desire; or Philip Larkin's musings on the subject (1988). I will restrict myself to not-knowing as absence, and the kinds of metaphors through which that lack is marked; and to not-knowing as 'a refusal to take notice of', and to the moral and political implications of such an attitude. The latter sense of ignorance involving the intentionality of the actor places the analysis firmly in the political domain: consider, for example, the power of pretending not to know as seen in the figure of Agatha Christie's Miss Marple, whose self-deprecating public proclamations of ignorance mask a nuanced understanding far more complex than that of the unfortunate, plodding local police inspector. These ways of knowing and not-knowing are a precondition, I argue, for the organization and distribution of relations of learning within specific contexts.

Mark Hobart picks up on the theme of the mutuality of knowledge and ignorance by arguing that the growth of knowledge entails the growth of ignorance. Indeed, he asks (Hobart 1993: 20), is ignorance always to be construed in the same way? Ignorance, he continues, 'differs in degree and kind according to the presuppositions of different knowledges' (1993: 21). If we are concerned with varieties of ways of knowing, should we also be attentive to differences in the ways of ignorance? These considerations have consequences for how perceived ignorance is overcome, and how the processes of knowledge production and learning are manifested in concrete social relations and institutions.

One example drawn from my fieldwork in Senegal may illustrate this point, and act as a counterpoint to our conceptions of ignorance. From two linguistic roots in Pulaar are derived a number of terms referring to states of ignorance. The first is *hump/kump*, which gives verbal forms that can be translated as 'to be or to remain unknown', 'to lack information about' or 'news on' a particular subject, event, or person. A substantive form, '*kumpta*', can also mean 'mystery', something that remains unknown; and '*humam binne*' refers to an ignorant person, one who is not informed – a term that carries a pejorative connotation.

The second linguistic root is '*majj*', as in the word '*majjere*', meaning 'misconception' or ignorance linked to a lack of learning: for example, a proverb suggests 'ignorance will remain with he who does not respect his teacher'. But it can also take a verbal form indicating 'to be lost', or 'to go astray'. This sense has numerous connotations for a people amongst whom the concept of the 'path' is central:[8] for those who are pastoralists it refers to the '*lawol pulaaku*' – the way of life of pastoralists; for those who are sedentary and historically more Islamized than the former, it is used figuratively to indicate the '*lawol Allah*', the path of Allah, of the Muslim religion and its prescriptions. Being lost or going astray in this latter context resonates with the idea of an ignorance connected with a deviation from Allah, the ultimate source of Islamic knowledge. Going astray from the way of the pastoralist, in the former sense, means to leave behind the qualities of fortitude, reserve, and forethought, no longer to herd cattle or follow the disciplines of this way of life. Not knowing here refers to deviation from some sort of true or proper path.[9]

The two senses of ignorance indicated above, coalescing around the linguistic roots *hump/kump* and *majj*, also give on to particular consequences for learning. The first sense of 'to remain unknown' or 'to lack information about' provides the grounds for a series of knowledge practices that are aimed at bridging the gulf of ignorance with respect to earthly, human, and spiritual matters. Forms of divinatory practice, for instance, ways of 'seeing' into the constellations of events and future possibilities, are the sciences that address this form of ignorance. The manner in which relations of learning are organized with respect to these esoteric sciences involves intimate master-disciple links that exclude others from the dissemination of this form of knowledge.[10] The perpetuation of ignorance in certain sectors of the population – a necessary condition for the construction of local expertise – is highlighted by the creation of restricted yet intense relations of learning in forms of either craft apprenticeship or religious disciple-hood among those selected to take part in these sciences.

The second sense of ignorance, as in 'going astray', implies an element of human agency, of wilful neglect on the part of the pupil, or of a lack of awareness of direction, both geographical and moral. To lose one's way, either as a pastoralist or as a religious disciple, is a failure of human responsibility, and is not only a symptom of ignorance, but produces further ignorance in its train, by straying from a recognized path of knowledge. There are thus moral and spiritual consequences to this form of not-knowing. Indeed, one of the consequences of pastoralists leaving the path of cattle-herding to settle as agriculturalists is the lament from those who remain as herders about the growth of ignorance about nomadism as a life-style.

Finally, the root 'majj' can take an adjectival form to refer both to those who are lost in a literal sense, and to those who are ignorant, indeed illiterate – that is, not versed in the language of the Qur'an. It was also used in the past to refer to domestic serviles held in bondage, whose social condition was considered little higher than that of domestic animals. This rank of people were considered totally lacking in the knowledge of the freeborn social rank, and they were excluded from the networks of knowledge trans-mission among either the literate Muslim cleric class or the artisan and musicians ranks, for whom knowledge was passed on by means of bodily training and oral instruction.

Claims to knowledge and accusations of ignorance can be illustrated by the Sene-galese case of Haalpulaar bondsmen (maccube), who took up weaving as part of their duties towards the household of their master. As craftsmen, they were considered distinct from the 'caste' of weavers (mabube), and were not credited with any form of esoteric knowledge associated with the craft as practised by the recognized hereditary craftsmen. Nonetheless, during my fieldwork in the 1980s, a number of bondsmen weavers constructed their own versions of weaving origin myths that mirrored those of the mabube (Dilley 1987). These versions retained certain similarities with mabu myths, such as the idea that weaving was discovered by humans through an encounter with spirits (jinn) practising the craft in the bush. However, one of the significant differences was that it was Malal, the bondsman of Juntel – the mabu mythical ancestor – who made the discovery, and not Juntel himself, a key figure in mabu definitions of their own pedigrees.

It would seem that the bondsmen, recognizing the attributions of ignorance ascribed to them by others, responded by claiming a form of knowledge that would stand as an alternative account to mabu constructions of themselves as craft experts. These accounts, however, were dismissed by mabu weavers as presumptuous, as misguided attempts by bondsmen that were based on a misconception of the true and proper origins of weaving. Such attempts were regarded as the products of those who were lost, and their claims to knowledge were further evidence of their ignorance.

A second set of examples in a similar vein illustrate how claims to knowledge and accusations of ignorance are articulated in relations first among mabube weavers themselves, and second between these weavers and Islamic clerics (toorobe).[11]

It was suggested during my apprenticeship to a mabu master weaver that I should consult an old and venerable weaver in a village in Fuuta Toro, in the north of Senegal. I subsequently spent some time with the old man, and recorded his versions of weaving origin myths. These were radical reinterpretations of stories I had become familiar with, and they cast the origins of weaving back to the time of Eve (the spinner of thread) and Adam (the weaver of cloth). The figure of the Prophet Muhammad also appeared, and he was portrayed as chiding those who would mock weavers for prac-tising their craft – an honourable profession now with a prestigious ancestry. Juntel, the mythical ancestor, had similarly been transformed and recast as a 'saint' in an Islamic tradition that stretched back to the beginning of time. On returning to my master weaver, I discussed with him the version the old man had recited to me, and he was shocked to hear of this reinterpretation. This version strayed from *mabu* orthodoxy, and had become an Islamized rendering of weaving's origins. It was fallacious, he claimed; the old man was losing his senses. He had become lost in his sense of direction of *mabu* ancestry and had fabricated a myth that confused two separate paths to knowledge: namely one of the craft specialist and the other of the Islamic cleric, each with its own set of restricted learning practices.

The other example involves a discussion that took place between a cleric and my master weaver at a naming ceremony held at a house just outside Dakar in 1981. The meal had been served and the guests, most of whom had finished eating, were relaxing in the shade of a tree in the courtyard. A lively exchange ensued when the cleric, having heard of my interest in weaving, brought up the idea that the craft had originated with the spider, whose example had inspired humans to develop the craft after observing the its web.[12] My master vehemently opposed this suggestion, arguing that weaving came from the *jinn* in the bush, and that the weavers had taken it from them.

This clash of knowledge claims produced accusations of ignorance by both parties with regard to their respective adversaries in the exchange. Each one argued from a position of knowledge, which they had differently acquired by means of their own social specific processes of knowledge transmission. Each man accused the other of straying from his own specialized province of knowledge; his adversary had evinced an ignorance, it was claimed, by deviating from the proper pathways of local expertise. More generally, it could be suggested that by tendering an opinion of the affairs of *mabu* weavers, the cleric was breaching quite purposefully (for performance effects in front of the anthropologist) a gulf of ignorance that should ideally lie between the business of weaving and the affairs of the clerics.

Thus it would seem that constructions of ignorance inform the ways in which the relationships of learning and the dissemination of knowledge are organized. In the first case, domestic captives and those of servile status in the past were beyond the pale of learning, and were subjected to moral evaluations that placed them on a lower rung of humanity. Ignorance is therefore a function of social positioning, and the imperative to overcome it or not hinged on what can be seen both as a response by those who were consigned to a position of ignorance in society, and as a social responsibility of those who controlled the relations of exclusive and restricted learning. The dynamics of claims to knowledge and the counter-attributions of ignorance in the cases above illustrate the way in which definitions of expertise, and the social relations that produce it, cast a shadow of not-knowing on others who are denied the possibility of knowing in a social domain considered to be outside their ken.[13]

Bodily knowledge and craftwork

How can we understand the mutuality of knowledge and ignorance with respect to specialist craft occupations, such as those I have described elsewhere in my ethnography of Senegalese 'caste' specialists (see Dilley 1989; 1999; 2000; 2004)? The training of an apprentice involves the instilling of particular ways of movement and bodily dispositions that mark the skilled practitioner off from other non-artisans in society. And the sets of skills learned by specialist 'caste' members are regarded as exclusive to them alone. The practitioners of specific craft occupations are born into particular social groups, and they are conceived as having innate predispositions to learn their socially allotted artisan skills. These dispositions are linked intimately to conceptions of persons, which are differentiated on the basis of social status and group membership (see Dilley 2000). Not knowing these forms of knowledge is a function of social position and the local division of labour; furthermore, it is linked to the exclusivity of opportunities for learning esoteric craft lore, and to a distaste for specific trades by the freeborn agriculturalists and Islamic clerics, for whom certain manual tasks are considered degrading and shameful.

Ignorance is thus a precondition of a hierarchical social system that is based on the exclusive, hereditary transmission of learning within bounded social groups. Ignorance is written in to the social organization of such societies. It is not one's place to know the skills and trade secrets of another social group, and the consequences of breaching this social demarcation of knowledge and ignorance are severe: madness and derangement, the results of misappropriated knowledge. This exclusion from domains of knowledge extends to the possibility that knowledge acquired casually through an acquaintance with craft specialists by virtue of close interaction with them in the everyday life of a village community would be denied. For example, a non-weaver who lived adjacent to my master weaver, and with whom he was on good terms, once displayed to me a sound competence in weaving by sitting and practising at my loom. He did this discreetly, at a moment when no one was around to witness the act. He was convincing too in that he mouthed *mabu*-like 'incantations', which normally accompany the practice of weaving. He had obviously picked up these skills through his close acquaintance with the master weaver during his frequent visits to the household, but he would never admit to them or exhibit them in the company of his fellows. This seemed to me to be a blatant act of bravado on his part to try to impress me, the anthropologist, struggling to learn the craft. This contrived or pretended ignorance is linked to the social standing of the respective parties, and it constitutes a political act of 'refusing to know' for reasons of cultural politics, prestige, and moral integrity. Ignorance is developed and maintained in the gulf between social statuses not only by means of the learning relations that formally exclude non-craftsmen from artisan trades, but also as a function of hierarchical difference between members of different social groups.

The mutuality of forms of knowledge and ignorance form the conditions of possibility of a social system based upon a social distribution of different kinds of knowing and of kinds of skills required of particular kinds of person. The forms of learning through which knowledge is re-created and skills passed on to others are therefore intimately connected to differences in knowing and not-knowing. Furthermore, the social significance of secrecy is that it develops around itself a cultural politics of ignorance. A specific example of this relates to witchcraft, a knowledge of which should not be publicly acknowledged by individuals. It would be dangerous for them to do so, for they would fear the consequences of accusation, ostracism, or worse. This might even extend to a denial of knowledge of anatomy or physiology, for such expertise is again the domain of the witch.[14]

One final point about skilled craft practitioners: where craft occupations are hereditary, the lack of practical ability or the inability to master a particular skill set by a person born into an artisan family provides a point of discussion in local debates about knowing and not-knowing, or not having the ability to know. With respect to Senegal, those who succeed in mastering the range of relevant practical skills are considered to manifest the essential qualities of what it is to be a weaver, blacksmith, woodcarver, and so on – that is, their 'weaverness' or 'smithness', as it were. These qualities are conceived as being linked to particular lines of descent traced back to the mythical originators of a trade. Those who lack the ability to master such skill sets, who do not know how to practise their natal craft, who lack the *savoir-faire*, are thought not to possess the moral and constitutional qualities that make up the quintessential artisan. They are in some way lesser exemplars of craft being. We might interpret this as being related to not-knowing by the senses, a lack of bodily awareness and sensitivity, or a lack of opportunity to develop these skills through human experience and practice. But it might be better to conceive of this way of ignorance as being more 'ontological' than 'epistemological'. By this I mean that this form of not-knowing relates to the whole being of the person, not just to an inquiring mind or an ability to sense the world. This kind of bodily ignorance does not lead on to a particular set of local learning strategies: the person is constitutionally flawed and no corrective action can alleviate the predicament.

These reflections are perhaps instructive for our own sense of how we perceive bodily knowledge as an object of anthropological inquiry. While this area of knowledge is broadly discussed in the discipline, we rarely learn much about what the absence of bodily 'knowledge' might entail – namely 'bodily ignorance'. One construction of this problem might envisage a kind of not-knowing by the senses, in which the person has not had sufficient exposure to a range of human experience to amass a knowledge of the world and an ability to act within it. Another construction of the problem might hinge on a more ontological interpretation: namely that not-knowing how to act, how to hold oneself, or how to use one's body in culturally appropriate ways indicates not a straightforward ignorance as such, but instead a sense that the person possesses less than human qualities, however those might be defined locally. The weaver who cannot weave is a lesser kind of weaver-person than one who can.

One of the most vivid examples of the lack of bodily mastery that comes to mind is that of Kaspar Hauser:[15] his enigma, as portrayed cinematically by Werner Herzog, was not so much how he experienced the world and his own humanity in the absence of learned ways of thinking, but how his lack of bodily knowledge led to him initially being classified as something less than human, part of a freak show for nineteenth-century entertainment. Unable to sit upright, to walk, to communicate or interact in social relations at the outset, he lacked the appropriate ways of behaving and comportment in society. My point is that in the absence of culturally specific bodily techniques and mastery of bodily forms, this ignorance or not-knowing, if we can call it such, is construed in ways that indicate fundamental moral problems of definition about what it is to be human. An absence of 'bodily knowledge', as we coin it, is not simply a form of ignorance; it is often related to questions of being. Perhaps anthropologists should be cautious about labelling this a form of 'knowledge' in the first place.

A number of contributors to this collection deal at length with the question of bodily knowledge, and these treatments beg the question as to what might be conceived as bodily ignorance in each case. The term 'embodied knowledge' requires an account of how knowledge might be 'inscribed' on the body either organically or behaviourally in order to address the problem of bodily learning. Downey, for example, discusses 'inconsistencies' across a range of achievements by different individuals learning capoeira, and talks of 'incomplete forms of bodily knowledge' (p. S32). 'Some students simply never got that good, even though they had the same opportunities to learn and train' (p. S32). The 'remarkable mimetic ability of our species' (p. S28) would appear differentially distributed among individuals in some specific respects at least. A sense of how these differences were conceived, discussed, and debated by students and masters alike could shed light in this case on the question of 'bodily ignorance', or an inability to integrate novel bodily postures and gestures into an existing cultural repertoire of movements.

My fieldwork experience in confronting my own 'bodily ignorance' revolves around how I came to be a reasonably skilled weaver in Senegal.[16] Not knowing the appropriate ways to behave for a novice anthropologist is a commonplace experience during fieldwork, and this problem is highlighted specifically when trying to learn a new set of body techniques. But rarely are such ways of incompetence rendered by those we work with as anything more than a 'cultural' mismatch. The anthropologist arrives in the field, after all, as a fully socialized person embodying the habits of another society, and there is a mismatch between one's own habitual practices and those of the host community – a mismatch that is often the focus of much ribbing and joviality. Successful fieldwork hinges on a realignment of that mismatch over time as the fieldworker progressively assimilates the appropriate body techniques of his or her host community.

My apprenticeship involved adapting and honing my body movements in order to gain a sense of bodily co-ordination so as to perform what might be described as the 'dance of weaving': that is, to develop a sense of rhythm and contrapuntal movement of hands, arms, and legs necessary to weave in a smooth, flowing, and precise manner. The learning of these techniques was regarded by my teacher, I would argue, as less to do with the overcoming of bodily ignorance on my part, and more to do with the emergence of me as a person who was progressively becoming part of a line of ancestry or pedigree that issued from my master, whom I recognized as a 'father'. His was the first name in the pedigree of sixteen generations I had to memorize as part of an initial stage in my training. I took this to be a question of ontology, not of epistemology.

The area in which my master recognized my ignorance was in my attempts to learn the body of esoteric weaving lore associated with the craft. Initially he played on my not-knowing, in part because he was not sure of my motives or level of commitment, by saying that he would answer whatever questions I might care to pose regarding these matters; but he would not volunteer unsolicited information on them. Not knowing what this lore entailed, or whether it even really existed as such, prevented me from posing appropriate, relevant, or focused questions that he would answer. My ignorance was a gulf to be bridged in this attempted engagement with my master's knowledge of craft affairs. Only slowly and delicately, and through the trust that is built up between two people over time, was this chasm negotiated and overcome in some small measure.

Knowledge and ignorance in French colonial practice[17]

If we turn to a different ethnographic example, this time taken from late nineteenth- and early twentieth-century French colonialism, another set of issues arises in relation to not-knowing and ignoring. I seek in what follows to focus on the social and political significance of knowledge and ignorance within the colonial administration of French West Africa. What ways of knowing were employed by military officers and colonialists in their attempts to overcome not-knowing about their new environment and the peoples who populated newly colonized regions? How did they come to an understanding of local affairs in order to administer and control territories and peoples? What were the consequences of their political and economic goals for those knowledge practices, and for the emergence of strategic areas of not-knowing within the colonial administration? The relationship between power and knowledge has been well worked following on from Foucault's contributions to this problem (Foucault 1979; 1989). But the relationship between power and ignorance appears to be much less explored, and what follows below is an attempt to address some issues around this problem.[18]

The first and most urgent knowledge practices of French colonialists during the nineteenth-century military phase of annexation of West Africa were related to the necessities of gaining an upper hand over local adversaries. The areas of inquiry were, for instance, mapping and topography, and gathering basic information on local populations, their resources, and their military capabilities. Colonial concerns about ignorance lay squarely in the domain of securing domination through military might – a domination founded upon a limited scope of knowledge governed by the dictates of an expansionist colonial enterprise. The structural inequalities of the colonial order created 'lop-sided structures of the imagination' (Graeber 2006), by means of which only limited knowledge was necessary for the imposition of military authority. Vast areas of ignorance could be maintained without posing too much threat to the emerging colonial administration. Claims of ignorance and moral discourses of outrage were constructed, however, by those subject to French rule as well as by the colonizers themselves. By the start of the twentieth century, the 'burden of interpretative labour' was shifting away from local populations trying to make sense of the changes to their social lives, and onto the shoulders of the colonialists, who developed new techniques of knowledge acquisition and defined new objects of inquiry; for they were now confronted by the limits of their own ignorance for the smooth administration of vast territories of West Africa by restricted resources of manpower. The emergence of colonial ethnography was the result. Inquiry now focused on the problematic of how to grasp local understandings of social and cultural relationships, the impact of ecological constraints on modes of livelihood and social adaptations to the environment, and so on. With the establishment of a civil colonial administration, the aim was to administer local populations through a more informed sense of what indigenous custom and practice was all about. The structures of inequality shifted from a military to an administrative mode, and with it the 'lop-sided structures of the imagination' balanced themselves more evenly. The colonialist now had a need to understand what was happening in more complex ways. In particular, new objects of knowledge emerged and new methods for the production and dissemination of this knowledge were created.

Ignorance, morality, and colonial politics
Ignorance was an uneasy bedfellow of the colonial enterprise. The military and colonial mission was predicated on a claim to superior knowledge of various sorts: scientific rationalism, technological mastery of arms and machines, economic know-how about the exploitation of resources for industrial production, and so on. It was also fuelled by a sense of intellectual and moral progress, by developments in education and religious understanding, and by the civilizing mission of an enlightened European power (Conklin 1997). Yet lurking behind this pretence of mastery was a sense of ignorance, of not-knowing. Ignorance was a function of 'not knowing' plain and simple, as well as 'shutting one's eyes to' aspects of local culture that challenged preconceived ideas and

deep-seated prejudices. These ways of not-knowing related to specific and important domains: for example, the environment and landscape, the geography and topography of regions yet to be annexed; the people who populated these landscapes; the languages they spoke.

To take the example of language as one area for closer examination: officers such as Henri Gaden learned *in situ* the languages necessary for colonial government and administration. Always keen to get hold of any published works on local vernaculars, he none the less honed his own linguistic skills through local studies of language, and emerged over the course of his life as an important linguist of West African tongues. The image that captures the experiential form of learning on the spot is the '*broussard*', the practical man of action living in the bush. Until the next generation of college-educated men arrived in West Africa, the *broussard* was a kind of ideal type of colonial officer – he was an unencumbered bachelor willing to spend time alone in remote up-country stations; a person whose knowledge was acquired by means of immediate, sensory experiences. The *broussard* absorbed a knowledge of local affairs by a range of practical adaptations to the climate and territory; he picked up a *savoir-faire* to deal with local conditions that could not be matched, it was argued, by other ways of learning. There was no explicit methodology taught to officers to explain how this learning was to occur in the bush: that is, how officers were to absorb the lessons that their postings to remote locations might teach them. The practical expression of this ideal, along with his own methods of putting them into practice, led to Gaden gaining an immediate experiential, bodily, and sensory knowledge of place and population. This is a knowing by means of the senses.

By the 1920s a new generation of trained, professional colonial administrators were graduating from the École Coloniale. Graduates of the Paris-based École were trained in African languages, ethnology, and culture before being posted overseas (Cohen 1971). Gaden's contempt for this new breed of official, expressed in his later years, is all too evident: they had no bush experience, no knowledge or understanding of local cultural complexities, no feel for the place or its people. These claims of ignorance by him on the part of his colleagues must be set within a context of political, ethical, and personal transformations, since they can be read, too, as strategic and individually motivated accusations that carry a moral burden. However, a different set of knowledge practices had been developed for this new generation of colonial administrators – a knowing by the mind that was not founded upon first-hand sensory experience. By means of different ways of knowing, the new recruits threatened the older methods of experiential learning.

Henri Gaden grappled with the problem of making sense of his immediate West African experiences. He was a young military officer, replete with nineteenth-century bourgeois prejudices of Africa and Africans, a one-time racist colonial novice with an unshrinking severity and judgemental eye. By the end of his life – which he played out in Senegal, where he remained in his retirement until his death and surrounded in his household by his Senegalese wife and children – he was recast as a respected figure of authority, a person of learning and stature in the eyes of his adopted community. He underwent a remarkable personal transformation. His initial dismissive attitudes towards those around him were gradually weathered away by successive encounters with the people of the region, such that his 'refusal to take notice of' what was around him gave way to an ability not to close his eyes to increasingly personal encounters with those he came to know.

The recognition of domains of ignorance by Henri Gaden led him to adopt a variety of ways of coming to know West Africa, its peoples, and its languages. Experiential learning was his first route towards greater understanding of local contexts, and this was the basis for his increasingly academic treatments of the new objects of ethnographic inquiry that he discovered around him. The shifts in political context after the First World War also brought about redefinitions as to what counted as knowledge for the colonialists. New and different sets of knowledge practices were introduced into West Africa in the 1920s by college-based recruits trained in Paris for colonial service overseas. Gaden's accusations of ignorance on the part of these new administrators are stark and condemnatory. In the confrontation of different knowledge systems, the claim of ignorance becomes a moral weapon for those caught up in conflict. Moreover, the self-parody of those who feign to be uninformed of new knowledge techniques, which is what Gaden did, can also have a subtle political effect: bemusement and bewilderment in the face of novel knowledge practices can be a powerful tool for those who knowingly resist change.

Conclusions

Henri Gaden's struggle with not-knowing West Africa helped him develop methods to address the absence or lack of knowledge that was problematic for him and for the colonial enterprise. His personal transformation suggests that his refusal to take notice of aspects of the world was eventually overcome; he could no longer ignore that which had become necessary to know. I return here to a reworking of Miss Marple's feigned ignorance for social and political effect. Not being able to resist the urge to couple Mark Hobart and Miss Marple, let me quote him on a moral and political dimension of ignorance: 'Ignorance, however, is not a simple antithesis of knowledge', he tells us. 'It is a state which people attribute to others and is laden with moral judgement' (1993: 1). Ignorance is therefore not an absolute or neutral condition; its construction is always linked to moral judgement and evaluation. This point has also been made above in relation to the examples of craft practice in Senegal.

Ignorance is not a simple absence, a plain lack of knowing. It is an absence that has effects in terms of what is construed as knowledge, and of what social relations of learning are established in order to address the consequences of absence. If knowledge provides a sense of certainty about things, and has a reassuring effect regarding our place in the world, ignorance, by contrast, can suggest uncertainty and a discomfort about the world. In game theory, knowledge provides a basis for certainty about the outcomes of interactions; in market theory, 'perfect' knowledge of market conditions, under a particular reading of such phenomena, affords market players a foundation and certainty in their transactions. We can luxuriate in the comfort of knowing; anxiety is the product of types of not-knowing. Ignorance is a social fact that is to be apprehended by anthropological methodology; it is not just a philosophical or theological problem. As indicated above, Murray Last has pointed to the difficulty in ethnography of handling what is known among a people, let alone what is not known. He goes on to say: 'To discuss ... the extent of not-knowing is presumptuous in the extreme; nonetheless to ignore the existence of not-knowing ... only negates our very claim to know another ... culture' (Last 1992: 394). The presumptuousness of this present discussion is not to be denied; but the importance of tackling this dilemma for the anthropology of knowledge and for the current trend of 'knowledge transfer' must none the less be emphasized persuasively.

Marchand's introduction calls for an 'interdisciplinary approach' to anthropology and knowledge. If I have met this call at all, it is by drawing on ideas from the disciplines of philosophy, theology, and history in trying to define what direction an anthropological study of knowledge and ignorance might take. My insistence in the first instance is that forms of knowledge and knowing must be construed in relation to conceptions of ignorance, for this mutual relationship informs the kinds of learning practice that emerge to address the perceived lacunae. Varieties of ways of knowing, acquiring knowledge, or 'being knowledgeable' (Ingold) are contingent upon how ignorance and not-knowing are framed. Second, I have problematized the concept of bodily knowledge, for if it is to be seen as such, it is not clear what shape bodily ignorance, its counterpart, would have; indeed, how this should be studied further, and what consequences might flow from this, also require attention.

The interdisciplinary perspectives strongly developed by some of the papers in this collection involve the way in which cognitive sciences, in the broadest possible sense, might extend and develop an anthropological approach to the relationship between the human body, the social environment, and ways of knowing. I have steered clear of this 'cognitive turn'. It would appear from my perspective that an account of ignorance is required in such analyses, such that the forms of knowledge and knowing being discussed by them should be seen in the light of the shape they are given by not-knowing, or ignorance. If 'knowledge resides in modality specific neuro-cognitive systems', and if much of 'cultural transmission is ... explained in terms of what is, in effect, a high-fidelity neural copy machine' (Cohen, this volume, p. S199), then we must take care, as Cohen and others also attempt to do, not to suggest by such an account that ignorance is an absence of certain types of neural pathway, a lack of cognitive circuitry, and so on. The 'cognitive turn', whether in simple or more sophisticated versions, must not allow ignorance to appear to be the analogue of the blank space left by philosophers after Ferrier's initial indications on the subject.

The accompanying conceptions of knowledge that are entailed here appear to be particularly susceptible to metaphors drawing from modern information technology: acquisition, storage, retrieval, transmission. This sort of formulation contrasts with the direction suggested by Marchand in his introduction, which highlights the idea of making knowledge by drawing from images associated with processes of craft production and human creativity. From such a perspective, knowing is a fluid active process ('making knowledge', Marchand), one that is in flux; or is in a state of becoming (Ingold), the outcome of a simultaneous moving and knowing. Knowledge is not to be reified as object. Whether the future of anthropological scholarship on human knowledge lies in an area of 'data-generated' 'testable hypotheses' (Cohen) drawing on, for example, the specification of 'material properties' of the 'social environment' is beyond the scope of this present chapter to assess. But what I hope to have shown in my reflections above is that a phenomenologically informed account of social, cultural, political, and moral relations (rather than inner cognitive states) in which claims to knowledge and ignorance are made would seem to suggest a means of holding true to a sense of fluidity in the contingent fabrication of our objects of inquiry.

NOTES

[1] Last argues that the origin of not-knowing lies in the break-up of traditional medicine as a system in Hausaland; my arguments attempt to establish the potential of ignorance as the grounds for knowledge, and the moral and political consequences of ignorance.

[2] See Marchand's Introduction to this book on his call to situate how people know and what people know in the frame of broader social relations.

[3] To quote Ferrier more fully: 'This section of the science is properly termed the Epistemology ... It answers the general question, "What is Knowing and the Known", or more shortly "What is Knowledge" ' (1854: 48); and 'We must examine and fix what ignorance is – what we are, and can be, ignorant of. And thus we are thrown upon an entirely new research, constituting an intermediate section of philosophy, which we term the agnoiology ... the theory of true ignorance' (1854: 51).

[4] See Harris (2007) for a similar discussion.

[5] See *http://www.newadvent.org.cathen* for some of the ideas which have informed this section.

[6] By illuminating the limits of knowledge (both theirs and ours), and of the forms of interpretation placed upon persons, events, and relationships in different locations in Chambaland, Fardon (1990) reveals the theoretical and methodological relationship between anthropological treatments of knowledge and the hitherto little-discussed domain of ignorance.

[7] See Herzfeld (2007) for a discussion of these issues.

[8] See Ingold in this volume on the idea of the path as a route by which knowledge is created through journeying along it.

[9] The disorientation of a wayfarer who loses his or her way makes for a topic that is suggestive of the possibility of not-knowing, of becoming unknowledgeable, in the context evoked by Ingold in this volume.

[10] See Dilley (2004) for further details.

[11] See Dilley (1987) for a more complete ethnographic account of these events.

[12] The spider is an important figure in Islamic thought, and a chapter (*sura*) is dedicated to it in the Qur'an.

[13] The politics of interpretation and counter-narratives of claiming particular kinds of knowledge can be seen in the example described by Cohen (in this volume): 'If a particular person harboured negative feelings toward a particular medium, those attitudes appeared to influence behaviour toward that medium also when possessed'. This seems to be a perfectly convincing explanation in terms of the politics of social interrelationships to account for the subsequent differences in local interpretations of possession, and of 'how these patterns arise'.

[14] See Last (1992), who reports this to be the case in Hausaland, Nigeria.

[15] Kaspar Hauser was a mysterious teenage foundling who appeared on the streets of Nuremberg in 1828 carrying a letter from an anonymous author. He died of stab wounds in 1833 at about the age of 21, although the circumstances of his death have never been conclusively uncovered. His life-story and speculations about his origins have been the subject of a range of literary, cinematic, musical, and historical works, Werner Herzog's 1974 film *The enigma of Kaspar Hauser* being just one example. The mystery still remains to this day as to who he was and the reasons behind his solitary incarceration from an early age until his release in Nuremberg.

[16] See Dilley (1989; 1999) for further details.

[17] This section relates to a new project I am conducting that focuses on a French Colonial Officer and administrator, Henri Gaden (1867-1939). A fuller version of the historical ethnography I present here has been published in Dilley (2007). The argument in this section highlights the implications of the conceptions of ignorance for emerging knowledge practices.

[18] Foucault's concept of *episteme* and the place he grants to knowledge within both his archaeological and genealogical method are suggestive about how ignorance might be conceived within his approach; this might be called 'epistemic ignorance'. His archaeology of knowledge is a kind of history that reveals the conditions that make a certain form of thought possible and necessary, by outlining specifically the conditions of possibility within a particular discursive formation for the emergence of specific objects of knowledge. These might be, for example, the recent invention of 'Man' as a subject, or the soul of a prisoner and the medicalization of madness as objects of knowledge. If structuralism uncovers unknown knowns, then Foucault's history of epistemic transformations suggests the possibility of unknown unknowns: that is, objects of knowledge yet to be uncovered and posed as problematic areas of inquiry. This is another rendering of ignorance: namely 'epistemic ignorance', not knowing the objects of knowledge according to ways of thinking in other places or in other times (see also Foucault 1984).

REFERENCES

COHEN, W. 1971. *Rulers of empire: the French Colonial Service in Africa*. Stanford: Hoover Institution Press.
CONKLIN, A.L. 1997. *A mission to civilize: the Republican idea of Europe in France and West Africa, 1895-1930*. Stanford: University Press.
CRICK, M. 1982. Anthropology of knowledge. *Annual Review of Anthropology* 11, 287-313.

Dilley, R.M. 1987. Tukulor weaving origin myths: Islam and reinterpretation. In *The diversity in the Muslim community: anthropological essays in memory of P.A. Lienhardt* (ed.) A. Al-Shahi, 70-9. London: Ithaca Press.

——— 1989. Secrets and skills: apprenticeship among Tukolor weavers. In *Apprenticeship: from theory to method* (ed.) M.W. Coy, 181-98. Albany, N.Y.: SUNY Press.

——— 1999. Ways of knowing, forms of power: aspects of apprenticeship among Tukulor Mabube weavers. *Cultural Dynamics* **11**, 33-55.

——— 2000. The question of caste in West Africa, with special reference to Tukulor craftsmen. *Anthropos* **95**, 149-65.

——— 2004. *Islamic and caste knowledge practices among Haalpulaaren, Senegal: between mosque and termite mound.* Edinburgh: University Press (for the International African Institute).

——— 2007. The construction of ethnographic knowledge in a colonial context: the case of Henri Gaden (1867-1939). In *Ways of knowing: new approaches in the anthropology of experience and learning* (ed.) M. Harris, 139-57. Oxford: Berghahn.

Fardon, R. 1990. *Between God, the dead and the wild: Chamba interpretations of ritual and religion.* Edinburgh: University Press (for the International African Institute).

Ferrier, J.F. 1854. *Institutes of metaphysic: the theory of knowing and being.* Edinburgh: Blackwell.

Foucault, M. 1979. *Discipline and punish: the birth of the prison* (trans. A. Sheridan). London: Peregrine.

——— 1984. *The Foucault reader* (ed. P. Rabinow). Harmondsworth: Penguin.

——— 1989. *The order of things: an archaeology of the human sciences.* London: Tavistock.

Graeber, D. 2006. Beyond power/knowledge: an exploration of the relation of power, ignorance and stupidity. The Malinowski Lecture, 25 May, London School of Economics and Political Science (available on-line: *http://www.lse.ac.uk/collections/LSEPublicLecturesAnd Events/pdf/20060525-Graeber.pdf*, accessed 13 January 2010).

Harris, M. 2007. Introduction: 'ways of knowing'. In *Ways of knowing: new approaches in the anthropology of experience and learning* (ed.) M. Harris, 1-26. Oxford: Berghahn.

Herzfeld, M. 2007. Deskilling, 'dumbing down' and the auditing of knowledge in the practical mastery of artisans and academics: an ethnographer's response to a global problem. In *Ways of knowing: new approaches in the anthropology of experience and learning* (ed.) M. Harris, 91-110. Oxford: Berghahn.

Hobart, M. 1993. Introduction: the growth of ignorance? In *An anthropological critique of development* (ed.) M. Hobart, 1-30. London: Routledge.

Kundera, M. 2002. *Ignorance: a novel,* London: Faber and Faber.

Larkin, P. 1988. Ignorace. In *Collected poems* (ed. A. Thwaite), 107. London: Faber and Faber.

Last, M. 1992. The importance of knowing about not-knowing: observations from Hausaland. In *The social basis of health and healing in Africa* (eds) S. Feierman & J. Jansen, 393-406. Berkeley: University of California Press.

10

Anthropology of knowledge

EMMA COHEN *Max Planck Institute for Evolutionary Anthropology and Max Planck Institute for Psycholinguistics*

In their various roles as perceivers, learners, recorders, communicators, and theorists of knowledge, anthropologists have long recognized the central importance of bodily experience in human knowledge. As learners of varied forms of cultural knowledge, they maintain and demonstrate the importance of 'being there' as experiential participants and observers. As communicators of knowledge, they are challenged to transcribe their experiences into forms of knowledge that are faithful to the richness of the data. And as fully engaged participants in the myriad aspects of human behaviour across variable cultural and learning contexts, anthropologists are uniquely positioned to generate precise descriptive and theoretical accounts of the making of diverse kinds of knowledge. The chapters in this volume illustrate these aspects of 'embodied' anthropological inquiry, enhancing our appreciation not only of the diversity of learning environments with which anthropologists now engage, but also of the challenges that any explanatory account of knowledge-making faces.

Three challenges are especially clear. First, these chapters conjointly demonstrate that to address satisfactorily the broad framing questions, concerning 'how we know' and 'how we come to know', we need more than a single explanatory account. As the contributors have so vividly shown, *what* we know takes many different forms. The social and cognitive mechanisms and processes by which different forms of knowledge are generated are multiple, involve different activating conditions, and produce different outcomes. Second, the generation of explanatory accounts of knowledge-making across these diverse forms necessarily requires the joint engagement of multiple disciplines and modes of inquiry. If we truly aspire to understand 'how we come to know', to espouse theories of knowledge acquisition, storage, retrieval, and communication processes, and to account for the importance of bodily and mental states in learning and performance, we simply cannot afford to ignore the vast and increasingly sophisticated scholarship on such issues in neighbouring disciplines. Third, we need precise empirical questions and testable hypotheses that are both generated from and generative of relevant data. The testing of precise hypotheses about the social and cognitive mechanisms underpinning and facilitating the transmission of knowledge may not immediately strike one as a particularly 'anthropological' challenge. Without clarity, precision, and methodological rigour, however, theoretical claims ultimately remain empirically intractable, unsubstantiated, and, therefore, of obscure value to the whole enterprise.

Many more general observations could be listed. The challenges are great. In this brief discussion, however, I will attempt to support these three observations, not simply as a synoptic take-home message, but as a series of guiding principles for future anthropological scholarship on human knowledge. Rather than abstract and address each of the above three points in turn, I will demonstrate their inter-reliance in practice, focusing on a central theme of this book, 'How do bodily factors influence the making of human knowledge?' The preceding chapters offer rich descriptive analyses that point to the pervasiveness and centrality of 'embodied knowledge' in cultural transmission, and that characterize the social complexity of transmissive processes (see also Hutchins 1995; Lave 1988). But what of the mechanisms that establish and channel such knowledge? To echo Downey, what are the material dimensions of the learning process? How do these permit and constrain the transmission of culture? In the space available, I will attempt to offer some general statements, partial answers, and guiding principles relevant to these questions.

Grounded cognition

Cultural transmission – i.e. the emergence, acquisition, storage, and communication of ideas and practices – is powerfully influenced by the physical context in which it occurs. More specifically, what we know depends upon the brains, bodies, and environments in and among which transmission occurs. Disciplines differ with regard to the variable emphasis they place on neuro-cognitive, bodily, and social-historical factors in cultural transmission. Increasingly, however, researchers across the human and social sciences are recognizing that the bodily, cognitive, neural, and social mechanisms that permit and constrain knowledge transmission are conjointly operative and mutually contingent.

In cognitive scientific models, the traditional view that knowledge resides neurally independently of the mode-specific route by which it was acquired is gradually losing ground. In recent years, a novel framework has emerged, which presents cognitive processes such as perception, conception, attention, memory, and motivation, as 'grounded' in their physical context (Barsalou 2008). According to this view, knowledge resides in modality-specific neuro-cognitive systems (e.g. those that process vision, movement, audition, emotion, motivation, etc.) and is re-activated via the partial simulation of the cognitive and bodily states, social interactions, and environmental situations that contributed to its acquisition. For example, there is evidence to suggest that in order for pianists to identify whether a musical recording is of their own playing, they tacitly and internally simulate the motor actions that compose the performance (Repp & Knoblich 2004). Importantly, these recent approaches do not conflate brains, bodies, and environments, or see all or any forms of knowledge as equivalently dependent on each, but rather they recognize specific and varied causal linkages among them. Specific body states, for example, have been shown to produce specific cognitive states (e.g. the activation of smiling musculature by clenching of a horizontally aligned pencil between one's teeth produces positive affect), and specific social stimuli produce specific cognitive states (e.g. perceiving another's laughter can produce positive affect in self) (see Barsalou, Niedenthal, Barbey & Ruppert 2003).

How might this scholarship contribute to our understanding of the micromechanisms underpinning human knowledge? The ethnographic analyses presented here compellingly demonstrate the centrality of bodily states in the making of knowledge: for example, in how learning to listen, learning to weave and embroider, and learning to refine and attune one's sense to a novel skill domain (Makovicky, Portisch, Rice, Venkatesan). The complementary scholarship on grounded cognition, and investigations of implicit cognitive and behavioural phenomena, further indicate that cognitive, affective, and bodily states are intimately interconnected across an exceedingly broad and diverse range of knowledge forms. Research into the tacit linkages between concepts and bodily states demonstrates that embodied knowledge pervades even basic-level conceptual categorization. In a well-known study by Bargh, Chen, and Burrows (1996), when social stereotypes associated with particular words were tacitly primed, embodied effects were produced. Adults primed with the word *elderly*, for example, took longer to walk from the laboratory to the elevator than adults in a control condition. The priming of the stereotype associated with *elderly*, particularly the assumption that the elderly tend to move slowly, appeared to generate corresponding bodily effects in the participants. Similar effects were obtained in another study by Aarts and Dijksterhuis (2002), in which participants were primed with the names of fast or slow animals (such as *cheetah* or *turtle*).

Barsalou explains such effects in terms of what he calls 'modal re-enactment'. According to this account, knowledge is not stored in some sort of neural filing cabinet, detached from the structures that are activated in its acquisition. Rather, the retrieval of knowledge entails the partial re-enactment of the very situation(s) that led to its encoding. Even retrieval of the most basic information pertaining to everyday objects and entities entails simulation of the situation of 'being there' with those objects and entities. Barsalou and colleagues, for example, asked research participants to produce properties for objects that would typically be found either above them (e.g. bird) or below them (e.g. worm). When producing properties for objects above them, participants were more likely to look up, and to lift their faces and hands upwards, than when thinking about objects typically found below them (see Barsalou *et al.* 2003).

These findings, and those of an expanding body of evidence, support the view that simulations underlie conceptual processing. In other words, the neural systems that produce experiences are activated in their subsequent representation – the modality-specific states activated by an affective, visual, and motor experience, such as a bungee jump, are used in subsequent performances, descriptive commentaries, and so on, of that experience. This account can help to explain why the re-description of such kinds of experiences in propositional language fails adequately to communicate many of their most keenly felt dimensions, or why in the everyday telling of jokes and stories we often end up resigning to the conclusion that 'you had to be there' (or succumbing to the temptation to embellish).

Applying and developing theories, findings, and methodologies from this new framework of 'grounded cognition', anthropologists can strive to identify more precisely how body, brain, and environment inform and constrain the making of knowledge. What we mean by 'embodiment', as a term and perhaps even an 'approach' or 'paradigm' in anthropology, is all too frequently obscured in protracted chains of metaphorical reinterpretation and re-formulation. Of course, the examination and refinement of our analytical concepts are essential to establishing their interpretative utility. If we wish not only to describe and interpret, however, but also to *explain* how the body is implicated in knowledge acquisition, problematized concepts must eventually be supplemented with operationalized concepts. As Downey (this volume) argues, to account for how knowledge is acquired, we need to engage with the organic matter of the body, with specific material, physical, and neurological dimensions, and how these impact perceptual, conceptual, behavioural, and social phenomena, and vice versa. In his introduction, Marchand lists numerous scholars in the cognitive sciences, including anthropology, who have already done so. Considerable scope exists for sustained and more widespread involvement in such an enterprise.

Many anthropologists, of course, are uncomfortable with the idea of simply borrowing findings from cognitive sciences on the factors contributing to patterns of knowledge transmission. The relevant questions may not have been helpfully framed and investigated, and sample populations used are often unrepresentative along various important dimensions. Consequently, anthropologists are increasingly developing their own – or collaborative – scientific research programmes born out of their fieldwork observations (e.g. Astuti 2001; Astuti & Harris 2008; Barrett & Behne 2005). Recognizing that factors underlying patterns of transmission observed may not readily be discovered or confirmed through immersive participation and observation, direct interview, and other standard ethnographic techniques, these anthropologists have adapted and incorporated methods developed outside of anthropology that probe for out-of-awareness knowledge and reasoning biases. Appreciating more fully the range of factors – cognitive, social, environmental, etc. – that govern behaviour, anthropologists can develop plausible accounts for patterns of behaviour that may otherwise remain unsolvable puzzles. Allow me to illustrate with an example from my own work.

The cognition of possession

Following fieldwork with a group of Afro-Brazilian spirit mediums in Belém, northern Brazil, numerous phenomena puzzled me as I reflected upon the behaviours and statements of my research participants. One such puzzle concerned the apparent inconsistencies in the ways in which my friends in the field talked about and behaved around possessed individuals. Possession (*incorporação*), I was frequently told, involves the entry of a spirit into a person's body, specifically the person's head. When the spirit comes into the person's body, the person leaves, and where the person is thought to go depends upon whom one asks. Some, for example, suggested that they lie down and sleep; others said that they fly away; others said that they remain in the spot they were at the moment the spirit entered their body. In contrast, there is a broad consensus on what possession entails for the body and for the spirit. The spirit inhabits the body temporarily, taking control of it and using it in the service of mediumistic activities, such as healing and counselling. Subsequent behaviours are said to be attributable to the intentions, desires, and so on, of the spirit, not of the medium.

These descriptions of possession, however, often conflicted with observers' commentaries about particular behaviours in particular possession episodes. Mediums were often teased for dancing or singing inadequately or for behaving inappropriately while possessed. People's interactions with mediums when possessed displayed striking continuities with their interactions with mediums when *puro*, or not possessed. For example, if a particular person harboured negative feelings toward a particular medium, these attitudes appeared to influence behaviours toward that medium also when possessed.

The community leader (*pai-de-santo*) once related a story in which a number of core members (*filhos-de-santo*) committed severe infractions of the house rules while possessed. He described how four *filhos*, possessed with spirit entities, helped themselves to alcoholic drinks that belonged to the house. The infraction was two-fold: consumption of alcohol was strictly forbidden in the house, and the alcohol consumed on this occasion was specifically and exclusively reserved for ritual libations to the spirit entities of the house. The *pai-de-santo*'s telling of the story revealed a certain level of ambivalence about whom to blame – the *filhos*, or the spirit entities possessing them.

He began by naming names, not of spirit entities but of *filhos*. Then, he itemized his reactions to the situation:

> First, I think that it wasn't necessary for the entities to do this. '*Look, I want to drink – ah, it's not ok – alright then, I'll go away*'. Fine! Second, the entities know the regime of the house. Third, they were stealing. Sure, this family [*of spirits*] is said to be fond of their drink, but ... I couldn't get over it and I'm still not over it.

Moments later, the blame seemed to be reside more in the direction of the *filhos*:

> Look, the most important people of the house – in terms of hierarchy – were involved. The most interesting thing is that the spirit entities know that these people cannot drink ... I just don't understand this at all.

And by the end of his record of the incident, it was quite clear that his disappointment was chiefly with the *filhos*:

> I thought that I was composing a stable, rigid, obedient society ... I thought that I could die in peace – that the community would continue on, but now I do not have this assurance. If I die, what is going to happen? ... I thought that I had a group of *filhos-de-santo* who were faithful, and sincere, but unfortunately this was not the truth. A betrayal within a house means a lot to me, especially since I have open communication [lit. 'an open game'] with the *filhos-de-santo*.

An obvious question, then, concerns the ways in which various forms of knowledge, at various levels of awareness, interact and inform one another in reasoning about possession. Possession, in the abstract, entailed that the *filhos* were no longer present as social agents, having been displaced from their bodies by incorporeal spirit entities. In actual possession episodes, and real-time interpersonal interactions, however, it appears that this abstract definition of possession did not consistently inform people's representations of agency, intentionality, and responsibility. Other anthropologists have reported similar patterns, but few have attempted to explain precisely *how* these patterns arise. Niko Besnier, for example, states that 'spirits and their world cannot be understood through a search for a *resolution* of such ambiguities and contradictions; rather, these qualities must be perceived as constitutive of the very nature of spirits' (1996: 76, original emphasis).

I suggest that a range of cognitive scientific findings can facilitate the development of an explanatory understanding of apparent contradictions in what people say, and in what people do, not only in possession scenarios, but across variable social, cultural, environmental, motivational, and emotional contexts. Explanations of such phenomena are often hastily dismissed for their purported imposition of coherence and rigidity on 'fluid', 'shifting', 'complex', and 'conflictual' cultural processes and discourses. Yet a considerable and growing literature investigating how human psychology reacts with bodily, social, and environmental stimuli now points to the presence of significant constraints and predictable biases on human reasoning.

The perception and interpretation of possession scenarios are guided by a set of implicit mental tools that deal with social perception in a broad range of interpersonal contexts. Through further ethnographic and experimental research on the cognition of possession, psychologist Justin Barrett and I discovered that the abstract definition of possession – that entailing a displacement of the medium's agency upon the entry of the spirit – does indeed appear to be underpinned by strong cognitive biases. As a result, the structure of this concept appears to be significantly more memorable, for example, than comparable possession concepts (e.g. that entail the merging of host and spirit agency in the host's body). This may explain, in part, widespread incidence cross-culturally of such displacement concepts (see Cohen & Barrett 2008a; 2008b).

In real-time perception of possessed individuals, however, a different set of cognitive mechanisms is activated, biasing individuals toward alternative representations of possessed individuals. Neuroscientific and psychological evidence on the processes underpinning the perception of faces, for example, indicates that the observation of the face of a known individual activates affective and semantic information that the observer holds regarding that individual (Leveroni et al. 2000; Shah et al. 2001). Because the pathway of activation – from systems involved in face perception, to those involved in face recognition, and ultimately person recognition – is automatic, we cannot readily attribute new identities to familiar faces. In our observations of how people represent possession episodes, we should therefore expect ambivalence and ambiguity in what observers say and do.

Drawing from our understanding of the implicit and explicit cognitive processes involved in person recognition, novel predictions can be generated concerning the variable importance of different bodily and behavioural cues for processes of person perception in possession and related contexts (e.g. actor type-casting). What bodily and behavioural transformations are likely to enable people more readily and consistently to represent a person as 'no longer present' and their body as now inhabited by a different identity? We might predict, for example, that the wearing of facial masks would produce interestingly different effects from situations in which such accoutrements are not used. What kinds of motivational and emotional factors, and other interpersonal expectations, are important for explaining the ambivalence with which the *pai-de-santo* understood the behaviour of the possessed *filhos* described above?

These questions are possibly interesting, but they are certainly tough to answer. How people reason about possession is produced by the interaction of brain, body, and social environment, and varies according to the ways in which elements of these three domains are differently configured across different contexts. This is not tantamount to an incoherent and impenetrable chaos, however. The material properties of each of these dimensions have variable, predictable, and often measurable effects on the making, storage, retrieval, and communication of knowledge. Anthropologists cannot always depend upon other disciplines to investigate how these dimensions contribute to the patterns of behaviour and cultural transmission they observe. Rather, generating plausible accounts of the complexities of knowledge-creation and -activation often requires a concerted, collaborative interdisciplinary effort, and the sharing of method-ological tools, data, and theoretical insights.

From fieldwork to fMRI?

Talk of the centrality of bodies and brains in knowledge transmission, together with appeals to neuro-cognitive theories on simulated re-enactments, and neuroscientific evidence on person recognition processes, may give the impression that the explanatory approach I am advocating necessarily requires that, at a certain point, we throw away our notepads and pencils for expensive brain-scanning gadgetry and white coats. The choice, however, is not between social, cultural, and historical phenomena, on the one hand, and brain mechanisms, on the other; nor do traditional fieldwork methods and flashy scanning methods even remotely constitute the complete battery of potentially relevant techniques available. Conventional methods in the psychology of learning and knowledge, including systematic observational techniques and eye-tracking, reaction-time, implicit priming, and recall studies, are highly relevant to perennial anthropo-logical concerns and questions about the transmission of culture.

Take imitation, for example. Imitative learning has been a central focus of research in developmental psychology. Despite the richness and importance of findings in this area, the neuroscientific discovery that imitative capacities are neurally grounded in a specially dedicated class of brain cells, called mirror neurons, has fast become one of cognitive science's most successful exports to the social sciences. Mirror neurons have received special attention, in particular, in discussions of skill acquisition and cultural transmission more broadly (including in this collection). That they operate uncon-sciously and automatically is often taken to suggest that learned motor behaviours are simple emulations, or behavioural copies, of observed behaviours in others. Much of cultural transmission is, by extension, explained in terms of what is, in effect, a high-fidelity neural copy machine. Research with infants, however, suggests that imitation does not consist only of re-enactments of demonstrated action. Rather, imitative behaviours are frequently selective, and the inferential processing biases that govern selection are firmly in place early in infancy.

In a series of simple but groundbreaking studies György Gergely, Gergely Csibra, and colleagues first demonstrated not only that 12-month-old infants are able to attribute goals to observed actions, but that they can also assess the efficiency with which the goal is achieved via the specific act, and according to the physical constraints upon the agent acting (Gergely, Nádasdy, Csibra & Bíró 1995; Csibra, Gergely, Bíró, Koós & Brockbank 1999). They then investigated whether considerations of efficiency would influence 14-month-old infants' imitative behaviours. In an adaptation of a seminal study by Andrew Meltzoff, in which actions demonstrated by an adult actor were re-enacted by infants after a one-week period, Gergely, Bekkering, and Király (2002) showed that 14-month-olds tend to re-enact a goal-directed action only if they perceive the action to be an effective means of achieving the intended goal. Infants watched an actor switch on a light box using her forehead. In one condition, the actor's hands were free while she executed the action, and in the other condition, her hands were occupied (pretending to be cold, she had wrapped a blanket around herself, which she held with both hands). Experimenters report a significant difference in the number of infants who copied the demonstrated action between the two conditions. When the demonstrator's hands were free, 69 per cent of infants re-enacted the head action. When the demonstrator's hands were occupied, only 21 per cent of the infants copied the head action, with the remainder choosing instead to turn on the light with their hands. The experimenters conclude that 'the early imitation of goal-directed actions is a selective, inferential process that involves evaluation of the rationality of the means in relation to the constraints of the situation' (Gergely *et al.* 2002: 755).

Developmental studies such as these suggest that emulation – or simple behavioural copying – is a component capacity in cultural learning, but that it is recruited alongside additional cognitive capacities that enable us to detect goals and assess the relative efficiency and relevance of variable routes to achieving those goals (all of which may be facilitated through the activation of mirror-neuron circuits, see Barsalou 2008: 623; Gallese, Keysers & Rizzolatti 2004). Where the functional rationale for a demonstrated behaviour is unknown, however, actions are more likely simply to be emulated. This is because, to the naïve observer, the relevant elements of the action may not be readily distinguishable from the irrelevant components. Gergely and Csibra (2006) suggest that selective transmission of relevant knowledge is enhanced by demonstrators, or teachers, through a variety of what they call 'ostensive-communicative cues'. Such cues include eye contact, contingent reactivity, gaze shifting, pointing, behavioural demonstration, eyebrow flashing, and so on. Gergeley and Csibra propose a bilateral human-specific pedagogical inclination to 'teach' each other, or to transmit relevant information via the use of these ostensive cues, and to learn from each other, or to be receptive to such cues (Gergely, Egyed & Király 2007). Such a 'pedagogical stance', if borne out, would be an extremely important component of any account of cultural transmission, and, indeed, of human sociality at large. Ethnographic evidence on whether ostensive-communicative cues are as widespread as this view suggests will surely be required to test these hypotheses. In those cultural contexts and learning situations where ethnographers have reported the absence of direct propositional teaching, do we none the less encounter a range of ostensive-communicative cues in transmission? Is the repertoire of such 'pedagogical tools' broadly similar, and are there recurrences in the patterns of activation of various components of the repertoire?

These tools and findings can demonstrate the relevance and importance of methodological pluralism beyond fieldwork and brain scans. This issue is more than methodological, however. By leaping from culture to brains and back, and bypassing the cognition in between, we risk missing what is happening at the psychological and behavioural levels. Explaining phenomena at the socio-cultural level in terms of the patterns of activation of neurons in individual brains is analogous to explaining a computer hardware failure in terms of the atomic structure of the materials of which it is composed. It is at the level of the psychological mechanisms, processes, regularities, and biases that constitute (and that may be constituted by) the individual and distributed ideas, expectations, intentions, behaviours, beliefs, feelings, attitudes, and so on, that make up a socio-cultural environment that we will potentially discover factors that meaningfully account for macro-cultural patterns. If we are to concentrate our collaborative efforts, then, in any domain of the broad aggregate of disciplines and specialisms that is cognitive science, an alliance with psychology is likely to be a particularly fruitful one.

Because of the complexity of human culture, sociality, behaviour, and thought, questions about the factors contributing to patterns of knowledge transmission are rarely settled with any single set of tools or findings. How we come to know necessarily entails complex and contingent interactions among brains, bodies, and environments.

There is an important role for anthropologists in identifying these interactions – not only as sensitive interpreters of human behaviour, but as methodical describers of human behaviour as it may be witnessed through a potentially broad variety of techniques. The contributions to this volume offer both rich data and probing questions for accounts of bodily knowledge, moving anthropology toward a position from which the discipline can further its collaborative engagement with relevant theories and findings in the cognitive sciences on cognition, embodiment, learning, and knowledge. As I have attempted to argue, the generation of insightful interpretative analyses of behaviour need not be the end-point of the ethnographic process. Faithful descriptions and analyses can engender data-driven questions and hypotheses about the causal mechanisms and processes that enable us to 'come to know'. Ultimately, however, 'being there' and the importance of sustained participant-observation in the generation of descriptive portrayals of human behaviour is powerfully upheld by emerging 'grounded cognition' models of human knowledge. A rich understanding of local concepts and categories as they inform ideas and practices, and the progressive departure from exclusively ethnocentric (mis)understandings, is best achieved via direct and repeated exposure to the linguistic, social, bodily, motivational, and affective contexts in which these concepts and categories appear. The chapters in this volume are surely strong testimony to this fact.

REFERENCES

AARTS, H. & A. DIJKSTERHUIS 2002. Category activation effects in judgement and behaviour: the moderating role of perceived comparability. *British Journal of Social Psychology* **41**, 123-38.

ASTUTI, R. 2001. Are we all natural dualists? A cognitive developmental approach. *Journal of the Royal Anthropological Institute* (N.S.) **7**, 429-47.

——— & P. HARRIS 2008. Understanding mortality and the life of the ancestors in rural Madagascar. *Cognitive Science* **32**, 713-40.

BARGH J.A., M. CHEN & L. BURROWS 1996. Automaticity of social behaviour: direct effects of trait construct and stereotype activation on action. *Journal of Personality and Social Psychology* **71**, 230-44.

BARRETT, H.C. & T. BEHNE 2005. Children's understanding of death as the cessation of agency. *Cognition* **96**, 93-108.

BARSALOU, L.W. 2008. Grounded cognition. *Annual Review of Psychology* **59**, 617-45.

———, P.M. NIEDENTHAL, A.K. BARBEY & J.A. RUPPERT 2003. Social embodiment. In *The psychology of learning and motivation*, vol. 43 (ed.) B.H. Ross, 43-92. San Diego: Academic Press.

BESNIER, N. 1996. Heteroglossic discourses on Nukulaelae spirits. In *Spirits in culture, history and mind* (eds) J.M. Mageo & A. Howard, 75-97. New York: Routledge.

COHEN, E. & J. BARRETT 2008a. When minds migrate: conceptualizing spirit possession. *Journal of Cognition and Culture* **8**, 23-48.

——— & ——— 2008b. Conceptualizing spirit possession: ethnographic and experimental evidence. *Ethos* **36**, 245-66.

CSIBRA, G., G. GERGELY, S. BÍRÓ, O. KOÓS & M. BROCKBANK 1999. Goal attribution without agency cues: the perception of 'pure reason' in infancy. *Cognition* **72**, 237-67.

GALLESE, V., C. KEYSERS & G. RIZZOLATTI 2004. A unifying view of the basis of social cognition. *Trends in Cognitive Science* **8**, 396-403.

GERGELY, G., H. BEKKERING & I. KIRÁLY 2002. Rational imitation in preverbal infants. *Nature* **415**, 755.

——— & G. CSIBRA. 2006. Sylvia's recipe: the role of imitation and pedagogy in the transmission of human culture. In *Roots of human sociality: culture, cognition, and human interaction* (eds) N.J. Enfield & S.C. Levinson, 229-55. Oxford: Berg.

———, K. EGYED & I. KIRÁLY 2007. On pedagogy. *Developmental Science* **10**, 139-46.

———, Z. NÁDASDY, G. CSIBRA & S. BÍRÓ 1995. Taking the intentional stance at 12 months of age. *Cognition* **56**, 165-93.

HUTCHINS, E. 1995. *Cognition in the wild*. Cambridge, Mass.: MIT Press.

LAVE, J. 1988. *Cognition in practice*. Cambridge: University Press.

Leveroni, C.L., M. Seidenberg, A.R. Mayer, L.A. Mead, J.R. Binder & S.M. Rao 2000. Neural systems underlying the recognition of familiar and newly learned faces. *Journal of Neuroscience* **20**, 878-86.

Repp, B.H. & G. Knoblich 2004. Perceiving action identity: how pianists recognize their own performances. *Psychological Science* **15**, 604-9.

Shah, N., C. Marshall, O. Zafiris, A. Schwab, K. Zilles, H.J. Markowitsch & G.R. Fink 2001. The neural correlates of person familiarity: a functional magnetic resonance imaging study with clinical implications. *Brain* **124**, 804-15.

Index

Printed and bound by CPI Group (UK) Ltd, Croydon, CR0 4YY

13/04/2025

14656567-0001